Beyond Civilization and Barbarism

The Bucknell Studies in Latin American Literature and Theory
Series Editor: Aníbal González, Yale University

Dealing with far-reaching questions of history and modernity, language and selfhood, and power and ethics, Latin American literature sheds light on the many-faceted nature of Latin American life, as well as on the human condition as a whole. This series of books provides a forum for some of the best criticism on Latin American literature in a wide range of critical approaches, with an emphasis on works that productively combine scholarship with theory. Acknowledging the historical links and cultural affinities between Latin American and Iberian literatures, the series welcomes a consideration of Spanish and Portuguese texts and topics, while also providing a space of convergence for scholars working in Romance studies, comparative literature, cultural studies, and literary theory.

Selected Titles in Series

Carlos Alberto González Sánchaez, *New World Literacy: Writing and Culture Across the Atlantic, 1500–1700*
Elisa Sampson Vera Tudela, *Ricardo Palma's Tradiciones: Illuminating Gender and Nation*
Andrew R. Reynolds, *The Spanish American Crónica Modernista, Temporality, and Material Culture*
Adriana Méndez Rodenas, *Transatlantic Travels in Nineteenth-Century Latin America: European Women Pilgrims*
Brendan Lanctot, *Beyond Civilization and Barbarism: Culture and Politics in Postrevolutionary Argentina*

For a complete list of titles in this series, please visit www.bucknell.edu/universitypress

Beyond Civilization and Barbarism

*Culture and Politics in
Postrevolutionary Argentina*

Brendan Lanctot

Lewisburg
BUCKNELL UNIVERSITY PRESS

Published by Bucknell University Press
Copublished with Rowman & Littlefield
4501 Forbes Boulevard, Suite 200, Lanham, Maryland 20706
www.rowman.com

10 Thornbury Road, Plymouth PL6 7PP, United Kingdom

Copyright © 2014 by Brendan Lanctot

All rights reserved. No part of this book may be reproduced in any form or by any electronic or mechanical means, including information storage and retrieval systems, without written permission from the publisher, except by a reviewer who may quote passages in a review.

British Library Cataloguing in Publication Information Available

Library of Congress Cataloging-in-Publication Data Available

ISBN 978-1-61148-545-5 (cloth : alk. paper)—ISBN 978-1-61148-546-2 (electronic)

∞™ The paper used in this publication meets the minimum requirements of American National Standard for Information Sciences Permanence of Paper for Printed Library Materials, ANSI/NISO Z39.48-1992.

Printed in the United States of America

Contents

List of Illustrations		vii
Acknowledgments		ix
Note on Translations		xi
Introduction: Interrogating the Common Ground		1
1	Writing, Affect, and the Portraiture of Power	17
2	Graffiti, Public Opinion, and the Poetics of Politics	59
3	Visual Culture and the Limits of Representation	89
4	The Machine in the Pampa, or Writing as Technology	123
Conclusion		159
Bibliography		163
Index		171
About the Author		179

List of Illustrations

Fig. 1.1	Lithograph of Juan Manuel de Rosas, 1835 (detail)	18
Fig. 1.2	Portrait of Juan Manuel de Rosas, c. 1840	47
Fig. 1.3	Medallion depicting Juan Manuel de Rosas	48
Fig. 1.4	Masthead of "Carta del viejo Francisco," 1835	52
Fig. 1.5	"Las esclavas de Buenos Aires muestran que son libres," painting signed D. del Plot, 1841	53
Fig. 2.1	Anonymous caricature of boy writing graffiti, c. 1822	69
Fig. 3.1	"Máquina para sacar vistas," sketch by Juan Manuel Besnes e Irigoyen, 1819	94
Fig. 3.2	"Tuti li mundi," Francisco de Goya, c. 1818–1820	100
Fig. 3.3	"Miran lo que no ven," Francisco de Goya, c. 1818–1820	101

Acknowledgments

The scope of this book crystallized as I was completing my doctoral dissertation at Columbia University. Carlos Alonso challenged me to articulate the broader implications of the diverse and ever-expanding corpus of nineteenth-century Argentine cultural artifacts that I was examining. During my dissertation defense, both Lila Caimari and Gabriela Nouzeilles offered pointed critiques that helped guide my subsequent investigations. Most importantly, Graciela Montaldo, as both my dissertation adviser and the reader of the early drafts of the pages that follow, always provided timely advice and calm encouragement that have been instrumental in the completion of this project.

Much of the writing and research of this project took place in and around Buenos Aires, and I want to thank both Columbia University and the University of Puget Sound whose support made this possible. In particular, summer grants from the University of Puget Sound in 2009 and 2012 allowed me to examine archival materials that proved crucial in formulating and supporting the central arguments of this book. Alberto Piñeiro and his collegues at the Museo Histórico de Buenos Aires Cornelio de Saavedra, Araceli Bellota of the Complejo Museográfico Provincial "Enrique Udaondo," and the Department of Documentation of the Museo Histórico Nacional generously assisted me in tracking down images, and the librarians of the Academia Nacional de la Historia, the Biblioteca Nacional, and the Museo Histórico Sarmiento were all of great help in locating often elusive sources.

A Martin Nelson Junior Sabbatical Fellowship provided me the opportunity to complete this manuscript, and my colleague Harry Vélez-Quiñones graciously shared a workspace that helped make this undertaking a bit more agreeable. Indeed, I want to thank all my colleagues in Hispanic studies—Pepa Lago Graña, Mark Harpring, Catalina Ocampo, Oriel Siu, and Alicia Ramírez Dueker—for their encouragement and for fostering a warm environment for teaching and scholarship. I owe particular thanks to Curt Wasson for his careful, perceptive reading of a draft of chapter 3.

Melissa and Maddock punctuated this labor with love, and I dedicate these pages to them.

Portions of chapters 2 and 3 have already appeared in print: "Graffiti and the Poetics of Politics in Rosas's Argentina (1829–1852)" (*Hispanic Review* 78.1 [2010]: 49–70) and "El gabinete óptico de la ideología: visualidad y política en la época de Rosas (1829–1852)" (*A Contracorriente* 7 [2009]: 91–110, republished in *Pensar el siglo XIX desde el siglo XXI: nuevas miradas y lecturas*, ed. Ana Peluffo [Raleigh, N.C.: Editorial A Contracorriente, 2012]). I thank the University of Pennsylvania Press and Editorial A Contracorriente for permission to republish these articles in revised form.

Note on Translations

All translations in *Beyond Civilization and Barbarism* are mine.

Introduction

Interrogating the Common Ground

On November 20, 2010, President Cristina Fernández de Kirchner of Argentina stood before a newly unveiled monument to Juan Manuel de Rosas (1793–1887) and gave a brief, fiery speech in observance of a new federal holiday, the Day of National Sovereignty. The televised ceremony took place on a bluff overlooking the Paraná River, where troops loyal to Rosas, the all-powerful governor of Buenos Aires from 1829 until 1852, had tried to block the upstream passage of a French and English flotilla on that same day in 1845. Toward the close of a year filled with celebrations for the bicentennial of Argentine independence, the public ritual identified the emblematic but divisive strongman of Argentina's turbulent postrevolutionary period as an exemplary defender of the sovereign nation conceived in the Revolution. As the massive, bright red metallic bust of the *caudillo* made abundantly clear, Rosas remains a larger-than-life figure in collective memory.

At the same time that President Kirchner celebrated the tactical defeat at the Vuelta de Obligado as a symbol of resistance to foreign incursions on Argentine soil, she also pointed to an internal discord that had proven an equally formidable threat to national unity. Paraphrasing a recently published book of popular history, Kirchner insisted that the cannon blasts of Rosas's troops "se vienen sucediendo a lo largo de la historia, en esta división de los que amamos y queremos a nuestro país y de los que muchas veces, sin darse cuenta o dándose cuenta, se convierten en serviles y funcionales a los intereses foráneos" [continue resounding throughout our history in that division between those of us who love and adore our country, and those that many times, with or without realizing it, become servants and instruments of foreign interests].[1] Beyond the partisan bent of such a pronouncement, the rhetoric of Kirchner's speech draws on a powerful myth that has long permeated Argentine politics, cultural production, and everyday life. In the broadest sense, Kirchner rehearses the received idea that Rosas's tenure initiated a transcendent conflict dividing the Argentine nation between friends and enemies, between a "we" and an internal, seditious other; Argentina has always been a "house divided against itself."[2]

Over the course of more than a century, this fiction has proven as versatile as it is durable, providing a common script for countless and often contradictory assessments of the postrevolutionary period. These accumulating representations of the past, used as proxies for ideological debates in the present, ground a cultural discourse in which "las oposiciones han sido constantemente redefinidas, alterando los polos del enfrentamiento, pero que se ha conservado el básico sistema binario de oposiciones entre dos orientaciones doctrinales" [the oppositions have been constantly redefined, the poles of confrontation alternating, but the basic system of binary oppositions between two doctrinal orientations has been maintained].[3] Thus, in the mid-twentieth century, Peronists defended *descamisados*, or shirtless workers, against sellout oligarchs, while during the most recent military dictatorship (1976–1983), the disappeared victims of state terror became "the linchpin in different, often ideologically opposed narratives that tie into, or run into, the national fantasy founded on radical differentiation."[4] It is as if Argentina has not only been incapable of resolving the basic internecine conflict of the postrevolutionary era, it has also been condemned to echo, restage, and reify the violent narrative of its origins.

To be certain, the enduring myth of absolute opposition echoes the vehement partisan rhetoric that marked the debates of postrevolutionary Argentina. Supporters of Rosas and the loosely organized Confederación Argentina made ubiquitous the regime's official, compulsory slogans *¡Viva la Santa Federación!* [Long live the Holy Federation!] and *¡Mueran los salvajes, asquerosos, inmundos unitarios!* [May the savage, disgusting, vile Unitarians drop dead!]. In publications, public ceremonies, and through the scrutiny of everyday habits, dress, and speech, the regime and its adherents celebrated an unmediated bond linking its leader to the poor and working classes, as it insisted on the sharp division between themselves and a feckless, Europhile minority that opposed them. In turn, a small group of dissident intellectuals sustained a withering critique of Rosas that only gathered intensity as the majority of this so-called Generation of 1837 sought exile in neighboring countries. This resistance produced what would become the most famous expression of Argentina's foundational myth: a frenetic, unclassifiable text published serially in a Santiago de Chile newspaper, titled *Civilización y barbarie, vida de Facundo Quiroga i aspecto físico, costumbres y ábitos de la República Argentina* [*Civilization and Barbarism, Life of Facundo Quiroga and the Physical Aspect, Customs, and Habits of the Argentine Republic*]

(1845). Written by the journalist and educator Domingo Faustino Sarmiento, *Facundo*, as it is commonly known, is a central work of the Latin American literary canon, and its axiomatic phrase of "civilization and barbarism" is widely recognizable as shorthand for the experience of modernity throughout the continent. Yet in the immediate context of its publication, it was a hurried diagnosis of Rosas's power that cast opposition to his regime as an existential crisis: "[d]e eso se trata: de ser o no ser *salvaje*" [that is the question: to be or not to be *savage*].[5] In Sarmiento's view, Rosas systematized the despotic, personalist rule of provincial strongmen like the slain Facundo Quiroga (the ostensible subject of the eponymous book) and thus embodied a backward mode of existence rooted in rural customs and the legacy of the Spanish Empire. In stark contrast to *rosismo*, Sarmiento championed an urban elite as the promoters of a strong centralized state who could impose the rule of written law and import wholesale the ideas and industry of modernized Western Europe. Of course, in insisting on the radical difference between his imagined community and the current (dis)order, Sarmiento's thesis is perfectly homologous with the pronouncements of his enemies, employing the same schema of a deontological clash between two diametrically opposed forces.

These dividing lines, originally written as contingent responses to a crisis of political legitimacy following Independence, later provided the point of departure for a national literature and competing nationalist historiographies. In the wake of Rosas's deposal in 1852, the substantial body of work written in protest of his regime "agigantó y volvió más espesa la sustancia de un conflicto típicamente maniqueo, y la literatura posterior, desgajada de las bases históricas y sociales que le dieron origen continuó, reviviendo en la conciencia colectiva las viejas tensiones del conflicto" [greatly enlarged and thickened the substance of a typically Manichean conflict, and subsequent literature, detached from the historic and social conditions that gave rise to it, sustained it, reviving the old tensions of the conflict in collective memory].[6] This transformation was in no small part due to their authors, the *letrados* known of the Generation of 1837, who would occupy prominent roles in directing the newly chartered national state. Juan Bautista Alberdi's political tract *Bases y puntos de partida para la organización política de la República Argentina* (1852) provided the blueprint for its Constitution of 1853, while Bartolomé Mitre (1862–1868) and Sarmiento (1868–1872) served successive terms as president of the Republic. These victors not only wrote accounts of the previous era, they also oversaw the expansion of a system of public education whose schools taught this official history. In the state-sanctioned account of events, the two decades dominated by Rosas were a dark age, memorable primarily for the visionary, heroic resistance of a handful of intellectuals, and thus was an aberration that interrupted a nation-building project initiated with the Revolution. Rosas was vilified and, ultimately, deemed only worthy of being forgotten.[7]

In the twentieth century, though, as new social demands and a shifting global economy weakened traditional elites' grip on the liberal state, historians began to reevaluate the legacy of Juan Manuel de Rosas and the postrevolutionary period. Particularly in the 1930s, as national literature and history were becoming professionalized as academic disciplines, there appeared a profusion of titles dedicated to the era of the so-called *Restaurador de las leyes* [Restorer of Laws]. Often written by children of immigrants, these works tend to be nationalistic and conservative, and their composite image of Rosas as a prescient defender of national interests and traditional values found a large audience that extended beyond specialists and university students.[8] In these accounts, Sarmiento and his Generation of 1837 appear less as heroic, forward-thinking architects of modern Argentina than as misguided intellectuals subservient to the nations of the northern Atlantic. The Rosas that emerges in this so-called revisionist history, it must be noted, is hardly stable, shifting over time in response to new sociopolitical crises (such as the rise and fall of Yrigoyen or Perón) and alternately assumes a popular or aristocratic character.[9] Regardless of these variations, revisionism provided a foil to the "official history" that preceded it. The rival strains of nationalist historiography, however, derived from the common narrative of absolute difference, and their interpretations of the past contested one another according to equivalent terms of opposition. The controversy generated by these conflicting views is still revived from time to time in popular representations (as evinced by President Kirchner's 2010 speech and the monument to Rosas), even though academic inquiries into the postrevolutionary period long ago shifted their focus to other questions. Nevertheless, even if the cannon blasts from the Battle of the Vuelta de Obligado and the vehement slogans of the epoch do not resound with the same intensity as before, the binary logic cleaving these nationalist myths continues to organize our understanding of nineteenth-century Argentina. In practical terms, the works of dissidents, destined to become foundational texts of the national literary canon, and the abundant yet long-ignored discursive production of the Rosas regime and its supporters are still largely treated as two wholly distinct, parallel corpora.

More broadly still, "civilization and barbarism" has echoed throughout Latin American intellectual history and still exerts a strong, if ghostly presence on our current critical discourse. Dislocated from the immediate circumstances of *Facundo*'s publication, the phrase has come to function as "una figura retórica hueca, un tropo que debido precisamente a su esencial vacuidad tiene paradójicamente la capacidad de potenciar y apuntalar una colección heterogénea de discursos" [an empty rhetorical figure, a trope that, precisely because of its essential emptiness, paradoxically has the capacity to bolster and underpin a heterogeneous collection of discourses].[10] In other words, it has become a default template for examining a seemingly inexhaustible variety of confrontations and conjunctures. "Civilization and barbarism" continues to appear with predictable regularity in the titles of conference papers, course syllabi, and the introductory paragraphs of journal articles dedicated to any number of topics. Indeed, the *sombra terrible de Facundo* [terrible specter of Facundo] even haunts works that disavow the modernizing projects advocated by Sarmiento and his fellow nineteenth-century *letrados*. For example, at the beginning of *The Exhaustion of Difference: The Politics of Latin American Cultural Studies* (2001), Alberto Moreiras remarks how "discursive battles brought two armies face-to-face who had been born into themselves out of their mutual opposition: two instances or vectors of force whose dissimilarity or heterogeneity was a direct result of the need to cut or divide a territory that had previously been indifferently occupied."[11] Taken out of context, the quote might very well read like a plausible, if against-the-grain take on culture and politics in postrevolutionary Argentina, somewhat anticipating the central argument of my project. Yet the quote refers to a dispute that pit proponents of cultural studies against defenders of literary studies during a 1996 conference in Rio de Janeiro. Applied to an instance of present-day academic in-fighting, the martial imagery is plainly hyperbolic, underscoring Moreiras's point that contemporary Latin Americanism has in fact fragmented in a number of complex ways. In a deeper sense, the irony of the phrase points to what Moreiras later calls the indistinction "between Latin Americanist reflection and its field of reflection."[12] There is, in other words, no "beyond civilization and barbarism" in the sense that our locus of enunciation provides a position of pure exteriority from which we can rethink nineteenth-century Latin American culture and politics by trying to ignore or reject outright the binary logic of its axiomatic phrase.[13]

At the same time, cultural studies make it possible to think beyond civilization and barbarism and *Civilización y barbarie* (that is, *Facundo*) in another, more inclusive sense. For in questioning the hierarchy of aesthetic categories and by examining the sociopolitical conditions that shaped their emergence, this "indiscipline" compels us to consider the more extensive terrain on which the adversaries of postrevolutionary Argentina collectively inscribed the terms of conflict.[14] Instead of retracing familiar dividing lines, *Beyond Civilization and Barbarism* asks how social actors used a variety of cultural forms to promote and debate competing political projects. Examining how rivals wrote about, for example, popular audiovisual spectacles demonstrates a shared preoccupation with questions of representation, common tropes, and a marked anxiety about the relationship between Latin America and Western Europe. The side-by-side readings of antagonists' texts support my central contention that the ideological positions and divergent worldviews of postrevolutionary Argentina were mutually intelligible and sustained one another and, hence, must be studied together; the supporters and opponents of the Rosas regime were complicit in articulating the basic relation of modern Argentine politics, that division between friends and enemies. We could say, then, that this antagonism is neither a "real opposition" nor a "contradiction," but the "failure of difference" or "the 'experience' of the limit of the social."[15] Looking beyond questions of difference, it becomes apparent that the politics and cultural life of the period as a whole—and not just a handful of prophetic intellectuals—were modern, inasmuch as they were grounded in the concepts of republicanism and popular sovereignty. Indeed, an overarching concern with the *pueblo*, or people, is the figure binding the various cultural artifacts studied in these pages.

Perhaps unexpectedly, Juan Manuel de Rosas himself offers advice on how the archive of the postrevolutionary period might be reread. Exiled in Southampton, England, after his defeat at the Battle of Caseros in 1852, Rosas maintained a steady correspondence with contacts in his native country. In a letter dated October 3, 1862, Rosas writes to José María Roxas y Patrón, ostensibly to discuss legal proceedings relating to the confiscation of his property in Argentina. Yet the bulk of the letter concerns the act of reading, namely the former dictator's habits and tastes, and concludes with a request that Roxas y Patrón continue sending documents that date from his governorship. Rosas describes himself as an impatient and fickle reader, commenting that "[e]s preciso que lo que lea sea muy interesante, o muy importante, o muy necesario, para que pueda continuar leyendo sin dormirme, una, dos, o más horas. Por eso es que he leído tan poco en libros durante mi vida. *He leído muchísimo, acaso más que nadie*, pero ha sido lo más en cartas, oficios, y demás manuscritos" [it is necessary that what I read be very interesting, or very important, or very necessary, for me to keep reading for an hour or two or more without falling asleep. That is why I have read so few books in my life. *I have read a great deal, perhaps more than anyone else*, but this has mostly consisted of letters, notices, and other manuscripts].[16] This self-portrait, strikingly at odds with official depictions circulated during Rosas's tenure, is less the gaucho Martín Fierro than Funes el memorioso, Borges's tormented, omnivorous reader who is incapable of forgetting. As the shift in verb tense indicates, Rosas stresses that writing and reading were indispensable instruments of his power.

At first, Rosas praises Roxas y Patrón's erudition and expresses a desire to "comprar a Gibbon y la historia de Grecia, pr. Goldsmith" [purchase Gibbon and the history of Greece by Goldsmith] and seems to regret that he lacks the disposition for reading longer, literary works.[17] Yet as he shifts to the question of his historical legacy, he returns to the ceaseless readings of his former life, and insists that their importance has not waned, but increased over time. In this context he mentions the *Archivo Americano y Espíritu de la*

Prensa del Mundo [*American Archive and Spirit of the World Press*] (1843–1852), a government-sanctioned publication that circulated favorable news of the regime in Spanish, English, and French. These pages, which Rosas was known to edit personally from time to time, have acquired a value that exceeds their original purpose:

> Aunque no registrara, tantos, tan importantes, y tan valiosos documentos de la época de mi administración y aun desde mucho antes de ello, hay no poco que entender, y que recordar con la lectura, de algunos de ellos que al leer el índice de cada tomo se pueden elegir, para leerlos cuando se quiera, cuando se necesite, o cuando haya tiempo, o ya sea buena voluntad, y un buen viento pampero. (*Correspondencia*, 229)
>
> [Even if it did not contain so many, so important, and such valuable documents from the period of my administration and even from well before it, there is more than a little to be understood and remembered from the reading of some of these (documents), which can be chosen upon reading the index of each volume, and they can read whenever one wishes, whenever one needs, or when there is time, or good will, and a strong wind is blowing off the pampa.]

Evoking idle moments and nostalgia ("a strong breeze off the pampa"), Rosas claims that the *Archivo Americano* provides a crucial testimony of his rule that is only discernible through a selective and even arbitrary rereading. There is, in other words, a deeper understanding of the postrevolutionary period to be gleaned from this and other similar sources, one that remains obscured if one focuses solely on their original, expressly partisan function. By enumerating the various possible circumstances under which one might feel compelled to consult the *Archivo Americano*, Rosas highlights how new contexts demand new modalities of reading. In other words, Rosas advocates that artifacts such as this can and must be read—and reread—nonsequentially and with the same seriousness (and, at times, the same idleness) that one might devote to literary texts.

There is a powerful and unintended implication at work in the letter to Roxas y Patrón that exceeds its author's immediate concerns. In effect, Rosas justifies the need to consider a much expanded corpus of postrevolutionary Argentina, one which would require that canonical works such as *Facundo*, José Mármol's historical novel *Amalia* (1851), Esteban Echeverría's long poem *La cautiva* (1837), and Juan Bautista Alberdi's satirical articles published in the newspaper *La Moda* (1837–1838) be considered alongside pro-Rosas writings that include the Neapolitan intellectual Pedro De Angelis's biography of Rosas and the prolific gauchesque verse of the gazetteer Luis Pérez, in addition to anonymous broadsheets. This cuts directly against the grain of the received idea that Argentine literature emerged in opposition to Rosas, which reiterates a narrow conception of the literary that is corollary to

Sarmiento's thesis: in the final chapter of *Facundo*, Sarmiento trenchantly states, "[s]i quedara duda, con todo lo que he expuesto, de que la lucha actual de la República Argentina lo es sólo de civilización y barbarie, bastaría probarlo el no hallarse del lado de Rosas un solo escritor, un solo poeta de los muchos que posee aquella joven nación" [if there remained any doubt, with everything that has been exposed, that the present struggle in the Argentine Republic is nothing more than that of civilization and barbarism, it would be sufficient proof to note that there is not one writer, not one poet of the many that the nation possesses, to be found on Rosas's side].[18] Indeed, given the polysemy of the term "literature" in nineteenth-century Latin America, fiction, poetry, essays, and other, difficult-to-classify texts ought to be studied in conjunction with journalism, advertisements, government publications, and personal correspondence.[19] Moreover, due to their instrumental role in articulating relations between different social actors, this corpus also must include different graphic forms, popular spectacles, and public rituals as constitutive elements of the cultural and political discourse of the Rosas era.

Recent studies on nineteenth-century Latin America have made it possible to glimpse the common discursive terrain of Rosas's Argentina. In the *Cambridge History of Latin America*, published in 1985, Frank Safford noted a "paucity of systematic research into the politics of the period after independence" and lamented the "distorted view" of this process, which relied almost exclusively on the accounts of "a few articulate members of the political elite struggling for the possession of the national state."[20] In the intervening decades scholars working in the fields of history, literature, and cultural studies have broadened the scope of their inquiries to examine how an array of social actors, including subaltern subjects, participated in processes that preceded, exceeded, and resisted the consolidation of state power and national identities. This body of work does not ignore the centrality of the nation-state in the nineteenth century, but questions the teleological narratives that accompanied its rise by adopting more flexible geographic frameworks and considering "otro tipo de relaciones [que] continuaron operando y recomponiendo el escenario de la modernidad" [other relations that continued to operate and recompose the scene of modernity].[21] Whether examining local situations or adopting a transnational, transatlantic, or hemispheric focus, these studies make apparent how many of the standard topics, tropes, and schemas that long governed the study of the nineteenth century were constituted during this very period in response to a reconfiguring global market, the deployment of new technologies, and the protracted transition from monarchical empires to nation-states.

In *Republic of Capital: Buenos Aires and the Legal Transformation of the Atlantic World* (1999), historian Jeremy Adelman documents the efforts of local politicians, jurists, merchants, and other interested parties to adapt to these changes. His scrutiny of the economic life from the Bourbon reforms of the late seventeenth century through the consolidation of the nation-state in the 1860s leads him to argue that "Argentina was not an exception to a liberal norm derived from an idealized view of a North Atlantic model" but rather "a more extreme and openly conflictual process of legal construction of market relations" because "the political machinery to consolidate a liberal regime was itself so contested."[22] Indeed, as Adelman explores more broadly in *Sovereignty and Revolution in the Iberian Atlantic* (2006), a range of social actors discussed questions of authority and legitimacy across the ocean and over shifting geopolitical boundaries, well before the mature expression of patriotism or revolutionary designs. Within a vacuum of power, the alliances formed during independence collapsed, and these concerns became especially pressing and drove rival factions to "essay" and negotiate a variety of possible arrangements.

As the title of Adelman's later book suggests, and as Elías Palti explores in *El tiempo de la política: El siglo XIX reconsiderado* (2007), what competing projects held in common was the question of defining popular sovereignty. It follows, then, that the act of constructing a *pueblo*—or people—was an essential operation for any claim to power following the collapse of the Spanish Empire. Moreover, as various studies have argued, the *pueblo* was not simply a symbol or nascent discursive figure, but also a signifier referring to various collectives responsible for new expressions of public opinion beyond the closed network of private correspondence and print media among elites of the revolutionary era, as per the influential work of François-Xavier Guerra.[23] Consequently, those vying to found and control nascent institutions in the decades following Independence needed to appeal directly to largely illiterate populations for support. On a theoretical level, as depicted and addressed through various cultural forms, the *pueblo* illustrates how hegemony and subalternity worked in tandem: "hegemony with the power of allocating meaning, subalternity as a relentless place of contestation and reallocation of meaning."[24]

In a hemispheric context, Argentina's transition from colony to nation-state was especially acrimonious for a host of reasons, including the weakness of state institutions, their sensitivity to the reconfiguration of the Atlantic economy in the late eighteenth century, and the force of militias and local strongmen. It became imperative for elites vying for power to engage the various social groups who had participated in the wars of independence, including members of the lower classes who were entirely excluded from political participation under the colonial system. In a time of interprovincial wars, the powerful landholder and militia leader Juan Manuel de Rosas came to power in 1829 following an uprising that led to the controversial execution of Manuel Dorrego. Rosas, like his predecessor Dorrego, identified with the Federalists, a political party that favored a weak national state and a high degree of provincial autonomy. After a brief hiatus in the early 1830s, Rosas resumed the governorship of Buenos Aires in 1835, endowed with the *suma del poder público*, or absolute powers, and did not relinquish control until his defeat at the Battle of Caseros in 1852. As head of its richest and most powerful province, and by decree of the 1831 Pact of San Nicolás, Rosas was leader of the constitution-less Argentine Confederation.

Though increasingly the target of attacks from the Generation of 1837, and facing pressures from other provincial caudillos as well as European powers, Rosas proved capable of maintaining the support of not only the Federalist elite but also the rural and urban poor. Contrary to the longstanding image of Rosas as a despot who ruled solely through brute force, scholars including Noemí Goldman and Marcela Ternavasio have argued how the Rosas regime sought legitimacy and popular adhesion through plebiscites, postrevolutionary political institutions, centrally planned public ceremonies, and rituals of state power. Moreover, while *rosismo* may not have engendered or espoused a consistent political philosophy, the regime and its supporters justified and promoted their actions through a modern political language of republicanism, as Jorge Myers convincingly demonstrates in *Orden y virtud* (1995). Beyond print media, Ricardo Salvatore's *Wandering Paysanos: State Order and Subaltern Experience in Buenos Aires During the Rosas Era* (2003), Pilar González Bernaldo's *Civilidad y política en los orígenes de la Nación Argentina* (2001), and Regina Root's *Couture and Consensus: Fashion and Politics in Postcolonial Argentina* (2010) document the unprecedented expansion of the political into new social spaces and everyday life.

In tandem with new historical perspectives, literary and cultural studies have amply shown how the foundational works of Argentine literature, many of which were penned in opposition to the Rosas regime, in fact derive much of their creative force from the adversaries and cultural traditions they so vehemently oppose. Notably, Carlos J. Alonso, Roberto González Echeverría, Josefina Ludmer, Julio Ramos, and Diana Sorensen, among others, have deconstructed the standard reading of Sarmiento's *Facundo* that places Rosas and Sarmiento, speech and writing, city and country, civilization and barbarism, and a host of concatenated terms in stark opposition. In other words, consistent with the latent hypothesis of Ángel Rama's influential but often misread essay *La ciudad letrada*, the intellectual elite embodied by Sarmiento sought to reclaim a traditional, privileged position by engaging, assimilating, or suppressing alternative and subaltern cultural practices. As a consequence, the *letrado* archive contains a fragmented and suppressed narrative of dissent and otherness that remains to be explored. Moreover, reinterpreting David Viñas's statement that resistance to Rosas was the origin of Argentine literature, scholars such as Ricardo Piglia, Graciela Montaldo and Jens Andermann have demonstrated how these works are indissociable from the political; they cannot be read in isolation, because they never possessed the autonomy to which they aspired. Indeed, scholarly inquiries have seemingly examined the Generation of 1837's corpus to the point of exhaustion, to the point that Sorensen felt compelled to open *Facundo and the Construction of Argentine Culture* (1996) by asking "Yet another book about *Facundo?*"[25]

Though these different lines of scholarly inquiry by and large still trace the partition maintaining the writings of the Generation of 1837 and *rosista* discourse separate, in synthesis they sketch the contours of a common space on which mutually intelligible terms of opposition took shape. Taken as a whole, they suggest that politics in postrevolutionary Argentina consisted not of a clash between a vestigial colonial worldview and an ideology imported wholesale, if belatedly, from the metropolis, but rather centered on a dispute over efforts to configure and control fledgling governing bodies and political subjects. Indeed, as the comparative readings of the following chapters demonstrate, the antagonists of the period grappled with the common, vexing question of the *pueblo*, which they regarded alternately as a source of legitimacy, an interlocutor, and an inescapable, if potentially threatening collective agent for change. In spite of their professed ideological differences, these actors conjointly delimited a cultural and political landscape with a stark and apparently unbridgeable frontier that cleaved it in two.

Such notions resonate strongly with political theorist Ernesto Laclau's rethinking of populism. As Laclau first explored in *Politics and Ideology in Marxist Theory* (1977) and developed more fully in *On Populist Reason* (2005), "populism" should not be understood as a particular form or style of government, but rather as a logic intrinsic to all modern politics. He critiques the tendency to identify, often in pejorative fashion, a motley array of political regimes as populist and signals how conventional definitions of the term are built upon an untenable distinction between "empty" rhetoric and action, between saying and doing. Populism, Laclau argues, is an operation employed by a variety of regimes (including those that might never be labeled "populist") articulated on a broad discursive terrain that is not "essentially restricted to the areas of speech and writing, but any complex of elements in which *relations* play the constitutive role."[26] In its most basic sense, populism is "one way of constituting the very unity of the group"; it does not "stand for" or represent a preexisting entity (read "the people"), but posits an equivalence between various demands such that different sectors of a given society may aspire to represent themselves as a totality. This, in turn, creates "a frontier of exclusion [that] divides society into two camps."[27] Populism, then, shapes social relations according to logics of equivalence and difference as a way of asserting the hegemony of a political project.

Understood in this sense, it is neither anachronistic nor teleological to speak of populism with respect to postrevolutionary Latin America. Instead, we might say, the term refers to a specter that has always haunted the liberal state, even before this specter had a name. Laclau's conception of populism, in other words, helps us to survey the common discursive terrain of postrevolutionary Argentina without retracing the frontier marked by civilization and barbarism, or without repeating notions of Argentine exceptionalism vis-à-vis the rest of Latin America. Indeed, given that my expanded corpus demonstrates a collective concern for how to represent, form, and inform the *pueblo*, it becomes apparent that Argentina presents a highly polarized variation of a fundamental political question that precedes any constituted republican power and may ultimately exceed and disrupt it. By scrutinizing shared practices, instead of emphasizing, once again, the opposing positions staked out within a tightly circumscribed cultural field, *Beyond Civilization and Barbarism* demonstrates how the struggle for power in Rosas's Argentina was rhetorically and institutionally modern. In this respect it constitutes a case study and offers a working hypothesis as to how a variety of cultural forms imagined, elicited, and conditioned popular involvement in competing hegemonic projects throughout postindependence Latin America.

To chart the common discursive terrain shaped by the antagonists of postrevolutionary Argentina, each of the four central chapters of *Beyond Civilization and Barbarism* focuses on a specific cultural practice. The first, titled "Writing, Affect, and the Portraiture of Power," centers on paintings, lithographs, and other visual depictions of Juan Manuel de Rosas that circulated during the period, as well as portrayals of the caudillo written by his supporters and opponents. These artifacts demonstrate how his regime conspicuously employed writing as a medium and a symbol of authority. Indeed, while it has long been common to remark on the ubiquity of Rosas's image during his tenure, I argue that this portraiture was not a byproduct or cover for coercion, but an instrument of power in its own right. To do so, I first consider two pro-regime biographies from 1830, Rosas's first full year as governor: Luis Pérez's biographical poem, published in his newspaper *El Gaucho*, and Pedro De Angelis's "Ensayo histórico sobre Rosas" [Historical Essay about Rosas], which appeared in *El Lucero*. Though intended for different audiences, these texts emphasize Rosas's adherence to the political institutions of the fledgling provincial government and the affective bonds he shared with his citizens. While the portraits of Rosas that appear in Sarmiento's *Facundo* and Mármol's *Amalia* predictably vilify him, they nonetheless coincide with the encomiastic texts in underscoring the dictator's savvy for representing popular support. A variety of graphic images of the *Restaurador de las leyes* moreover suggests how the regime conspicuously insisted on the importance of writing in forging affective bonds with a variety of subjects, including the rural poor and the Afro-Argentine population of Buenos Aires.

Chapter 2, "Graffiti, Public Opinion, and the Poetics of Politics," takes as its point of departure the famous scrawl *on ne tue point les idées* [ideas cannot be killed] that begins Sarmiento's canonical *Facundo*. A protest against the Rosas regime, the French phrase is typically regarded as a foundational act of Argentine literature, unintelligible to the ignorant soldiers who discover it. By contrast, I demonstrate how Sarmiento's inscription is, in fact, wholly legible as a gesture in the context of the democratization of public opinion in the 1820s and 1830s. Indeed, I contend that, while the content of the phrase projects erudition, its enunciation mimics popular protests employed by subaltern subjects during this period. After a close reading of this graffiti, as well as other instances in Sarmiento's writings, I then examine a poem written on a wall facing the central plaza of Buenos Aires, commemorating Rosas's assumption of absolute powers in 1835. The written and spoken word played an important role in the civic festivals that the Rosist state began to stage, from this point on, with increasing regularity. These "Argentine graffiti" thus conjointly indicate how writing possessed an iconic power that extended far beyond the reduced circle of literate citizens. At the same time, these inscriptions also reveal how those vying for power did not merely appeal to popular audiences for support, but also were compelled to mimic and appropriate the voice of the *pueblo*.

The third chapter, titled "Visual Culture and the Limits of Representation," surveys a variety of written sources, including journalism, advertisements, memoirs, and personal correspondence to examine the social function of popular audiovisual spectacles, including magic lantern shows, phantasmagoria, and optical cabinets. Drawing on Jonathan Crary's *Techniques of the Observer* (1992), I analyze these practices as both a cultural phenomena and as discursive figures imbued with metaphorical meanings. As in the preceding chapters, I engage in a close reading of texts written by ideological opponents: a series of satirical pieces published in Luis Pérez's newspaper *El Torito de los Muchachos* (1830) and the Uruguayan polymath Andrés Lamas's "Visiones de la óptica" (1838), a precursor of fantastic literature that appeared in a Montevideo newspaper published by exiled dissidents. In both instances, an optical device not only serves as the focal point for a critique of contemporary customs, it also registers the incipient desire and the accompanying anxiety to represent, order, and maintain surveillance over national subjects. As works of Echeverría and Sarmiento attest, these apparatuses appear constantly in the writings of the era, functioning as aporias that signal the constitutive exclusions framing the various, competing images of the nation, omissions that political language and publicity attempt to conceal.

The fourth chapter of this study is called "The Machine in the Pampa, or Writing as Technology." Having examined the common ground of Rosas's Argentina in the preceding chapters, here I reconsider the cultural discourse of modernity that the Generation of 1837 articulated in their now-canonical writings. Collectively the works of Alberdi, Echeverría, and Sarmiento insist on the need to deploy machine power to fill the cultural and economic void of the *desierto*. That is, the commonplace of the empty pampa as the emblematic site of Argentine nationhood is predicated on its imminent overwriting. In their Faustian vision of progress, literature itself becomes itself a technology, a "mode of revealing" (Heidegger) that seeks to establish new social bonds and political affiliations, at that same time that it imagines the conditions for its own obsolescence. In other words, given the impossibility of securing immediate popular support, these *letrados* sought to import and implement the technological means for making a modern *pueblo* that could, in turn, manufacture consent and legitimacy for their civilizing projects.

NOTES

1. Pacho O'Donnell, *La gran epopeya: El combate de la Vuelta de Obligado* (Buenos Aires: Grupo Editorial Norma, 2010); Cristina Fernández de Kirchner, "Palabras de la Presidenta en el acto por el Día de la Soberanía Nacional," accessed May 20, 2013, www.casarosada.gov.ar/discursos/4006.
2. Nicolas Shumway, *The Invention of Argentina* (Berkeley: University of California Press, 1991), 299.
3. Ángel Rama, "Argentina: Crisis de una cultura sistemática," *Inti: Revista de Literatura Hispánica* 1, no. 10 (1979): 52.
4. Diana Taylor, *Disappearing Acts: Spectacles of Gender and Nationalism in Argentina's "Dirty War"* (Durham, N.C.: Duke University Press, 1997), 147.
5. Domingo Faustino Sarmiento, *Facundo: Civilización y barbarie* (Madrid: Alianza, 1988), 42.
6. Adolfo Prieto, *Proyección del rosismo en la literatura argentina; seminario del Instituto de Letras* (Rosario, Argentina: Universidad Nacional del Litoral, 1959), 37.
7. In 1857 Bartolomé Mitre published his *Galería de celebridades argentinas* [Gallery of Argentine Celebreties], a collection of short biographies accompanied by lithographs that sought to establish a pantheon of liberal heroes, including José de San Martín and Juan Lavalle. The volume not only lacks a biography of Rosas, Mitre conspicuously avoids mentioning his name in the introduction. He identifies caudillos such as José Artigas, Facundo Quiroga, José Félix Aldao, and Estanislao López as the type of men who don't warrant inclusion in the volume, because "se presentarán a sus ojos con el resplandor siniestro de aquella soberbia figura de Milton, que pretendía arrastrar en su caída las estrellas del firmamento" [they will appear before one's eyes with the sinister splendor of that haughty figure of Milton, who in his fall tried to pull the stars from the firmament] (3). Rosas, the *interdit*, thus becomes the invisible foil to whom those included are inevitably compared.
8. Diane Quatrrocchi-Woisson, *Un Nationalisme de déracinés: L'Argentine, pays malade de sa mémoire* (Paris: Editions du Centre national de la recherche scientifique, 1992), 44–45.
9. Tulio Halperín Donghi treats this topic at length in *El revisionismo histórico argentino como visión decadentista de la historia nacional* (Buenos Aires: Siglo Veintiuno, 2005).
10. Carlos Alonso, "Civilización y barbarie," *Hispania* 72, no. 2 (1989): 57.
11. Alberto Moreiras, *The Exhaustion of Difference: The Politics of Latin American Cultural Studies* (Durham, N.C.: Duke University Press, 2001), 7.
12. Moreiras, *The Exhaustion of Difference*, 98.
13. This is, in effect, the critique that Abril Trigo levies in his review of *The Exhaustion of Difference*: "es precisamente en su retórica, en su exposición argumental y en su lógica discursiva, donde es preciso analizar críticamente su pensamiento crítico, que en la mejor escuela deconstructivista, pese a declararse contrario a todo tipo de lógica binaria y de sutura epistemológica, opera sobre la base de una sistemática oposición de contrarios y se riza constantemente sobre el rizo del pensar" [it is precisely in its rhetoric, in the exposition of its argument and in discursive logic, where it is necessary to analyze his critical thought critically, which like the best school of deconstructive thought, in spite of declaring itself opposed to any

Introduction

kind of binary logic or epistemological suture, operates according to a systematic opposition of differences and constantly wraps itself up in its own thinking] (1024).

14. I am borrowing the term "indiscipline" from W. J. T. Mitchell, whose uses it to describe the emerging field of visual culture: "[i]f a discipline is a way of insuring the continuity of a set of collective practices (technical, social, professional, etc.), 'indiscipline' is a moment of breakage or rupture, when the continuity is broken and the practice comes into question" ("Interdisciplinarity and Visual Culture," *The Art Bulletin* 4 [1995]: 541).

15. Ernesto Laclau and Chantal Mouffe, *Hegemony and Socialist Strategy: Towards a Radical Democratic Politics* (London: Verso, 2001), 124–25.

16. Juan Manuel de Rosas, *Correspondencia de Juan Manuel de Rosas* (Buenos Aires: Eudeba, 2005), 224; italics added.

17. Rosas, *Correspondencia*, 225.

18. Sarmiento, *Facundo*, 349–50. This is not to suggest that Rosas's opponents denied the fact that the Federalist regime produced a great deal of writing, but simply that it refused to consider them works belonging to the same cultural field as their own. See, for example, "Literatura mashorquera," where Esteban Echeverría admits that "se ha formado también en ese Buenos Aires una literatura de Rosas, y las inteligencias deben seguir el impulso que Rosas quiera darle y moverse en la órbita que les trace" [a pro-Rosas literature has also emerged in Buenos Aires, and those intellects must follow the impulse that Rosas wishes to give it and move in whatever orbit he traces] (*Obras Completas* V, 141).

19. As Beatriz González-Stephan notes, multiple definitions of the term "literature" coexisted in nineteenth-century Spanish America. In its broadest sense, literature was homologous to the printed word. The term "literature" thus came to denote "conocimientos generales, conocimientos pertenecientes al campo de las *humanitas* (historia, filosofía, gramática, geografía, filología, teología, oratoria y bellas letras)" [general knowledge, knowledge relating to the field of humanities (history, philosophy, geography, philology, theology, oratory, and fine arts)] (*Fundaciones: Canon, historia y cultura nacional*, 242). "Literature" also vaguely referred to the "arte de expresarse bien, pero, sobre todo, arte de escribir" [the art of expressing oneself well, but, especially, the art of writing] (243) and, in a more restrictive sense, "los géneros específicamente estéticos, con un consenso generalizado en considerar como prácticas 'estéticas' sólo aquellos discursos en verso" [the specifically aesthetic genres, with a general consensus of considering as "aesthetic" practices only those discourses in verse] (244). Lastly, literary historians defined the field according to its practitioners, in the sense that "estuvo relacionado con la cultura del hombre de letras, el 'hombre culto', aquel que produce letras impresas" [it was related to the culture of the man of letters, the 'cultured man,' that who produced printed works] (244). In practice, these four abstracted models overlapped, mapping an undefined literary field that was based on various forms of exclusion, particularly those of genre and gender.

20. Frank Safford, "Politics, Ideology, and Society in Post-Independence Latin America," in *The Cambridge History of Latin America: From Independence to c. 1870*, vol. 3, ed. Leslie Bethell (Cambridge: Cambridge University Press, 2008), 149.

21. Graciela Montaldo, "La desigualdad de las partes," *A Contracorriente: Revista de Historia Social y Literatura en América Latina* 7, no. 1 (2009):16.

22. Jeremy Adelman, *Republic of Capital: Buenos Aires and the Legal Transformation of the Atlantic World* (Stanford, Calif.: Stanford University Press, 1999), 12.

23. Such studies include Peter Guardino's *The Time of Liberty: Popular Political Culture in Oaxaca, 1750–1850* (Durham, N.C.: Duke University Press, 2005); Cecilia Méndez's *The Plebeian Republic: The Huanta Rebellion and the Making of the Peruvian State, 1820–1850* (Durham, N.C.: Duke University Press, 2005); and Gabriel Di Meglio's *¡Viva el bajo pueblo! La plebe urbana de Buenos Aires y la política entre la Revolución de Mayo y el rosismo (1810–1829)* (Buenos Aires: Prometeo, 2006). Guerra's work includes *Modernidad e independencias: Ensayos sobre las revoluciones hispánicas*.

24. Walter Mignolo, quoted in Moreiras, *The Exhaustion of Difference*, 268.

25. Diana Sorensen, *Facundo and the Construction of Argentine Culture* (Austin: University of Texas Press, 1996), 1.

26. Ernesto Laclau, *On Populist Reason* (London: Verso, 2007), 68.

27. Laclau, *On Populist Reason*, 74, 81.

Chapter One

Writing, Affect, and the Portraiture of Power

> Nada es más difícil, sino imposible, que lograr una perfecta unión entre las grandes masas, a quienes para lo mismo que las agitan sentimientos diversos, debe siempre suponérseles disposiciones opuestas.
>
> [There is nothing more difficult, if not impossible, than to achieve a perfect union among the masses, for much as diverse sentiments agitate them, one must always suppose them to be of opposing inclinations.]
>
> —Juan Manuel de Rosas in a letter to Juan Lavalle, July 14, 1829 [1]

On December 21, 1829, several weeks into his first term as governor, General Juan Manuel de Rosas presided over an elaborate funerary procession through the streets of Buenos Aires. The honored deceased was Rosas's popular Federalist predecessor Manuel Dorrego, who had been executed without trial the previous year in an uprising led by the Unitarian general Juan Lavalle. Once the rebellion had been put down, the provincial legislature decided to exhume Dorrego's body from its grave in the nearby countryside and give him a hero's burial in the Recoleta Cemetery of the capital city. The event, which the newspaper *El Lucero* described as "un espectáculo solemne, esplendido, grandioso [. . .] con una magnificencia jamas vista en esta capital" [a solemn, splendid, grandiose spectacle . . . of a magnificence never before seen in this capital], publicly introduced Rosas to his subjects and staged a symbolic transfer of sovereignty.[2]

If the spectacle was intended to mark the end to more than a decade of political instability and internecine violence following independence from Spain, Dorrego's funeral also signaled the emergence of a fundamental discursive strategy that Rosas and his supporters would employ throughout his lengthy rule. Various elements of the procession and the burial ceremony, as

Figure 1.1. Lithograph of Juan Manuel de Rosas, 1835 (detail) (*Courtesy of Museo Histórico Nacional, Argentina*)

well as the subsequent circulation of printed copies of Rosas's speech, the score of a funeral march composed for the occasion, and illustrations of the events, emphasized a bond connecting the new governor to the multitude that witnessed and participated in the spectacle.[3] Drums had summoned the inhabitants of the city and, according to the eyewitness account of U.S. diplomat John Murray Forbes, nearly the entire population of Buenos Aires watched the parade that included three thousand soldiers and militiamen.[4] At times two Indian chiefs and some fifty beggars pulled the funeral carriage as Rosas accompanied them on horseback, carrying Dorrego's sword.[5] The ceremonies concluded with a brief graveside address, in which Rosas declared that "[l]a mancha más negra en la historia de los argentinos ha sido ya lavada con las lágrimas de un pueblo justo, agradecido y sensible" [the darkest stain on the history of Argentines has now been washed away with the tears of a just, grateful, and sensitive people].[6] Even as the governor "arrogated to himself and personified the symbols of power," his discourse identified the people as the ultimate agent responsible for exacting justice and restoring the peace.[7] Through its outward expression of collective grief, the *pueblo* lays the ghost of Dorrego to rest and elects Rosas as his legitimate successor, prior to any formal legislative act. As part of an orchestrated series of civic rituals, the speech thus posits an indissociable link between state authority and the image of a "just, grateful, and sensitive people."

While frequent patriotic festivals provided a venue for dramatic and participatory representations of loyalty to the Federalist regime, written and graphic depictions of Rosas provided the principal means for disseminating his image and reasserting the link between caudillo and *pueblo* in everyday life, especially as his public appearances became scarce.[8] As José Mármol commented in 1851, the visage of the dictator "se encuentra en los salones y en las barberías, en la moneda, en las cintas, en los abanicos, a todos precios, y en un centenar de grabados diferentes" [is to be found in living rooms and barbershops, on coins, on ribbons, on fans, at any price, and in hundreds of different engravings].[9] Written portrayals that circulated in the pro-regime press complemented the proliferation of visual images; Esteban Echeverría, for example, protested that the newspaper *Archivo Americano* (1843–1851) constituted "una biografía continua, inagotable, del Restaurador, de ese hombre prodigioso" [a continuous, inexhaustible biography of the Restorer, of that prodigious man].[10] The caudillo himself insisted on the utility of both the written word and the dissemination of his likeness. Far from Buenos Aires, fighting indigenous populations during his interregnum in 1833, Rosas wrote to Felipe Arana and instructed him to have friends and associates enclose current issues of "periódicos de los nuestros" [newspapers of our side] with letters to their relatives on the campaign. He promises Arana that his wife and sister-in-law will do the same with the mothers of free Afro-Argentine soldiers and adds that "[a] esta clase de gente les gustan los versos, y también les ha de agradar el restaurador con el retrato" [this class of people likes verses, and portraits of the restorer will also be pleasing to them].[11] The anecdotal evidence points to a prolific discursive production, a portraiture of power that conveys a crucial relational aspect of the legitimizing strategies employed by the Rosas regime. Printed, painted, and impressed on countless surfaces, circulated freely or as an object of commerce, and displayed in various settings, ceremonial and quotidian, public and private, the composite text of voice, writing, and graphic images helped construct the social networks that sustained Rosas's power throughout the province of Buenos Aires and beyond.

Remarks about the ubiquity of Rosas's likeness, such as those of Mármol and Echeverría, have long been commonplace in histories of mid-nineteenth-century Argentina but treat these images as merely reflective of and ancillary to politics. By contrast, this chapter insists on the transitive dimension of textual and graphic depictions of Rosas, building upon recent studies that have shed light on the complex mechanisms informing the exercise of power in postrevolutionary Spanish America. I contend that the reproduction of Rosas's likeness was a crucial instrument of his regime's hegemony because it represented and helped constitute an affective bond that connected Rosas to the pueblo, the leader to his source of legitimacy. In this respect, the specter of populism that has long been associated with Rosas is not to be dispelled, but, per Ernesto Laclau's rethinking of the term, reconsidered as a modern political logic intrinsic to his rule. By virtue of its incessant circulation and numerous variations, Rosas's public image was the primary discursive figure that allowed his regime to address and resolve the "diverse sentiments" of new social actors in order to imagine "a perfect union among the masses," to borrow from Rosas's letter to his adversary Juan Lavalle.

As constituted through multiple portrayals, the figure of Rosas possesses a series of attributes that continue to inform collective memory. Whether in gaucho attire or a formal military uniform, he appears as a *primus inter pares*, a first among peers, a *patrón* whose authority stems from the common attributes he shares and the effect he cultivates with loyal subjects. Indeed, it is precisely Rosas's capacity to channel popular opinion—as well as a trenchant disregard for intellectual activity—that are grounded by two very different biographies published in 1830, Rosas's first full year as governor: Luis Pérez's biographical poem, written in a stylized rural vernacular, and Pedro De Angelis's essay, addressed to the literate elite of the capital city. While these two texts seek to subordinate their own medium to Rosas's deeds, the dissident intellectuals José Mármol and Domingo Faustino Sarmiento look to discredit the *Restaurador* in their works precisely by calling attention to how the manipulation of discourse is a central mechanism of his power. Ironically, though, these hostile depictions are consistent with a series of rarely studied pro-regime portraits that, by adapting a preexisting iconography of republican power, emphasize their subject's mastery of the written word. Moreover, as other contemporary artifacts indicate, Rosas's supporters brandished writing itself as an instrument of affect, not only as a medium or surrogate, but as a physical manifestation of their leader's authority. In synthesis, through writings about the caudillo and images of the caudillo writing, in the intersection of text and picture, a more nuanced portrait of Juan Manuel de Rosas's power becomes apparent. The figure that emerges from this analysis less sketches the defining features of its nominal subject, than it stages the constitutive relations of Rosist hegemony.

THE HISTORICAL TREATMENT OF ROSIST ICONOGRAPHY AND THE SPECTER OF POPULISM

For the so-called official history that accompanied the rise of the liberal state in the final decades of the nineteenth century, Rosas's portraits provided ample, if redundant evidence of despotism grounded in archaic forms of power. The most commonly cited example this abundant iconography is the likeness of the *Restaurador* displayed in the churches of Buenos Aires, apparent proof of an idolatry steeped in the prerevolutionary closeness between the church and the Spanish crown. Cataloguing other artifacts merely confirms the basic propagandistic function of portraiture. For example, "La iconografía de Rosas" ["The Iconography of Rosas"], a 1905 article published in the illustrated magazine *Caras y caretas*, summarizes its presentation of eighteen different images of Rosas by stating that "[e]sta gran variedad de retratos, medallas y cuños con la efigie del Restaurador, y leyendas donde se le ensalzaba como héroe y padre de la patria, ponen de manifiesto el terror que había logrado inspirar al pueblo por el gobernado[r] y demuestra palmariamente el estado de postración à que había llegado el pueblo de la república" [this great variety of portraits, medals, and coins with the likeness of the Restorer, and legends that held him up as a hero and father of the patria, make manifest the terror that was instilled in the people by the governor and demonstrate in exemplary fashion the state of prostration to which the people of the republic had been reduced].[12] Image and text, in other words, reiterate a single, base emotional response produced through the prior subjugation of its audience. Similarly, in *Rosas y su tiempo* (1907), José María Ramos Mejía examines a series of lithographs, paintings, and articles of clothing bearing Rosas's image before concluding that "[a]unque eficaz, la mitología del terror no fué, sin embargo, fecunda en sus variaciones y formas . . . sus recursos parecían limitados y, hasta cierto punto, vulgares" [though effective, the mythology of terror was not, however, fertile in its forms and variations . . . its techniques seemed limited and, to a certain point, vulgar].[13] Having provided verbal descriptions of what he promises is but a small sampling of a vast repertoire, Ramos Mejía stresses the banality of the regime's self-image, a crude aesthetic that is always derivative of other techniques of terror. If this vast iconography has "para la historia política, el valor de un verdadero documento escrito" [for political history, the value of a true written document],[14] the composite text confirms, time and time again, the preestablished hypothesis that Rosas's power was "simply the effect or the continuation of a relationship of domination."[15] As such, the traditional reading of Rosas's image operates according to the notion that his power was grounded in the subordination of discourse to action, of representation to force. Consequently the regime's iconography has little intrinsic value and would warrant no further scrutiny.

Throughout much of the twentieth century, so-called revisionist historians contested the official historiography that cast Rosas as a despot, but in doing so they did not upend the binary logic underpinning this image: Rosas may have been a man of his word, but he was first and foremost a man of action. Indeed, much as a previous generation had consecrated the works of Rosas's opponents as foundational texts of the national literary canon, revisionists deployed the anachronistic conception of an autonomous aesthetic sphere in defense of the regime. No longer seen as mere agitprop, the various depictions of Rosas became pioneering examples of national culture, proof that "no se limita a las artes plásticas: la música, el teatro, las ciencias y las letras alcanzan, entre 1830 y 1852, un considerable y jamás desechable desarrollo" [this was not limited to plastic arts: music, theater, the sciences, and letters attain, between 1830 and 1852, a considerable development that can never be disregarded].[16] There is in this respect an affinity shared by revisionism and the official history it challenged: whether dismissed as propaganda or elevated to the status of art, the representations of the caudillo reflect a political culture they did not substantially inform. Thus, while the figure of Rosas emerged in the twentieth century "dans la relation entre un homme acclamé par la foule et cette foule elle-même" [in the relation between a man acclaimed by the masses and those masses themselves] and onto which adversaries transposed their respective ideological positions, the depictions of Rosas produced during his rule only evidence a stable, predetermined relationship between caudillo and crowd.[17]

The pervasiveness of this notion can be detected in John Lynch's influential biography *Argentine Dictator: Juan Manuel De Rosas, 1829–1852* (1981) and the condensed profile of the *Restaurador de las leyes* in his later *Caudillos in Spanish America 1800–1850* (1992), two works that seek to explain the lasting presence of Rosas's figure in Argentine society from a position outside of national polemics. In this portrayal, the empty rhetoric of Rosist discourse acquires a proleptic function:

> [Rosas] anticipated the populist dictators of a later age, treating Argentines with that peculiar mixture of concern and contempt which was pure *rosismo*. Rosas had a talent for manipulating popular discontents and turning them against his enemies in such a way that they did not damage the basic structure of society. By such a skillful exhibition of demagogy and nationalism he was able to give an illusion of popular participation and create a sense of identity between *patrón* and peon. (*Caudillos in Spanish America*, 252)

Lynch's Rosas presides over an extensive clientelist system that operates independent of an illusory discourse of popular support. It follows, then, that the image of the people is merely an aftereffect, a plebian noise that does not disrupt the status quo because its various "discontents" remain singular and isolated enunciations.[18] What is populist about *rosismo*, and hence, what is most modern, is its treatment of the people, but this treatment is unsubstantial. In this respect, Lynch validates the tendency to associate Rosas with twentieth-century populists such as Yrigoyen and Perón, but qualifies the affinity by restricting it to a rhetorical dimension.

In other words, all its verbiage disguises the "essential bond" of Rosist power, which consists of "[t]he relation of a patron and client . . . based upon a personal exchange of assets between these unequal partners."[19] Rosas thus differs from twentieth-century populists because of his unbending conservatism: "[i]n spite of his overt populism, he stood for the preservation of the traditional social structure in its entirety"; or, while the regime indeed "had a popular base, it did not have populist objectives of any capacity for changing the social structure and redistributing wealth."[20] The play of differences that cleaves Rosas to twentieth-century leaders depends on a conception of "populism" that Lynch never explicitly defines. It would seem to be, roughly, a political system led by a charismatic, personalist ruler who employs manipulative, empty rhetoric to secure popular support in order to bring about a radical restructuring of the state. Paradoxically, then, the discursive operation by which the regime fashions its self-image is the thing that most strongly links Rosas to the populists he prefigures, but this dimension of his ruling style occludes a larger legacy of authoritarianism.

Over the past two decades historians have called into question the strong linkage between caudillo power and clientelism, a thesis that first gained traction in the North American and European academe during the 1960s. As Noemí Goldman and Ricardo Salvatore summarize in their introduction to *Caudillismos rioplatenses: Nuevas miradas a un viejo problema* (1997), recent scholarship has critiqued the reduction of postrevolutionary society to a network of client-patron relationships and the formula that caudillismo emerged as the result of a weak state apparatus, the general use of violence in disputes, and the dominance of a landowning class.[21] By focusing on specific contexts (including Artigas in Uruguay and the Argentine littoral, Facundo Quiroga and el Chacho Peñaloza in La Rioja, and, above all, Rosas in Buenos Aires) and themes such as finances, elections, political language, and civic rituals, these studies collectively demonstrate how, beyond the familiar mechanisms of favors, coercion, and manipulation, the maintenance of caudillo power also depended on reciprocal relations with a variety of social actors and by employing (and hence, reshaping and reinforcing) a precarious republican institutional order established in the years following independence from Spain. However, in calling attention to the rational and procedural aspects of this process, recent studies have tended to push aside the psychological and affective dimensions that concerned earlier studies of the postrevolutionary period. It is thus unsurprising that current nineteenth-century studies have paid little attention to iconography, particularly given its past use as evidence of Rosas's despotism.[22]

For a clearer sense of how the reconceptualization of caudillo power deconstructs the image of Rosas in traditional historiography (which in turn, signals the need to reexamine Rosist iconography), let us briefly consider Marcela Ternavasio's exemplary "Hacia un régimen de la unanimidad: Política y elecciones en Buenos Aires, 1828–1850" [Toward a Regime of Unanimity: Politics and Elections in Buenos Aires, 1828–1850]. In this essay Ternavasio demonstrates how Rosas and his supporters organized elections for members of the provincial House of Representatives as well as annual plebiscites that the regime used after 1835 to ensure the continuation of Rosas's mandate with absolute powers. Mobilizing new sectors to vote, a practice that their Unitarian opponents had instituted during the 1820s, the government retained suffrage as a principal means of legitimation, though did so by imposing a single list of candidates.[23] Officials at all levels, from Rosas himself to the low-level rural authorities known as *jueces de paz*, were involved in devising, printing, and distributing ballots, as well as ensuring the participation of citizens, "a efecto de que sea más numerosa la votación según corresponde a un asunto de tan elevada importancia" [so that the voting turnout is higher as is appropriate for a matter of such great importance], as an official memorandum from Rosas reminded local officials.[24] There existed, in other words, a coordinated process by which the regime adapted preexisting (but postrevolutionary) customs and a legal framework to produce—and reproduce—an image of widespread popular support. A host of formalized, informal, and even festive practices signals a not only a consistency between action and discourse, but, moreover, the unequivocally modern nature of this process.[25]

The investigations by Ternavasio, as well as those of Myers, Salvatore, Goldman, Bernaldo González, and others, make it apparent that the Rosas regime established, maintained, and modified its hegemony through a relation of forces that exceeded simple dominance. The immediate circumstance of his rise to power was not the disappearance of a remote, absolute authority (the Spanish crown), but rather the resulting struggles that pitted different local factions against one another (*unitarios* and *federalistas*) and, eventually, divided the latter party into *federalistas doctrinarios* and Rosas's camp, known as *federalistas netos*. In simultaneously fulfilling the roles of "apaciguador y representante de las masas que han irrumpido en la política" [pacifier and representative of the masses that had burst into politics],[26] Rosas resolved the demands of competing groups to the forge the image of "una perfecta unión entre las grandes masas" [a perfect union among the masses].[27] Through the figure of its leader, the regime asserted a lasting claim to popular sovereignty by employing a malleable image of a *pueblo*, a composite of social actors who had "burst into politics" at the beginning of the nineteenth century, including the rural poor, the sizeable Afro-Argentine population of the city, and women. To draw on Jacques Rancière's terminology, the regime inscribed within public discourse different parts of society who previously had no part, factions formerly excluded from the count of the state.[28] As such, elections, civic rituals, republican ideals, the scrutiny of everyday habits and dress, and, as we will argue, written and graphic portraiture did not simply repeat, reflect, or, inversely, conceal the exercise of force, but instead conditioned its usage within a precarious institutional order, effecting a shift in which "el sentido de la nación se desplaza furtivamente del Estado a la sociedad; desplazamiento semántico que coloca la sociedad y la representación que de ella se da en el corazón de las apuestas del poder" [the meaning of the nation was furtively displaced from the State to society; a semantic displacement which located society and its representation at the core of the struggles for power].[29]

The recent contributions of social and intellectual history thus suggest that the Rosas regime was not populist simply by virtue of its manipulation of the masses or vague, empty rhetoric, but because its discursive output endeavored to identify as the people as "a partial component which nevertheless aspires to be conceived as the only legitimate totality."[30] In other words, *rosismo* was populist in a more expansive and foundational sense: as the political theorist Ernesto Laclau defines the term, populism is a discursive act that is not inherent to a specific style or form of governance or leadership, but "an ontological condition of the political."[31] Seen from this perspective, the organization of elections and the subsequent dissemination of their results, always overwhelmingly in favor of Rosas, exemplify the operation by which a part of society comes to stand for the whole, thus rendering the different demands of voters equivalent. Rosas becomes the empty signifier that allows the *pueblo* to be named. That is, Rosas's figure (graphic and rhetorical) condenses a multiplicity and forms from it a singular, if contingent political identity.

If the handful of votes cast in opposition clearly posed no serious challenge to the prolongation of Rosas's mandate, they nonetheless served as a reminder of a fundamental idea held in common by friends and enemies of the regime: society remain starkly divided into two opposing camps. This partition illustrates the maintenance of "antagonistic frontiers within the social," the presence of an otherness that is at once threatening and necessary. Recent scholarship, looking beyond the familiar division of loyal Federalists and savage Unitarians (or, inversely, civilization and barbarism), stresses the logic of equivalence that in turn requires the exclusion of an internal other.[32] That is to say, the people did not exist in Rosist discourse as an undifferentiated or amorphous mass, but as the nodal point of an ensemble of relations; or, in Homi K. Bhabha's terms, "the people are neither the beginning nor the end of the national narrative; they represent the cutting edge between the totalizing powers of the 'social' as homogenous, consensual community, and the forces that signify the more specific address to contentious, unequal interests and identities within the population."[33]

According to Laclau, however, the play between logics of equivalence and difference is alone incapable of making a partial component of society stand as its whole. Indeed, as Laclau argues, "the complexes which we call 'discursive or hegemonic formations' . . . would be unintelligible without the affective component."[34] There is nothing intrinsic to language that explains why one particular component or another serves as the image of a legitimate totality; something in excess of language—but which is inseparable from it—ensures a "radical investment" that accounts for the force of a particular hegemonic relation.[35] In this respect it is clear that Laclau employs the term in a way that is distinct from theories that presuppose the autonomy of affect, as a kind of emotional intensity that "escapes confinement in the body whose vitality, or potential for interaction, it is."[36] Whatever its liberating potential may be, the "differential cathexes" that make affect manifest in discourse can be channeled and accumulated through and among various bodies, individual, corporate, political, and otherwise. For this reason Laclau argues that affect plays a fundamental role in the formation of the people from a partial object. Love, hatred, admiration, fear, and terror permit an assemblage of demands to coalesce around a particular figure, such as a charismatic leader. Affect does not follow power relations as a residual effect, as the traditional explanations of Rosas's dominance would have it. It is indispensable in constituting a people and, hence, helps shape the "internal antagonistic frontier separating the 'people' from power" that is a *sine qua non* of the political.[37]

Laclau's theory of populism, beyond justifying the persistence of an anachronistic label, provides a theoretical framework to analyze how the image of Rosas informs the hegemony of his regime. In concert with the other mechanisms of power, the written and graphic representations of the *Restaurador de las leyes* depict, often in didactic fashion, "differential cathexes"; that is, these texts register efforts by the regime and its supporters to organize the emotional intensities that gave shape and force to the affinities and antagonistic relations among social actors. In this respect, while Rosas is central figure of this corpus, its ultimate subject is the relation between leader and people. Depicted as a *primus inter pares*, Rosas stands in relation to an ideal collective as both a paternalistic figure and an equal, a fellow citizen whose dominance of the social order paradoxically depends on his demonstrative subjection to it. In other words, these depictions do not solely represent devotion to the leader, but instead stress common positive attributes that bind the caudillo and the pueblo, setting them apart from an internal opposition that threatens the constituted order.

ROSAS IN WRITING: TWO PRO-REGIME BIOGRAPHIES FROM 1830

Particularly in the first years of his mandate, print media played a significant role in the dissemination of the figure of Rosas. During his rise to power in 1829 and 1830 and again during the interregnum of 1833–1834, there appeared a spate of periodicals that sought to gain adhesion to Rosas by appealing to multiple sectors of society. That is, precisely in moments of unrest and despite the paucity of presses and printing materials, supporters of Rosas went to great lengths to disseminate their ideas to a broad and varied audience. In this context Luis Pérez published over thirty short-lived publications, including *El Gaucho, La Gaucha, El Negrito, La Negrita,* and *El Toro de Once.* Written typically in rhyming, metered verse and imitating the speech of the various audiences identified in their titles, these extra-official newspapers were intended to be read aloud and sung in public settings and sought to inspire fervent demonstrations of loyalty to the *Restaurador de las leyes.*[38] On July 31, 1830, the first number of Pérez's *El Gaucho* included the opening section of a biographical poem of Rosas. A few weeks later, the Neapolitan intellectual Pedro De Angelis published in his newspaper *El Lucero* an encomiastic "Ensayo histórico sobre Rosas," whose refined language was directed to the literate minority of the capital. Despite significant differences in structure and point of view, these two texts sketch the salient features of a prototypical image of Rosas. The figure that emerges is that of a skilled *estanciero* [rancher], whose rapport with his subjects and deep reverence for existing political institutions make him the ideal leader for the Argentine Confederation. These biographies also articulate a marked anti-intellectual attitude, a discourse against discourse, which values experience and action over theoretical thinking and anticipates the censorship and hostility toward letters and *letrados* that intensified during Rosas's second mandate.

Narrated in a rural vernacular by a literate gaucho named Pancho Lugares, Luis Pérez's biographical poem presents a Juan Manuel de Rosas who directly dialogues with his peons and soldiers, as well as with generals and heads of state. The poem appeared in installments over the course of the first forty numbers of *El Gaucho,* between August 7 and December 15, 1830, and consists of three parts: a testimonial of the narrator Pancho Lugares's first-hand encounters with Rosas; then, perhaps in response to the appearance of De Angelis's biography, a brief dialogue in which Panta the *nutriero,* or trapper, convinces Lugares to begin his story anew, taking into account that "algunas cosas / Me parece que has dejado" [some things / it seems to me you have left out];[39] and, finally, a longer, more impersonal narrative that roughly parallels De Angelis's text.[40] The first section of the poem is less an account of Rosas than it is an autobiography of Pancho Lugares, the *gacetero gaucho*. Gazetteer, and not *payador* or singer, because no sooner than he identifies his parentage and place of origin, Lugares boasts that "En el monte apredí á lér / Por mandato de mis padres. / Y supe lér y escribir, / Luego que cumplí doce años" [In the country I learned to read / as demanded my parents. / And I learned to read and write, / by the time I turned twelve].[41] The irregular spelling calls attention to the fact that in gauchesque literature the printed text was often "un mero mediador entre un modo de producción que, aunque manejando la escritura, trabajaba sobre órdenes orales, y un modo de difusión que se haría también oralmente mediante cantos o recitados antes los públicos analfabetos" [a mere mediator between a mode of production that, though employing writing, followed the dictates of speech, and a mode of dissemination that would also take place orally, whether sung or recited for illiterate audiences].[42] If, as Josefina Ludmer suggests, the gauchesque is "la alianza entre una voz oída y una palabra escrita" [an alliance between a heard voice and a written word],[43] Lugares functions as a fictional intermediary connecting the illiterate inhabitants of the countryside to Rosas himself. In the context of *El Gaucho*, this function extends to an even broader range of subjects: in "La lira de los negros," the Afro-Argentine Catalina, another recurring character in the newspaper, requests "Hacemi favol, ño Pancho, / De esplical mi tu papeli, / Polque yo soy bosalona / Y no puedo entendeli" [Do me the favor, Mr. Pancho, / Of explaining to me your paper / Because I'm dimwitted / And can't understand it].[44] The *gacetero* mediates between men and women, country and city, the literate and the illiterate and, in doing so, offers instructions on how to use newspapers.[45] Pérez's publications seek to form alliances between diverse sectors of society, at the same time that the distinct forms of address reinforce group identities, thus setting difference and equivalence into play.

The most notable subject with whom Lugares dialogues is of course Rosas himself. Immediately after boasting of his mastery of the written word, Lugares recounts the principal events of his life. Having worked as a horse tamer on one of Rosas's *estancias*, he is involuntarily conscripted and sent to fight in the war against Brazil, deserts, and eventually joins Rosas's militia. The details of his life, stock elements of gauchesque literature, acquire significance through his contact with the *Restaurador*, first as a peon and later as a militiaman. During Lavalle's 1828 uprising, Rosas personally requests that Lugares reconnoiter the movements of the ill-fated Dorrego and his troops. Displeased to learn that Dorrego remains nearby, Rosas insists that "usté, ñor Pancho, / Se ha de haber equivocado, / No ha de ser de nuestra gente / Con la que usté se ha topado" [you, Mr. Pancho, / Must be mistaken, / That can't be our people / That you've run into]. The sight of Dorrego's troops, however, confirms Lugares's observations and the gaucho recalls that "Velay lo tiene, Señor, / Le dije a D. JUAN MANUEL" [There you have it, Sir / I said to D. JUAN MANUEL].[46] The exchange not only foregrounds the presence of the narrator in the episode, but also presents a Rosas who is fallible, but ultimately willing to listen to Lugares. Rosas thus appears at the height of Lavalle's treason—in the midst of a losing battle—as engaging in a frank conversation with one of his subordinates.

A shift from singular to plural first-person narration after Panta the trapper's interruption broadens the scope of the poem as it follows Rosas from his formative rural upbringing to the moment of Lavalle's invasion of Santa Fe in 1829, when the poem abruptly concludes. This much longer section of the poem, appearing in installments over twenty-six issues of *El Gaucho*, recounts many of the same events of the earlier, autobiographical section, but shifts its focus to encounters between Rosas and a succession of embattled leaders who seek his advice, his diplomatic skills, and the support of his well-organized militia. While the distance between the speaker and the events narrated increases, there remains a tone of intimacy, as Lugares affectionately refers to Rosas as *el Viejo* and *el Rubio*, and reminds the reader that "Todo gaucho lo quería" [Every gaucho loved him].[47] Rosas's own voice frequently interrupts Lugares's narrative, often to declare fealty to the government of the moment: in 1820 he tells the Cabildo that "Soy un simple ciudadano; / Estoy a punto de obedecer / Como fiel americano" [I am a simple citizen; / I am on the verge of obeying / As a faithful American]. The legislators' response is immediate and unanimous, and no less emotional, as "al momento / Los ojos se le empaparon; / Y los cabildantes todos / Se tocaron y lloraron" [at the same time / his eyes filled with tears / And all the councilmen present / touched one another and cried].[48] Later, when the governor Martín Rodríguez is threatened, Rosas rushes to his aid and professes, "Si la junta lo ha nombrado, / Su nombramiento es legal / Y es mi deber respetarlo" [If the junta has named him / his appointment is legal / And it is my duty to respect it].[49] He repeatedly demonstrates a deep sense of obligation to a threatened government that he believes to be an authentic expression of popular will. The poem repeats this basic sequence of events each time a political crisis occurs: in response to a maverick political faction, Rosas organizes his peons into a militia and reluctantly departs from his beloved estancia; no sooner than the crisis is resolved, he returns once again to his lands. Rosas intervenes to suppress the periodic threats to the government and, in doing so, secures the same kind of admiration and affection that he has long enjoyed among the inhabitants of his properties.

The definitive proof of Rosas's allegiances comes in 1828, when he condemns Lavalle's uprising against the governor Dorrego. Much as he earlier predicts Bernadino Rivadavia's resignation ("al fin sentirán / Que el pueblo hace resistencia / Y *Rivadavia* por sí / *Dejará la presidencia*" [in the end they will sense / that the people resist / and *Rivadavia* on his own / *Will abandon the presidency*][50]), Rosas argues with his adversary and friend La Madrid that Lavalle has ignored popular will and, in doing so, will soon fall from power:

> Compadre, usté está engañado,
> La opinión no puede ser
> Quien a *Dorrego* ha quitado.
>
> Si ella estaba pronunciada
> De un modo tan general,
> De un motín escandaloso
> No tuvo necesidad.
>
> Uste bien conocerá
> Que un gobierno aborrecido
> Con facilidad se quita
> Y no es necesario ruido.
>
> Pero esto no es cierto, amigo,
> No hay tal aborrecimiento;
> Usté lo conocerá
> Sin que pase mucho tiempo.
> (*El Torito*, 33)
>
> [My friend, you are mistaken,
> It cannot be [public] opinion
> That has removed Dorrego.
>
> If it had been pronounced
> In such a general fashion,
> For such a scandalous mutiny
> There would be no need.
>
> You must know well
> That a detested government
> Is removed with ease
> And noise is not necessary.
>
> But this [opinion] is untrue, my friend,
> There is no such hatred;
> You will recognize this
> Before much time passes.]

Rosas identifies the pueblo as the agent responsible for effecting a transfer of power and insists that the existing state must respond to spontaneous demands from below. His exchange with La Madrid draws a sharp contrast between public opinion, which is "pronounced" as a readily intelligible, unified voice, and mutinous, meaningless noise, seemingly uttered by no one. He moreover links legitimate popular demands to affect—in this case, hatred—presupposing that it is manifest in such pronouncements. Accordingly, what threatens the state is not the emergence of the pueblo as a political actor, but a feckless class of political leaders, an elite that is incapable of resolving its own internal conflicts. Of course, in predicting the eventual collapse of Rivadavia and Lavalle's governments, the Rosas of *El Gaucho* is a keen interpreter of public will and, in effect, predicts his own ascent to the governorship of Buenos Aires. To extend the logic of Pérez's poem to the events surrounding the publication of *El Gaucho* in 1830, Rosas's assumption of extraordinary powers resolves a political crisis by placing the state in direct dialogue with the people, preempting the legislative body (and the elite that comprise it) responsible for granting these powers; caudillo and pueblo support one another reciprocally.

While the hero of Pérez's poem insists on the autonomous and constructive nature of public opinion, the Rosas of Pedro De Angelis's "Ensayo histórico" maintains public order by virtue of his ability to secure the loyalty of potentially rebellious masses. Following a brief history of Rosas's ancestors, De Angelis recounts Rosas's youth spent in the countryside as a result of the turmoil caused by the Revolution, an event that "hizo que los esclavos fuesen menos dóciles a la voz de sus amos" [made the slaves less docile in response to their masters' voices].[51] The period proved formative for the young Juan Manuel, who quickly displayed acumen for both hard manual labor and the administrative duties of his family's estancias, and soon became widely respected. This high regard was especially conspicuous "[e]n medio del espíritu de insubordinación que se había manifestado en todas las clases, por la insuficiencia de las leyes [y] la debilidad o tolerancia de los magistrados" [in the midst of a spirit of insubordination that had manifested itself in all classes, due to the inadequacy of the laws, and the weakness or tolerance of the magistrates].[52] The orderliness of the Rosas' estancias contrasts with the widening disorder of postrevolutionary society. Absent any meaningful figure of authority, social classes are left to their own devices and tend toward disintegration and chaos.

Yet like Luis Pérez, De Angelis ultimately attributes the weakness of the state to its ruling elite, one which fails to comprehend and control the general populace; insubordination is, in other words, not a cause but an effect of the failure of leadership. At the root of a state crisis is neither the absence of a legal framework nor the lack of its enforcement, but a disconnect between rulers and citizens. It is for this reason that Juan Manuel de Rosas emerges as the sole reputable, if unofficial, authority in the province of Buenos Aires:

> Desde que se había resuelto a vivir en sus tierras, había sentido la necesidad de granjearse el afecto de los habitantes del campo, sobre los cuales había tomado cierto ascendiente, participando en sus trabajos, mezclándose en sus diver-

siones, auxiliándoles en sus desgracias; mostrándose, en fin, justo, humano y compasivo con todos. (*Acusación y defensa de Rosas*, 193)

[Since he has resolved to live on his lands, he felt the need to cultivate the affection of the inhabitants of the countryside, over whom he had assumed a certain influence, participating in their work, mixing with them in their diversions, assisting them in their misfortunes; showing himself to be, in short, just, humane, and compassionate with all.]

Upbraiding the customs of at least a portion of the intended audience of *El Lucero* (the literate minority of the capital), De Angelis attributes Rosas's superiority to his ability to roll up his sleeves and associate with various elements of rural society in labor, leisure, and moments of adversity. It is through the resulting emotional bonds that Rosas can administer his estancia and organize militia forces effectively and, by extension, the nation. Affect, then, is a distinguishing feature of Rosas's authority, which ensures a social cohesion that gives written law its binding force. De Angelis further emphasizes that Rosas's continued popularity is due to "beneficios, a que los individuos corresponden a veces con gratitud, pero que los pueblos olvidan difícilmente" [benefits that individuals sometimes repay with gratitude, but which peoples forget with difficulty].[53] These benefits, then, cannot be reduced to purely economic terms (as per the clientist hypothesis), nor to the sum of the numerous good deeds to which the "Ensayo histórico" alludes. This is underscored by the detached narrative style of De Angelis's text, which never pauses to offer anecdotal evidence of individual encounters with its subjects, in the way Pérez's poem does.[54] The acts that pueblos cannot easily forget are not discrete, individual instances but the aggregate representation of such events; these can be recounted, but not counted in a quantifiable sense. Which is to say, it is through the cultivation of affect that the experience of the different pueblos has been rendered equivalent, in that they remain equally and mutually indebted to the countless *beneficios* and their consequences, those "innumerables . . . ejemplos que podríamos citar de los que volvieron a la buena senda, por los paternales cuidados del señor Rosas" [countless . . . examples that would could reference of those restored to the good path, thanks to the paternal attentions of señor Rosas].[55] Rosas's acts of paternalism are as effective (and affective) as compressed and transmitted through narrative as they are individually, if not more so.

Though in possession of a unique authority, the Rosas of De Angelis's "Ensayo histórico" also refuses to assert his charismatic power to circumvent the established institutional framework, even in a moment of crisis. During Lavalle's uprising in 1828, for example, Rosas "tuvo el dolor de saber del mismo señor Dorrego que sus tristes pensamientos se habían realizado, y que ya no quedaba más apoyo al gobierno legítimo que su espada, la cooperación del señor Rosas y la fidelidad de los milicianos" [was pained to learn from

Dorrego himself that his fears had come true, and that the legitimate government had no more support than his sword, Rosas's cooperation, and the loyalty of the militias].[56] The caudillo becomes the confidant of the man whom he will replace within a year and learns of how Dorrego foresees his own downfall. Despite the dire situation, Rosas maintains his unflinching fidelity to the state; as the enumeration of Dorrego's remaining sources of support emphasizes, Rosas stands beside a now-empty symbol of power without seizing it, the very sword that he will dramatically bear in Dorrego's funeral procession upon assuming the governorship. The contiguity between symbolic authority, an obedient civilian (here he is "el señor Rosas"), and a loyal militia (in opposition to the standing army in revolt) suggests a preordained, if unofficial transfer of power, one that is but postponed by Lavalle's treason. Linked by a conjunction, Rosas's cooperation and the militiamen's fidelity appear, respectively, as individual and collective expressions of the same basic adherence to the "gobierno legítimo."

While Pérez and De Angelis differ substantially in their representation of the people, they coincide with regards to the question of intellectual activity. In both texts, Rosas acquires his knowledge of the land and its people through personal experience, from laboring as a youth alongside the workers of his estancias. As Pérez has it, his superior intellect is wholly organic, derived from manual labor and explicitly divorced from the act of writing: "La esperiencia lo jue haciendo / Mas singular cada día; / Y así a los veinte y cinco años / Todo trabajo entendía . . . De plumario no digamos / Por que era el ilustrao del pago, / y ansi todos a el no más / Venian a consultarlo" [His experience was making him / More unique each day; / And so, by the age of twenty-five / He understood every job / . . . Let's not call him a penpusher / Because he was the enlightened man of the country, / and he was the only one / everyone would come to consult].[57] In similar fashion, De Angelis attributes Rosas's intellectual capacity to years of physical toil: "Don Juan Manuel . . . pasó sus primeros años en las faenas del campo, que contribuyeron a robustecerlo; y este desarrollo precoz de sus fuerzas físicas despertó también su inteligencia" [Don Juan Manuel . . . spent his first years in the tasks of the countryside, which contributed to strengthening him; and this precocious development of his physical abilities also awoke his intelligence].[58] As a result of this unsentimental education, Rosas develops a disdain for men of letters and their theories. Not surprisingly, of the two texts, Pérez's poem is more direct, as Rosas confides in his peons and frequently shares with them his outspoken opinions:

>De los *sabios* de la Tierra
>Guena opinión no tenía;
>*Estos no tienen acierto,*
>Siempre a solas nos decía.

> Estos nos han de enredar
> Con sus malditas teorías:
> Y si no, tenga espera
> Y lo verán algún día.
> (*El Torito*, 23)
>
> [Of the *wise men* of the Earth
> A good opinion he did not have;
> *These don't have all the answers*,
> He would always say to us alone.
>
> These are going to mix us up
> With their damned theories:
> And if not, just wait,
> And you'll see one day.]

These words, uttered between chores in the field, posit a total separation between the local reality and the "wise men of earth," whose confusing theories nonetheless seem to be gaining influence. The phrase "a solas" alludes to the sharp division of the political field between "friends" and "enemies," or the *plebs* that represent a totality and those excluded from participation in the Rosist state. In the context of the narrative, Rosas warns against the impending disaster of the Rivadavian reforms of the 1820s; in 1830, the threat is more diffuse. Given the internal fissures of the Federalist Party, contrarian ideas and intellectual activity in general are perceived as unproductive and potentially seditious. This wariness will over time convert into outright intolerance. As a result, even the earliest sophistries of the Generation of 1837, sprinkled with pro forma declarations of loyalty to the Federation and the Restorer of Laws, will provoke the suspicions of the government.

The critique of intellectuals, though muted, is equally present in De Angelis's text. In place of Rosas's own brash declarations, the Neapolitan contrasts Rosas's action with the passive grumbling of his adversaries:

> Los ociosos le reprochaban su contracción al trabajo; los intrigantes su odio a las revoluciones; los díscolos la sencillez y la severidad de sus costumbres; y no faltaban hombres *ilustrados* que le hacían un cargo de su interés por los indios.
>
> El señor Rosas nunca contestó a sus detractores; limitábase a confundirlos con la práctica de todas las virtudes, y con su respeto inalterable a las instituciones del país. (*Acusación y defensa*, 203)
>
> [The idle reproached him for his obligation to work; the schemers his hatred for revolutions; the unruly the simplicity and severity of his customs; and there is no shortage of *enlightened* men that take issue with his interest in the Indians.

Señor Rosas never answered his detractors; he limited himself to confounding them by putting all of his virtues into practice, and with his unwavering respect for the institutions of the nation.]

As De Angelis enumerates Rosas's positive attributes, he dismisses potential critiques by associating them not with ideological beliefs or party affiliations but with individuals of deficient character: the lazy, the disobedient, and the (over)educated. Rosas's opponents counter his actions with words; Rosas, in turn, contests them indirectly and through action. To say that Rosas never responded to his detractors is the logical inversion of his tendency to confide *a solas* with his supporters. It is therefore forced to claim that Pérez "agrega . . . rasgos explicables teniendo en cuenta el público a quien se dirigía y que serían impensables en el De Angelis: por ejemplo, Rosas se hace cargo y comparte la desconfianza del paisano hacia el saber del letrado" [adds attributes that can be explained taking into consideration the audience he addressed and that would be unthinkable in De Angelis's portrayal: for example, Rosas looks after the peasant and shares his distrust of the intellectual's knowledge].[59] Regardless of the differences in audiences, both Pérez and De Angelis contrast the practical, experiential knowledge that Rosas possesses with the empty rhetoric of his opponents.

Pérez and De Angelis's biographies present emblematic, if occasionally contradictory, images of Rosas, and, in doing so, they perform a discursive operation essential to the consolidation of his regime's power. They narrate from two distinct loci of enunciation, often in tension, "uno desde el espacio de la voz oída y el otro desde el espacio exterior del género [gauchesco], el de la palabra escrita" [one from the space of the spoken word and the other from the exterior space of the genre, that of the written word].[60] In this manner, they represent the social relations that structure federalist hegemony, both its affinities and its exclusions. Pérez employs a literate gaucho to tell his tale, a figure that negotiates a social hierarchy while maintaining it. The fictional narrator draws on his personal experience to write a story that may be read in a variety of ways, silently or aloud, alone or publicly, and set to music. De Angelis also subordinates the written word to action, albeit discretely, to exalt the figure of Rosas. The uneasy alliance between the voice of the gaucho and the illustrated scribe has its limits, though. As Ludmer reminds us, Pérez's newspapers were allowed to circulate only in specific circumstances, namely in 1829–1830 and 1833–1834, when Rosas needed to mobilize the rural masses.[61] On the other hand, De Angelis, a former tutor of European royalty and author of encyclopedia articles, would write and edit publications for Rosas until the very end of the regime.

Both the trajectory of De Angelis's own career and other texts that he authored, edited, and published in the regime-sanctioned newspapers of Buenos Aires demonstrate the ambivalence with which pro-Rosas discourse regarded itself. A survey of *El Lucero*, *La Gaceta Mercantil*, and *El Diario de la Tarde* reveals a proliferation of texts that employ a counterdiscourse, a performative use of language that seeks to conceal this very operation. On January 31, 1835, some ten months before Rosas returned to power, *La Gaceta Mercantil*—another publication in which De Angelis was involved—printed an anonymous article that reiterates, albeit in a more refined language, his harangue against wise men and their theories:

> Las teorías, lejos de servir en circunstancias extraordinarias, vienen a ser sumamente perjudiciales; porque ellas suponen una serie de acontecimientos regulares y ordinarios que es imposible tengan lugar en las oscilaciones políticas, cuando a cada momento se presentan sucesos singulares que crean necesidades urgentes y del momento... acción, acción es lo que se necesita."
> (qtd. in Myers, *Orden y virtud*, 269)

> [Theories, far from serving in extreme circumstances, come to be especially damaging; since they suppose an impossible series of regular and ordinary events take place during the fluctuations of politics, when in a given moment singular occurrences present themselves that create urgent necessities of the moment... action, action is what is needed.]

The article trenchantly rejects the notion that a set of rules, abstracted from historical events, have any bearing on the contemporary political situation. Discourse and event are placed in absolute opposition, suggesting that even a narrative approach to history, defended by the staid Andrés Bello in Chile during the historiography polemic of the early 1840s, is unacceptable. For the author of this article, the Argentine situation is unique and, implicitly, requires a leader who will respond to the political instability resulting from Rosas's absence: naturally, Rosas himself. These ideas themselves constitute what is truly unthinkable, or at least interdicted, for Rosas's supporters: theory—and, more specifically, a theory on (or against) discourse. Pro-Rosas writing, while excepting itself, thus articulates the same problematic that structures the conventional critique of populism: political discourse is mere rhetoric, a manipulation or distortion of a concrete reality. The irony is that, as Rosas and his supporters actively attempted to regulate writing through censorship and their own cultural production, discourse itself became a contested terrain, necessary to sustain the mutually intelligible antagonisms of political adversaries.

For the young *letrados* who gathered in Marcos Sastre's bookstore in 1837, aspiring to found a national literature and advocating a more prominent place for intellectual activity in the affairs of state, the cultural landscape of Rosas's Buenos Aires was less an empty space than a field staked out and monitored by the regime and its surrogates. As Pedro De Angelis's presence at the inaugural gathering of the Salón Literario suggests, Rosas and his government took a keen interest in the activities of potential dissidents, and its refusal to permit the publication of their proposed newspaper the *Semanario de Buenos Aires* (whose general editor, at least in name, was the son of Rosas's own aide-de-camp) indicated its reluctance to let their ideas circulate publicly. This, as well as the brief existence of Juan Bautista Alberdi's *La Moda*, a periodical that claimed to be concerned with only frivolous things like literature, music, and fashion, were not isolated incidents, but symptomatic of a tighter control over the outlets of public opinion. Following the flurry of newspapers that appeared during Rosas's interregnum, the number of new publications dropped sharply and the content of sanctioned papers such as *El Diario de la Tarde* and *La Gaceta Mercantil*, as well as the pro-Rosas, English-language *The British Packet*, largely restricted their content to commercial news and official government documents.[62] Rosas himself intervened frequently in controlling the discursive output of his regime, going so far as to make suggestions, additions, and line edits to De Angelis's articles for the *Archivo Americano*.[63] Which is to say, Echeverría's critique of the paper could be amended to describe the *Archivo Americano* as "continual *auto*-biography" of the Restorer of Laws. Indeed, writing could be said to be a distinguishing feature of Rosas's particular style of personalist rule, to the point that, post-1835, "Rosas pasó más tiempo haciendo uso de la pluma que del caballo" [Rosas spent more time making use of the pen than the horse].[64]

READING ROSAS

The Generation of 1837 sought to intervene in a discursive space in which Rosas was the dominant figure, both as the subject and a producer of his official image. In this respect, the caudillo became a "fenómeno *totalitario*" [*totalitarian* phenomenon] that forced his opponents to confront the dilemma of choosing between "la marginalidad o la integración, la huida o la penetración en y por la realidad, la abdicación, la crítica o la abstracción, al proponerles una figura cargada de referencias románticas por su origen popular, desmesura, connotaciones irracionalistas y hasta por sus violentos contrastes" [marginality or integration, flight or penetration of and by reality, abdication, criticism or abstraction, by presenting them a figure loaded with romantic references because of its popular origins, its excess, irrational connotations and even because of its violent contrasts].[65] To challenge his authority, in other words, required discrediting the authenticity of the social text of which Rosas was the ultimate author; confronting him on the terrain of discourse required dissidents to "sobreescribir su creación original por los *comienzos* de su propia letra" [overwrite his original creation with the *beginnings* of their own script].[66] Some attacks on the dictator simply called for his elimination, offering a perfect counterpart to Federalist slogans: the exiled liberals José Mármol, Esteban Echeverría, and Juan María Gutiérrez contributed to a magazine titled ¡*Muera Rosas!* [*May Rosas Die!*] (Montevideo, 1841–1842) that included graphic caricatures of a bloodthirsty, homicidal dictator, while the erstwhile Rosas supporter José Rivera Indarte justified regicide in his tract "Es acción santa matar a Rosas" ["It Is a Holy Act to Kill Rosas"] (1843). Other texts, however, sought not to demolish Rosas's figure, but instead deconstruct it by calling attention to how its mechanisms of legitimation contradicted the prevailing images the regime promoted of its leader.

Among these texts we can include José Mármol's novel *Amalia* (1855) and Sarmiento's *Facundo*. While these foundational texts have long been cited as early sources for casting Rosas "en términos de rígidos contrastes como la personificación del bien o del mal" [in terms of a rigid contrast between the personification of good and evil] and, as a consequence, led to "el verdadero registro de su gobierno" [the true register of his government] being subsumed by mythology,[67] a careful reading shows how *Amalia* and *Facundo* present a more complex figure than traditional interpretations would suggest. Specifically, they emphasize the relationship of Rosas to discourse and his use of writing as an instrument of power. In calling into question the authenticity of the composite image produced by pro-regime portrayals, they moreover insist on the essential falseness of the supposed affective bonds shared by the dictator and his followers.

José Mármol began to write *Amalia* in 1851 and interrupted its serial publication in *La Semana* of Montevideo when Rosas fell. Though written when Rosas's downfall was imminent, the novel centers on the year of 1840, when the regime responded to the French embargo of Buenos Aires and Juan Lavalle's invasion of the province with forceful and often violent measures. Throughout the novel, Mármol depicts Rosas as a reclusive, conniving despot, who manages a network of secret police, thugs, and informants from behind the walls his mansion. In a typical domestic scene, the *Restaurador de las leyes* interrupts a meeting with the English diplomat Mandeville to read a memo that his aide-de-camp Corvalán has given him:

> Rosas . . . se sentó, extendió el pliego sobre la mesa, y, apoyando la frente sobre sus dos manos, continuó leyendo, mientras a cada palabra sus ojos se inyectaban de sangre, y pasaban por su frente todas las medias tintas de la grana, del fuego y de la palidez.
>
> Un cuarto de hora después, él mismo había cerrado la puerta exterior de su gabinete y se paseaba por él a pasos agitados, impelido por la tormenta de sus pasiones que se hubieran podido definir y contar en los visibles cambios de su fisonomía. (*Amalia*, I: 149)

[Rosas ... sat down, extended the sheet of paper on the table, and, resting his head in his hands, continued to read, while with each word his eyes became more bloodshot, and his forehead flickered between bright red, fire, and pallor.
A quarter of an hour later, he himself closed the outside door to his office and paced with agitated steps, driven by the torment of his passions that could have been defined and recounted in the visible changes to his features.]

Throughout the novel, Rosas exhibits a volatile character, and those in his presence often endure his verbal and physical abuse. Here, however, though the act of reading inspires rage, Rosas does not direct it outward, but instead grows pensive. Normally surrounded by his advisors and adulators, Rosas withdraws, still visibly afflicted by the contents of the dispatch.

The scene contrasts sharply with the romantic idyll that characterizes the moments when the lovers Amalia Sáenz and Eduardo Belgrano read Byron and Lamartine to each other. These acts of reading, which have drawn their fair share of critical attention, not only exhibit the civilized tastes of the heroes of the novel, but also possess a specular quality in that these private acts of resistance to Federalist tyranny mirror those of the contemporary readers of the *folletín*.[68] The volumes of Romantic poetry, along with the other items in Amalia's house that Mármol exhaustively catalogs, permit the couple (and, by extension, its author and its sympathetic readers) to imagine, like the living rooms of their Parisian contemporaries, a "distant ... world but also, at the same time, in a better one, in which, although men are as unprovided with what they need as in the everyday world, things are free of the drudgery of being useful."[69] Not yet violated by Rosas's henchmen, Amalia's domestic space functions as a capsule of Unitarian aspirations. In this milieu, reading European authors brings the *tucumana* Amalia and the *porteño* Eduardo together, alluding to the remote possibility of a consolidated Argentine republic.[70]

Though Rosas, too, rarely leaves home, his is a site of constant comings and goings, a space that is at once domestic and public. It is also highly theatrical, where not only the buffoon Viguá performs, but where each new visitor must demonstrate his or her loyalty through gestures, declarations of loyalty, and style of dress. Reading, however, suspends the theatrical component of Rosist hegemony. Unseen by the reader, the message that Corvalán delivers Rosas announces the proximity of the Confederation's enemies. The response to the text echoes the way Mármol characterizes Rosas's rejection of the Generation of 1837, as described in an open letter to him that appeared alongside *Amalia* in the Montevideo newspaper *La Semana* in 1851:

Hijo legítimo de las ideas retrógradas, en los jóvenes no mirasteis sino muchachos; e *incapaces los ojos de vuestra inteligencia de extenderse más allá de las paredes de vuestro gabinete,* no comprendisteis que esos muchachos habían de crecer más, habían de ser hombres formales, y de más o menos valer en los negocios públicos o en los sucesos de la revolución. (*Manuela Rosas*, 268–69; italics mine)

[Legitimate son of retrograde ideas, you never saw in young men anything but boys; and as *your mind's eye was incapable of extending itself beyond the walls of your office*, you did not understand that these boys were to grow much more, they were to be gentlemen, and be more or less of value in public affairs and the events of the revolution.]

Contrary to the encomiastic portrayals of Pérez and De Angelis, Mármol contends in both his letter and *Amalia* that Rosas does in fact take into consideration the *díscolos* and *ilustrados* that oppose him. His defect, as Mármol would have it, is that he lacks perspicacity—he can only see what is directly before his eyes. Simply put, he is a bad reader, incapable of responding to his adversaries. Whereas *Amalia*'s hero, the crafty Daniel Bello, is a prolific correspondent and skilled interpreter of news and rumors, writing interrupts business as usual in Rosas's mansion.[71]

Rosas appears as an obsessive, if incompetent reader for only a brief scene in *Amalia*, but Mármol's portrayal echoes the ambitious and more extensive attempt to understand Rosas's power that Sarmiento undertakes in *Facundo*. Though it is ostensibly the biography of the provincial caudillo Juan Facundo Quiroga, the perspective that Sarmiento adopts in the work, at once panoramic and historical, allows him to address the much broader issue of caudillo power in postindependence Latin America. Deciphering the enigma that is Facundo promises to reveal the conditions that make *rosismo* possible. A sensation when it began to circulate among enclaves abroad and in Argentina, *Facundo* had a tremendous influence on shaping the figure of the dictator in the writings of the Generation of 1837, including *Amalia*. Indeed, the chapter of Mármol's novel "El caballero Juan Enrique Mandeville" reads like a fictionalized elaboration of this passage from *Facundo*:

> Rosas no *administra*, no gobierna en el sentido oficial de la palabra. Encerrado meses en su casa, sin dejarse ver de nadie, él solo dirige la guerra, las intrigas, el espionaje, la mazorca, todos los diversos resortes de su tenebrosa política; todo lo que no es útil para la guerra, todo lo que no perjudica a sus enemigos, no forma parte del Gobierno, no entra en la administración. (*Facundo*, 343–44)

[Rosas does not *administer*, he does not govern in the official sense of the word. Locked in his house for months on end, without letting anyone see him, he alone directs the war, the intrigues, the espionage, the secret police, all of the various mechanisms of his dark politics; all that which is not useful for war, all that does not damage his enemies, does not form part of the Government, it does not figure in the administration.]

For Sarmiento, the primary function of Rosas's government is the production of terror; its principal means of consolidating power is the maintenance of an instability attributed to its proscribed critics. Rosas, far from being a charismatic leader who shares with his people a strong affective bond, is distant and cold. He conducts the affairs of state remotely, far removed from the execution of the decrees that he issues. Sarmiento's Rosas is, in other words, a remote theoretician of state terror, the intellect responsible for sustaining a constant state of war that prevents the realization of the national projects proposed by Sarmiento and his peers.

Much as Rosas lurks in the shadows of his mansion, throughout *Facundo* he is a ubiquitous figure that stands in the *sombra terrible* of the caudillo of La Rioja. Facundo's atrocities nearly always prefigure acts by Rosas; whenever Sarmiento invokes the former's name, its distorted echo is likely soon to follow: Rosas's name appears no fewer than 275 times in the course of the text. Occasionally, Sarmiento addresses the caudillo of Buenos Aires directly—at one point he screams: "¡Rosas! ¡Rosas! ¡Rosas! ¡Me prosterno y humillo ante tu poderosa inteligencia!" [Rosas! Rosas! Rosas! I kneel and humble myself before your powerful intelligence!].[72] His presence is so strong that Sarmiento insists in his 1851 prologue-letter to Valentín Alsina that "sería agraviar a la historia escribir la vida de Rosas, y humillar a nuestra patria recordarla, después de rehabilitada, las degradaciones por que ha pasado" [to write Rosas's life would be an insult to history, and it would humiliate our fatherland, after its rehabilitation, to recall the dishonors it has endured].[73] He does not employ the "calculated fiction" that Mármol uses in *Amalia*, which imagines that the author "escribe su obra con algunas generaciones de por medio entre él y aquéllos" [writes his works at a remove of several generations from those events].[74] If fiction requires the imagined absence of Rosas, a reading set in the future perfect, *Facundo* and Facundo remain unintelligible without his presence.[75] As such, Sarmiento's work constitutes an antibiography of Rosas, as it seeks to undermine the prevailing image of the dictator.

Sarmiento trenchantly denies that *Facundo* is Rosas's biography because, immediately following the famous invocation of Facundo's spirit, he proceeds to explain the relationship between the murdered caudillo and the governor of Buenos Aires. Though Facundo was born only five years before Rosas, Sarmiento treats the two as if they belonged to two distinct generations of leaders. In this order of succession, Rosas derives the style and power of his rule directly from the *Tigre de los llanos* [Tiger of the plains]:

> Facundo no ha muerto; está vivo en las tradiciones populares, en la política y revoluciones argentinas; en Rosas, su heredero, su complemento: su alma ha pasado a este otro molde, más acabado, más perfecto; y lo que en él era sólo instinto, iniciación, tendencia, convirtióse en Rosas en sistema, efecto y fin; la

naturaleza campestre, colonial y bárbara, cambióse en esta metamorfosis en arte, en sistema y en política regular capaz de presentarse a la faz del mundo como el modo de ser de un pueblo encarnado en un hombre que ha aspirado a tomar los aires de un genio que domina los acontecimientos, los hombres y las cosas. Facundo, provinciano, bárbaro, valiente, audaz, fue reemplazado por Rosas, hijo de la culta Buenos Aires, sin serlo él; por Rosas, falso, corazón helado, espíritu calculador, que hace el mal sin pasión, y organiza lentamente el despotismo con toda la inteligencia de un Maquiavelo. (*Facundo*, 35–36)

[Facundo is not dead; he lives on in popular traditions, in Argentine politics and its revolutions; in Rosas, his successor, his complement: his soul has passed on to this other mold, more complete, more perfect; and that which in him was only instinct, initiation, tendency, has converted with Rosas into system, effect, an end; the nature of the countryside, colonial and barbarous, changed with this metamorphosis into art, into system, and into a regular politics capable of presenting itself to the world as a people's way of being, which is embodied in a man who has aspired to give off airs of a genius that dominates events, men, and things. Facundo, barbarous, valiant, audacious, was replaced by Rosas, son of sophisticated Buenos Aires, without being himself those things; by Rosas, ersatz, coldhearted, calculating spirit, who does evil without passion, and slowly organizes his despotism with all the intelligence of a Machiavelli.]

Facundo is pure shadow and spirit, preserved in the popular traditions that Sarmiento regards with an ambivalent mix of fear and admiration, particularly in the famous descriptions of the iconic figures of the pampa in the second chapter of the work, "Originalidad y caracteres argentinos" [Argentine originality and character]. Terrible as he may be, Facundo is, in a word, authentic. Rosas, by contrast, embodies the conversion of Facundo's unmediated barbarism into a systematic form of government. As such, Rosas is neither original nor genuine; he produces a false image of himself and his reign for public consumption. In terms of representation, he is the perfect inversion of Facundo: whereas the people remember the latter after the fact, the former represents himself to the people as a means of securing their allegiance. The Rosas that Sarmiento portrays here is a beneficiary of major historical changes—the transition from revolutionary society to a fledgling nation, tottering political institutions, and the increasing dominance of the city over the country. Rosas, the prodigal son of the city, appropriates the symbolic capital of the country and applies it as an instrument of control.

Thus, to discredit Rosas, Sarmiento employs a rhetorical strategy that is by now all too familiar: he repeatedly insists that the dictator has manipulated the people for his own designs. Time and time again he calls attention to the deliberate nature of Rosas's despotism and thereby undermines the state-sanctioned image of Rosas as a man of action and organic intellect. For Sarmiento, "Rosas no ha inventado nada; su talento ha consistido sólo en plagiar a sus antecesores, y hacer de los instintos brutales de las masas ignorantes un sistema meditado y coordinado fríamente" [Rosas has invented nothing; his talent consists only of plagiarizing his predecessors, and of making the brutal instincts of the ignorant masses into a coldly meditated and coordinated system].[76] Much as he asserts in the introduction, here he accuses Rosas of having copied the leadership style of earlier caudillos without having developed the social relations that give rise to these images. The irony that characterizes Rosist discourse therefore depends on the fact that the social actors that perform it—namely the "ignorant masses"—are unaware of its implications, while others, the leaders who produce it, are hypocrites. Rosist discourse is a calculated strategy whose primary objective is to produce unreason in the form of fear, ignorance, and submission:

> Es inaudito el cúmulo de atrocidades que se necesita amontonar unas sobre otras para pervertir a un pueblo, y nadie sabe los ardides, los estudios, las observaciones y la sagacidad que ha empleado D. Juan Manuel Rosas para someter la ciudad a esa influencia mágica que trastorna en seis años la conciencia de lo justo y de lo bueno, que quebranta al fin los corazones más esforzados y los doblega al yugo. (*Facundo*, 253)
>
> [It is astonishing the host of atrocities that must be heaped onto one another to pervert a people, and no one knows the ruses, the studies, the observations, and the sagacity that Don Juan Manuel de Rosas has employed in order to subject the city to that magical influence that, in six years time, upends respect for what is good and fair, that in the end breaks the strongest hearts and twists them into submission.]

Whereas official documents and proclamations purport to represent the people faithfully, speaking their same language, Sarmiento accuses the Rosas government of producing a wholly opaque discourse that conceals its motives and perverts its public. For the author of *Facundo* the people are an amorphous mass, bereft of distinguishing features; he hints at their internal divisions but never addresses them directly. As he questions the affective bonds that connect the masses to their ruler, Sarmiento does not condemn Rosas for treating the people as ignorant (this, for him, is a given); it is not the distance that separates the caudillo and his people that he criticizes, but the fact that Rosas abuses this position to construct a nation that is antithetical to Sarmiento's own aspirations.

The accumulating references to plagiarism, scheming, and deception not only emphasize the cunning intellect that distinguishes Rosas from his subjects, it also alludes to the tremendous discursive production required to maintain the popular image of the despot. Eventually Sarmiento comes to consider Rosas not as simply a strong-armed caudillo, but as a competing author as well:

> Ambos son escritores. Rosas produce volúmenes de notas oficiales al año, dirigidas a diez gobiernos sobre veinte pleitos pendientes; el otro [Sarmiento] produce volúmenes sobre educación popular, que es su manía favorita, inmigración, correos, industria y demás cosas necesarias para la prosperidad de los pueblos. (*Obras de D. F. Sarmiento*, XXXV: 35)
>
> [Both are writers. Rosas produces volumes of official notes each year, directed to ten governments about twenty pending cases; the other [Sarmiento] produces volumes about public education, which is his preferred obsession, immigration, mail service, industry, and other necessary things for the prosperity of peoples.]

A mere four years after the publication of *Facundo*, the text whose notoriety he would exploit throughout his political career, Sarmiento audaciously compares his works with the documents of the Rosas regime. The comparison is asymmetrical because Sarmiento does not refer to the content of Rosas's production. He contrasts the empty forms of the dictator's writings with the predominant themes of his work. If Rosas beats Sarmiento easily in terms of quantity, the subjects of Sarmiento's works are far more noble; that is, his criteria are more moral than aesthetic. Sarmiento censures Rosas for writing poorly to defend the perverse logic of his despotic rule, while Sarmiento's own body of work constitutes a continuous act of open resistance.

While Pedro De Angelis and Luis Pérez promote the image of a leader who exhibits a disdain for intellectual activity and, in turn, claim to subordinate their medium to the numerous acts that form the basis of a deep affinity shared by Rosas and his subjects, the depictions of José Mármol and Domingo Faustino Sarmiento insist on the artificial nature of the relations portrayed by pro-regime iconography, a counterimage that the official historiography of the turn-of-the-century liberal state will repeat and elaborate. Mármol presents the caricature of a tyrant who seems to suffer from a pathologically dysfunctional relationship with writing. A poor reader, he can neither interpret nor react to text in such a way as to maintain a credible visage of authority. In *Facundo* Sarmiento offers a more nuanced portrait of the caudillo, who craftily wields writing as an apparatus of power and then, with Machiavellian cunning, disguises this fundamental operation. In both cases, the dissident intellectuals make the implicit claim that they are shedding light on a hidden practice, as if revealing a secret mechanism of Rosas's power.

THE IMAGE-TEXT OF ROSAS WRITING

The irony of these denunciations is that, while they doubtlessly run counter to the prevailing image of Rosas as first among gauchos, they highlight a basic attribute that certain pro-regime portraits also emphasize. A host of paintings, lithographs, and medallions depict the *Restaurador de las leyes* together with writing implements, including feather pens, inkwells, and sheets of paper. There are minor variations among these portraits with regards to Rosas's pose and the details of his surroundings, but they generally depict their subject dressed in military regalia, beside a desk in an interior space that is presumably an office. The setting, Rosas's rigid posture, and the inclusion of written documents and captions commemorating specific historical events, such as military battles and the signing of treaties, present Rosas through a codified visual vocabulary of political and military authority, whose antecedents include colonial-era portraits of viceroys and other high-ranking officials of the Spanish crown, Antoine-Jean Gros, and Jacques-Louis David's paintings of Napoleon Bonaparte, and, in a more immediate context, José Gil de Castro's portraits of the high command of the Ejército de los Andes, many of which made their way to Argentina at the end of the Revolution, carried by the very subjects who had sat for them.[77] Like these portraits of the revolutionary heroes, the images of Rosas identify their subject as the executor and embodiment of a republican order. Contrary to the dichotomy that is central to the image of Rosas promoted by supporters and adversaries alike, portraits of Rosas-as-author insist on the reciprocity of action and discourse. In this respect, they do not simply conjure the juridical notion of sovereignty evoked by the nickname the "Restorer of Laws," but more broadly link Rosas's mandate to a variety of scriptural practices.

A lithograph attributed to Hippolyte Moulin (see figure 1.1, at the beginning of the chapter) is representative of these images. In this full-length portrait, Rosas stands in front of a tall desk. With his sword at his side and a bicorn hat resting on a chair beside him, the caudillo is decked in a military uniform that includes a sash, a medal, and a *divisa punzó*, the crimson insignia that became an obligatory accessory in Rosas's second term. In his right hand Rosas holds a feather pen and, in his left, a sheet of paper that reads "Expedición contra los bárbaros 1833" [Expedition against the barbarians 1833]. The desk exhibits an inkwell, a paper titled "Decreto" [Decree] with several blank sheets beneath it, and a map of the basin of the Río de la Plata. Identified by a caption as "El Exmo. Sor. Brigadier / Dn. Juan Manuel de Rosas / Restaurador de las Leyes / Gobernador y Capitán General de la Provincia de Buenos Aires 1835" [The Most Excellent Brigadier General / Don Manuel de Rosas / Restorer of Laws / Governor and Captain General of Buenos Aires Province 1835] the leader brandishes the account of a past military feat, an illustration signaling his sphere of influence, a legal document, and blank pages (awaiting further inscriptions) as credentials of his authority. Invested with different forms of knowledge (historical, military, geographic, legal), Moulin's Rosas lays bare precisely what Sarmiento accuses him of concealing in *Facundo*.

In Moulin's portrait image and text, visibility and legibility effect a kind of chiasmus, akin to what Louis Marin detects in portraits of Louis XIV, in which "pictures are texts that are legible from end to end and images that are resolved into signs; a narrative is in the end a visible image, and history takes on the consistency of a synopsis, map, or panorama to be contemplated."[78] Of course, this is not to say that Rosas aspired to the Sun King's transcendent absolutism, but that the portrait, as an embodiment of his power, simultaneously deploys symbolic and imaginary modalities of representation. Rosas's own absolute powers—the *suma del poder público* whose assumption the lithograph commemorates—is bound by the spatial and historical limits shown in the portrait, but within these boundaries his image re-presents his authority as present. In other words, the image-text operates according to the fiction that its composite image has an equivalent force to the central figure depicted therein. Or, in more radical terms, this iconography presumes an ontological sameness between the portrait and its subject: the representation of Rosas's power, in effect, puts into effect that power. Hence the crimson insignia, which often bore a portrait of the *Restaurador* together with Federalist slogans and was worn by members of different social classes, "helped create a ready-made identity" and "projected a unifying ideology" by making sovereignty present in the physical absence of the caudillo or state officials.[79] Thus the mob in Esteban Echeverría's canonical fiction "El matadero" kills but does not sacrifice the defiant Unitarian who emphatically refuses to wear the *divisa*; he becomes the bare life that signals the indistinction between violence and law.[80] What Echeverría's narrative suggests, then, is that Rosas's presence in letters, insignias, and, by extension, portraits, is more iconic than symbolic, a re-presentation of authority that neither conceals nor reflects the use of force, but in fact sanctions it.

Multiple depictions of Rosas-as-author attest to the variety of contexts in which the regime and its supporters asserted the linkage between writing and its power. An anonymous oil painting from 1840 (figure 1.2) shows Rosas's clumsily drawn right hand resting on a copy of the Mackau-Arana treaty, which brought an end to the French blockage of Buenos Aires on October 31 of that same year. With his left hand he holds a staff at this side (instead of a sword), as if to underscore the peaceful resolution brought about through diplomatic means. Though the basic elements of the portrait are the same as those displayed in Moulin's lithograph, the naïve or folkloric stylization of Rosas's flat, somewhat contorted figure might evoke the informal training of its artist or the spontaneous nature of its execution, as well as the space where such a representation might be displayed: while viceroys' portraits may have hung in government buildings and Gil de Castro's portraits of San Martín and his officials were originally destined for private use, this image of Rosas was in all likelihood destined for a popular audience for whom its text would be unreadable.[81]

A series of stamped metal reliefs that were distributed to schoolchildren as prizes in public ceremonies attest to the dissemination of this image to a

Figure 1.2. Portrait of Juan Manuel de Rosas, c. 1840 (*Courtesy of Museo Histórico Buenos Aires "Cornelio de Saavedra"*)

more specific audience (figure 1.3). As Mark D. Szuchman observes, these festivities persisted throughout the nineteenth century and "served as an expression of the state's asserted concern for education . . . [demonstrating] the strong nexus that joined the style and content of learning to the political

Figure 1.3. Medallion depicting Juan Manuel de Rosas (*Courtesy of Museo Histórico Buenos Aires "Cornelio de Saavedra"*)

values held by the governing authorities."[82] The medallions, which depict Rosas seated at a desk that includes the requisite writing materials, less commemorate a specific event or action by Rosas, than they function as a currency, a tender of Rosas's power that is placed into circulation in a ceremonial setting. Given the pedagogical nature of the event in which they are given, the medals articulate a relationship "between the diversification of the institution of force as power . . . and the self-legitimation of representation where force insists itself."[83] While the portraits of Rosas-as-author are bereft of the familiarity and compassion extolled in Pérez and De Angelis's biographies, the school prizes nonetheless insist on a basic social bond that traverses the limit between power and people, inasmuch as they function as ritualized objects of exchange. They represent the caudillo giving himself to his subjects, a performance of reciprocal relations expressed through letters.

Other artifacts produced by the adherents of the Rosas regime synthesize the different modalities of visibility and readability deployed in the written and graphic portrayals of Rosas we have seen thus far. If the biographies of Pérez and De Angelis employ writing as a medium to represent affective bonds, and a series of graphic depictions display writing as an instrument of power, an anonymous broadsheet from 1835, titled "Carta del viejo Francisco Junco de la Guardia de la Monte, al viejo Gregorio Chaparro de la ciudad" [Letter from old Francisco Junco of Guardia de la Monte, to old Gregorio Chaparro of the city] conflates these functions by narrating an exchange of letters. Published by the government-sponsored Imprenta del Estado, the *hoja suelta* purports to reprint a letter sent from a small town in the countryside to the capital. Written in rhyming, octosyllabic quatrains—a typical verse structure of gauchesque poetry—the text recounts its author's participation in a raucous celebration of Rosas's assumption of the *suma del poder público* in April of the same year. The tone, however, darkens as Junco warns Chaparro of treacherous Unitarian enemies who still inhabit the province. The depiction of Federalist enthusiasm thus doubles as a call for increased vigilance against threats to the regime from within. Given the timing of its publication, its treatment of current events, and its stylized language, the "Carta del Viejo Francisco Junco" encourages its own enthusiastic public reading and, in turn, demonstrations of loyalty to the reappointed Governor Rosas, much in the same way that Pérez's newspapers sought to stoke popular fervor in 1829–1830.[84]

With its opening verses, Junco's letter emphasizes how it relates exceptional circumstances through a personal form of communication. At a glance, its first stanza seems superfluous, as Junco essentially repeats the information contained in the title of the poem: "esta carta es para Usté / Pues aunque me haiga olvidao / Yo siempre le escribiré" [this letter is for You / Since although you've forgotten me / I will always write you].[85] Yet soon it becomes apparent that the epistolary form and, more generally, the act of writing are central themes of the text. Indeed, the magnitude of what Junco desires to recount exceeds a single letter, as he admits to Chaparro that "[t]anto que decirle tengo / De lo que pasa en el Pago, / Que con cinco ni seis pliegos / Me hace que tavia no lo hago" [So much I have to say to you / Of what is happening in the Country / That five or six pages won't suffice / So I haven't done it yet].[86] Junco promises that a fuller account is forthcoming, but limits himself in this letter to a singular occurrence, the receipt of a proclamation signed by Juan Manuel de Rosas himself.

Each of the first seven stanzas of Junco's "Carta" explicitly mentions either an object or an action relating to letters. The accumulating references imagine a network of readers that connects Rosas to Junco to Chaparro to the intended audiences of these different texts: the many letters, past and future, from the speaker to his friend, the "sobre escrito" [addressed envelope] containing the official document, Rosas's signature, and the proclamation (as physical object and as a text read aloud).[87] As the poem proceeds, it becomes clear that Junco is not referring to terms of domination and subordination, but the affective bonds validating the obligations of written law. For hearing the proclamation read aloud, he is overcome with emotion:

> ¡Cosa linda! amigo viejo;
> Que sermon ni que sermon,
> Conforme la ivan leyendo
> Tun... tun... me hacía el corazón.
>
> El se acuerda de toititos:
> De militar, del paisano,
> Y ansi nos mira como á hijos
> En siendo guen ciudadano.
>
> Ande hablar de la campaña
> No pude disimular,
> Cogi la esquina del poncho
> Y ya me largué a llorar.
> ("Carta del viejo Francisco Junco," 122)
>
> [What a beautiful thing, old friend;
> This was no kind of sermon,
> As they were reading it
> Tun... tun... my heart was beating.
>
> He remembers everyone:
> From the soldier to the peasant,
> And looks upon us all like sons
> As being good citizens.
>
> When talking about the country
> I couldn't hide it,
> I grabbed the corner of my poncho
> And I broke down crying.]

The onomatopoeic image of the speaker's heart gives way to an expression of admiration for the caudillo, whose words convey a general concern for the citizens he treats with a paternal affection. Reduced to tears, an act he seeks to conceal, Junco is momentarily isolated from his companions, but no sooner than they have finished reading the letter, "todos alli se abrazaron" [all those present embraced]. The fraternal Federalist embrace, however, does not last long, as the men take to the streets, where they again read aloud the proclamation and initiate a raucous celebration that includes exclamations, patriotic songs and fireworks, and lasts until morning. Once again, the speaker describes the collective act of reading, and again he stresses the visible emotion produced through the written and spoken word: "*¡Que viva nuestro Gobierno! / Repetían con calor, / ¡Viva el padre de los pobres! / ¡Que viva el Restaurador!*" [*Long live our Government! / They repeated with fervor, / Long live the father of the poor! / Long live the Restorer!*].[88] The printed artifact deploys a metanarrative of its own putative genesis, as it repeats Junco's letter, which recounts the events of the evening, which in turn revolve around the emotional readings of Rosas's decree. It thus insists on its own performative reading, not simply in the sense of "dramatic" or "participatory" but in that it aspires to produce an utterance asserting the legitimacy of Rosas's authority; in reading aloud the report of a fictitious or fictionalized instance, it not only represents a public act and its constitutive exchanges, but also appeals to its underlying legal framework.[89] The broadsheet is itself not law, but functions like a *sobre-escrito* [an over-writing] in that it contains and delivers the announcement of Rosas's new mandate (the reading of the proclamation) and the confirmation of the announcement back in the capital city (Junco's letter to Chaparro). As a call to action for loyal Federalists, the broadsheet's function is cathectic, in that it looks to convert emotional intensities and potentially transgressive, spontaneous violence into a series of codified actions that reinforce Rosist hegemony.

The woodcut image that accompanies the poem reinforces the centrality of writing in this operation (figure 1.4). The picture, which originally served as the masthead image for Luis Pérez's *El Gaucho* (also published by the Imprenta del Estado), depicts a man wearing a poncho, boots, and spurs, standing before what seems to be a fence or wall. At his feet one can clearly see a *rebenque*, or whip, while his crossed hands hold a feather pen and a sheet of paper. In the context of *El Gaucho*, this figure is presumably Pancho Lugares, the gaucho gazetteer who has interrupted his labors in the field to take up the pen in support of Rosas. In like fashion, one can associate the reused image with Francisco Junco, the author of the broadsheet's poem. However, taking into account that the figure divides the official slogans "Federación ó muerte" and "Viva el Restaurador de las leyes," one can also plausibly identify it as Rosas himself, the author of the document that inspires Junco's letter; beside the differences of costume and setting, the woodcut presents a similar figure to the portraits of Rosas-as-author we have seen. Moreover, as Raymond Monvoisin's 1842 portrait reminds us, the portrayal of Rosas in gaucho attire was not unprecedented. The broadsheet conflates the two authors and their writings, further underscoring the degree of identification that informs the affective bonds represented therein. The masthead of the "Carta del viejo Francisco Junco" implies a minimal distance between caudillo and citizen, in which the pen traces the limit that cleaves the people to and from power. Writing may serve as a visible symbol of the caudillo's

Figure 1.4. Masthead of "Carta del viejo Francisco," 1835

unique authority, but its conversion into the spoken word and its transmission through letters and other ancillary texts also render it a medium for affect. It is through the performance of affective relations—and the didactic representation of these public displays—that the Rosist pueblo constitutes itself from the partial components of postrevolutionary society.

If the 1835 broadsheet offers a textual version of the relationship between Rosas and the male inhabitants of the countryside, an 1841 painting signed

Figure 1.5. "Las esclavas de Buenos Aires muestran que son libres," painting signed D. del Plot, 1841

by D. de Plot presents a graphic depiction of an equivalent exchange between the *Restaurador* and another segment of the population that formed part of the Rosist pueblo: the Afro-Argentine women of the city of Buenos Aires (figure 1.5). With broken shackles beneath his feet, Rosas reads the 1839 proclamation abolishing slavery, while his audience listens and holds flags aloft bearing Federalist slogans. Overhead, an angel blows a clarion and announces that "[y]a no gemirá en el Plata en cadenas ningún esclavo. Su amargo llanto cesó desde que Rosas humano, de su libertad ufano, compasivo y generoso, prodigó este don precioso al infeliz Africano" [now in the River Plate no slave will cry in chains. His bitter wail ceased the moment the humane Rosas, staunch in defense of freedom, compassionate and generous, bequeathed this precious gift to the unhappy African]. If the tears of a just, grateful, and sensitive pueblo provided Rosas his mandate, per his eulogy for Dorrego, here Rosas's compassion brings an end to the cries of slaves. The scene condenses the series of exchanges that comprise the narrative of Junco's letter: framed by a caption and supertitle that reiterate the substitution of shackles for affective bonds, Rosas stands stiffly as he reads his own writing before a grateful audience, whose members display banners with written expressions of loyalty. The dramatic scene is slightly off-center: framed at its right margin by an aide-de-camp and a pavilion behind him, the placement of figures indicates that the public act is doubly an interpellation, in that it marks the inclusion of the women as political subjects and it interrupts other affairs of state that also demand Rosas's presence.

CONCLUSION

As this corpus of images makes evident, there is an important element of truth to the commonplace that Rosas's image was ubiquitous in mid-nineteenth-century Argentina. Regardless of the exact quantity of such images, what is certain is that a rhetoric of ubiquity is central to the textual and graphic representations of the governor of Buenos Aires. Rosas is made present, not through substitution, but through the repeated, synecdochal representation of affective bonds that precede and exceed the legal framework and state institutions to which this figure so demonstratively adheres. In the turmoil following the execution of Dorrego in 1828, Salvador María del Carril reported to Dorrego's executioner, Lavalle, that multiple lithographs and songs recalling the slain governor were circulating throughout the city. For this reason, he insisted, "si V. pudiera multiplicandose estar en la capital haria una cosa soberana" [you would do a sovereign thing if you could by multiplying yourself to be in the capital].[90] In following years, it would seem that Rosas succeeded in doing this "sovereign thing," making his presence felt simultaneously in the capital and throughout Argentine territory by means of disseminating his likeness in various formats and among various audiences. The multiplication of Rosas's portrait is a sovereign thing not in the sense that it provides some kind of ex post facto legitimation or "cover" for prior actions, but in that it constitutes a concurrent hegemonic operation. Beyond appealing to a juridical notion of sovereignty, the use of repressive force, and a complex of formal and informal mechanisms, the Rosas regime conspicuously endeavored to cultivate affective bonds among a variety of social actors. Writing, as medium and image, became the terrain on which these social relations were inscribed. As a result, any effort to contest Rosas's hegemony, as well as the efforts to maintain it, had to make public and publish their opposition through a variety of discursive practices and from multiple loci of enunciation.

NOTES

1. Juan Manuel de Rosas, *Correspondencia de Juan Manuel de Rosas* (Buenos Aires: Eudeba, 2005), 70.
2. *El Lucero*, December 23, 1829, 3–4.
3. In a letter from January 16, 1830, John Murray Forbes informs Secretary of State Martin Van Buren of some of these materials: "[a]compaño por este barco la oración fúnebre pronunciada por el doctor Figueredo, en la reciente ceremonia en memoria de Dorrego y relacionado con éste, un cierto número de *facsímiles* litográficos de sus cartas y otros escritos, producidos en la corta hora que se le acordó para preparase a morir. Esta colección, impresa en gran estilo, me fué enviada por el Gobierno y probablemente ofrece interés por las circunstancias de la tragedia a que se refiere" [I carry aboard with me the funeral oration read by Doctor Figueredo, in the recent commemorative ceremony for Dorrego, and related to this a certain number of lithographic facsimiles of his letters and other writings, produced in the short period

of time he was granted before dying. This collection, printed with great style, was sent to me by the Government and will probably be of interest given the circumstances of the tragedy to which it refers] (*Once años en Buenos Aires, 1820–1831: Las crónicas diplomáticas de John Murray Forbes* [Buenos Aires: Emecé, 1956], 572).

4. Forbes, *Once años*, 569.

5. Gabriel Di Meglio, *¡Viva el bajo pueblo! La plebe urbana de Buenos Aires y la política entre la revolución de Mayo y el rosismo (1810–1829)* (Buenos Aires: Prometeo, 2006), 306.

6. *El Lucero*, December 23, 1829, 4.

7. Jeremy Adelman, *Republic of Capital: Buenos Aires and the Legal Transformation of the Atlantic World* (Stanford, Calif.: Stanford University Press, 1999), 114.

8. Ricardo Salvatore examines in detail several such patriotic festivals in *Wandering Paysanos: State Order and Subaltern Experience in Buenos Aires during the Rosas Era* (Durham, N.C.: Duke University Press, 2003), 361–93.

9. José Mármol, *Manuela Rosas y otros escritos políticos del exilio* (Buenos Aires: Taurus, 2001), 260.

10. Esteban Echeverría, *Dogma Socialista*, ed. Alberto Palcos (La Plata, Argentina: Universidad Nacional de la Plata, 1940), 389.

11. Rosas, *Correspondencia*, 122.

12. "La iconografía de Rosas," *Caras y caretas*, May 13, 1905.

13. José María Ramos Mejía, *Rosas y su tiempo*, vol. 2 (Buenos Aires: Félix Lajouane, 1907), 269.

14. Mejía, *Rosas y su tiempo*, 269.

15. Michel Foucault, *Society Must Be Defended: Lectures at the Collège de France, 1975–76* (New York: Picador, 2003), 17. This is how Foucault defines the reductive "war-repression" conception of power in his inaugural lecture.

16. Fermín Chávez, *La cultura en la época de Rosas; aportes a la descolonización mental de la Argentina* (Buenos Aires: Ediciones Theoría, 1973), 12.

17. Diana Quattrocchi-Woisson, *Un Nationalisme de déracinés: L'Argentine, pays malade de sa mémoire* (Paris: Editions du Centre national de la recherche scientifique, 1992), 44.

18. "Was there an element of populism in Rosas's policy? If there was, it was only a by-product of his main object," in John Lynch, *Argentine Dictator: Juan Manuel De Rosas, 1829–1852* (New York: Clarendon, 1981), 64.

19. Lynch, *Argentine Dictator*, 108.

20. Lynch, *Argentine Dictator*, 100, 114.

21. Noemí Goldman and Ricardo Donato Salvatore, eds., introduction to *Caudillismos rioplatenses: Nuevas miradas a un viejo problema* (Buenos Aires: Eudeba, 1998), 15.

22. As Pilar González Bernaldo de Quirós remarks in a footnote in *Civilidad y política*, "Desdichadamente, no existe ninguna investigación sobre la construcción simbólica de la figura de Rosas" (233).

23. Marcela Ternavasio, "Entre la deliberación y la autorización: El régimen rosista frente al dilema de la inestabilidad política," in *Caudillismos rioplatenses*, ed. Goldman and Salvatore, 139–40.

24. Quoted in Ternavasio, "Hacia un régimen de unanimidad: Política y elecciones en Buenos Aires, 1828–1850," in *Ciudadanía política y formación de las naciones: Perspectivas históricas de América Latina*, ed. Hilda Sábato, 119–41 (Mexico City: Fondo de Cultura Económica, 1999), 135.

25. During Rosas's interregnum, *La Gaceta Mercantil* ran an article criticizing "la costumbre que se ha introducido en las elecciones de celebrar con música, cohetes y vivas a los nuevos diputados" [the custom that has been introduced in elections of celebrating with music, fireworks, and hurrahs for the new legislators] (April 29, 1833, qtd. in Ternavasio, "Hacia un régimen de unanimidad," 131).

26. Tulio Halperín Donghi, *De la Revolución de Independencia a la Confederación Rosista* (Buenos Aires: Paidós, 2000), 291.

27. Rosas, *Correspondencia*, 70.

28. Jacques Rancière, *Disagreement: Politics and Philosophy* (Minneapolis: University of Minnesota Press, 1999), 5.

29. González Bernaldo de Quirós, *Civilidad y política*, 21.
30. Ernesto Laclau, *On Populist Reason* (London: Verso, 2007), 81.
31. Laclau, *On Populist Reason*, 91.
32. Laclau, *On Populist Reason*, 154.
33. Homi K. Bhabha, *The Location of Culture* (New York: Routledge, 1994), 209.
34. Laclau, *On Populist Reason*, 111.
35. Laclau, *On Populist Reason*, 110.
36. Brian Massumi quoted in Clare Hemmings, "Invoking Affect: Cultural Theory and the Ontological Turn," *Cultural Studies* 19, no. 5 (2005): 562.
37. Laclau, *On Populist Reason*, 74. As Laclau later notes, "[s]ince the construction of the 'people' is the political act *par excellence* . . . the *sine qua non* requirements of the political are the constitution of antagonistic frontiers within the social and the appeal to new subjects of social change—which involves, as we know, the production of empty signifiers in order to unify a multiplicity of heterogeneous demands in equivalential chains" (154).
38. Though the details of Pérez's life are murky, William Acree provides a thorough overview of the gazetteer's activities in "Luis Pérez, a Man of His Word in 1830s Buenos Aires and the Case for Popular Literature," *Bulletin of Spanish Studies* 88, no. 3 (2011): 367–86.
39. Luis Pérez, *El Torito de los Muchachos, 1830*, ed. Olga Fernández Latour de Botas (Buenos Aires: Instituto Bibliográfico "Antonio Zinny," 1978), 22.
40. It should be noted that the first portion of the poem is sometimes published as a separate poem with the title "Historia de Pancho Lugares." See, for example, Jorge B. Rivera, ed., *Poesía gauchesca* (Caracas: Biblioteca Ayacucho, 1977).
41. Pérez, *El Torito*, 17.
42. Ángel Rama, "El sistema literario de la poesía gauchesca," in *Poesía gauchesca*, ed. Jorge B. Rivera (Caracas: Ayacucho, 1977), xxxvi.
43. Josefina Ludmer, *El género gauchesco: Un tratado sobre la patria* (Buenos Aires: Sudamericana, 1988), 138.
44. Luis Pérez, "La lira de los negros," in *Cancionero Federal*, ed. Héctor Pedro Blomberg (Buenos Aires: Anaconda, 1934), 17.
45. "Correspondencia," another poem published in the September 15, 1830, issue of *El Gaucho* fulfills a similar didactic function by describing different ways in which writing reinforces social relations between loyal Federalists. Written in the form of a letter from Lugares's uncle Pedro Nolasco to the editor himself, the texts narrates an encounter in which Pedro, having traveled from the capital city to the countryside, proudly shows Pancho's mother Juana a copy of the prospectus of *El Gaucho*. Yet Juana in unimpressed because, as she boasts, she already possesses the first three numbers of the paper and that "Hoy mismo con las vecinas / á Pancho lo festejé, / y con los cielos del gaucho / toda la tarde bailé" [Just today with the neighbors / I celebrated Pancho['s success] / and with gaucho songs [from the paper of the same title] / I danced the whole afternoon] (Rivera, *Poesía gauchesca*, 124). Thus the paper condenses onto the printed page a fictionalized version of the comings and goings between city and country: a gaucho from Montes comes to the city and prints a newspaper; his uncle brings the newspaper back to Montes, only to discover that the newspaper circulates freely among the entire community and read aloud in a festive atmosphere; the uncle writes a letter, sent to the gaucho in the city, who reprints the letter in the newspaper, which is destined, in turn, to circulate in the outlying countryside.
46. Pérez, *El Torito*, 20.
47. Pérez, *El Torito*, 23.
48. Pérez, *El Torito*, 22.
49. Pérez, *El Torito*, 26.
50. Pérez, *El Torito*, 30.
51. Pedro de Angelis, *Acusación y defensa de Rosas* (Buenos Aires: La Facultad, 1946), 190.
52. De Angelis, *Acusación y defensa de Rosas*, 193.
53. De Angelis, *Acusación y defensa de Rosas*, 202.
54. De Angelis insists that the "Ensayo histórico" maintains a sense of decorum that accounts for its omissions. He declares that the "vida pública [de Rosas] no presenta hecho

alguno que esté en oposición con estos elogios; y si no temiésemos ofender su modestia, encontraríamos en su vida privada muchas pruebas que los confirman" [Rosas's public life presents no fact that contradicts these praises; and if we did not fear offending his modesty, we would find many examples from his private life that confirm them] (205).

55. De Angelis, *Acusación y defensa de Rosas*, 193.
56. De Angelis, *Acusación y defensa de Rosas*, 204.
57. Pérez, *El Torito*, 23.
58. De Angelis, *Acusación y defensa de Rosas*, 190.
59. Ana María Amar Sánchez, "Las versiones de la historia: Gauchesca versus periodismo y ensayo histórico," *Filología* 22, no. 1 (1987): 169.
60. Ludmer, *El género gauchesco*, 111.
61. Ludmer, *El género gauchesco*, 111.
62. Félix Weinberg, "El periodismo en la época de Rosas," *Revista de Historia* 2 (1957): 84–85.
63. See Ignacio Weiss's introduction to *Archivo Americano y Espíritu de la Prensa del Mundo* (Buenos Aires: Americana, 1946), xxiv–xlvi, and Adriana Amante, "Género epistolar y política durante el Rosismo," in *La lucha de los lenguajes*, ed. Julio Schvartzman (Buenos Aires: Emecé, 2003), 494–95.
64. Marcela Ternavasio, "Estudio preliminar," in *Correspondencia de Juan Manuel de Rosas* (Buenos Aires: Eudeba, 2005), 33.
65. David Viñas, *Literatura argentina y política: De los jacobinos porteños a la bohemia anarquista* (Buenos Aires: Santiago Arcos, 2005), 15.
66. Jens Andermann, *Mapas de poder: Una arqueología literaria del espacio argentino* (Rosario, Argentia: Beatriz Viterbo, 2000), 36.
67. Lelia Area, *Una biblioteca para leer la Nación: Lecturas de la figura Juan Manuel de Rosas* (Rosario, Argentina: Beatriz Viterbo, 2006), 18.
68. See Andermann, *Mapas del poder*, 56–67; Graciela Batticuore, *La mujer romántica: Lectoras, autoras y escritoras en la Argentina: 1830–1870* (Buenos Aires: Edhasa, 2005), 52–67; and Thomas Bremer, "Historia Social de la Literatura e Intertextualidad: Funciones de la lectura en las novelas latinoamericanas del siglo XIX (el caso del 'libro en el libro')," *Revista de crítica literaria latinoamericana* 24 (1986): 31–50.
69. Walter Benjamin, *Reflections*, ed. Peter Demetz, trans. Edmund Jephcott (New York: Schocken, 1986), 155.
70. Here I am summarizing Doris Sommer's interpretation of the novel in *Foundational Fictions: The National Romances of Latin America* (Berkeley: University of California Press, 1991), 83–112.
71. See, for example, the scene where the young Bello confidently counters the hopeful speculations of the Unitarian leaders exiled in Montevideo, part 3, chapter 3.
72. Domingo Faustino Sarmiento, *Facundo: Civilización y barbarie* (Madrid: Alianza, 1988), 266.
73. Sarmiento, *Facundo*, 52. It is notable that in 1857, that is, following the fall of Rosas, Sarmiento contributes to Bartolomé Mitre's *Galería de celebridades argentinas*, a collection of short biographies accompanied by lithographs that sought to establish a pantheon of Unitarian and liberal heroes, including San Martín and Lavalle. The volume not only lacks a biography of Rosas, Mitre conspicuously avoids mentioning his name in the introduction: though he refers to the type of men who don't warrant inclusion in the volume, who "se presentarán a sus ojos con el resplandor siniestro de aquella soberbia figura de Milton, que pretendía arrastrar en su caída las estrellas del firmamento" [appear before their eyes with the sinister splendor of that haughty figure of Milton, who sought as he fell to tear the stars from the firmament] (3). In the following paragraph, Mitre lists several such men—Artigas, Quiroga, Aldao, López—but never names Rosas, the most obvious of these figures. Rosas, the *interdit*, thus becomes the invisible foil to whom those included are inevitably compared.
74. José Mármol, *Amalia*, vol. 1 (Buenos Aires: El Elefante Blanco, 1997), 29.
75. As Piglia says, without Rosas, Sarmiento is unable to write ("Sarmiento the writer" 127).
76. Sarmiento, *Facundo*, 112.

77. The two portraits of Napoleon I'm referring to specifically are Gros's "Napoleon as First Consul" (1802) and David's "The Emperor Napoleon in His Study at the Tuileries" (1812). As Laura Malosetti Costa observes, Gil de Castro's portraits are formulaic and draw heavily on late colonial portraiture (114).
78. Louis Marin, *Portrait of the King* (Minneapolis: University of Minnesota Press, 1988), 121.
79. Regina A. Root, *Couture and Consensus: Fashion and Politics in Postcolonial Argentina* (Minneapolis: University of Minnesota Press, 2010), 12.
80. For Giorgio Agamben, the poet Pindar is "the first great thinker of sovereignty" because he reveals that "*the sovereign nomos is the principle that, joining law and violence, threatens them with indistinction*" (*Homo Sacer*, trans. Daniel Heller-Roazen [Stanford, Calif: Stanford University Press, 1998], 31). While there is not mention of a likeness of Rosas in "El matadero," the narrator does signal the importance of writing, when he describes the slaughterhouse as "un edificio tan ruin y pequeño que nadie lo notaría en los corrales a no estar asociado su nombre al del terrible juez y a no resaltar sobre su blanca pintura los siguientes letreros rojos: 'Viva la Federación', 'Viva el Restaurador y la heroína doña Encarnación Ezcurra', 'Mueran los salvajes unitarios'" [a building so dilapidated and small that no one would notice it from the corrals if it were not associated with the name of the terrible judge and these following red slogans did not stand out from its white paint: 'Long live the Federation,' 'Long Live the Restorer and the heroic Doña Encarnación Ezcurra,' 'May the savage Unitarians die'] (Esteban Echeverría, *Obra escogida*, ed. Beatriz Sarlo and Carlos Altamirano [Caracas: Ayacucho, 1991], 130).
81. Laura Malosetti Costa, "¿Verdad o belleza? Pintura, fotografía, memoria, historia," *Revista Crítica Cultural* 4, no. 2 (2010): 114.
82. Mark D. Szuchman, "Imagining the State and Building the Nation: The Case of Nineteenth-Century Argentina," *History Compass* 4, no. 2 (2006): 121.
83. Marin, *Portrait of the King*, 33.
84. After a heated public debate with Pedro De Angelis in 1834, Pérez fell out of favor with the regime and was imprisoned. While his fate thereafter is uncertain, what is clear is that his feverous journalistic activities did not contribute to the tumult surrounding Rosas's return to power (Acree, "Luis Pérez, a Man of His Word," 385).
85. "Carta del Viejo Francisco Junco," reprinted in Chávez, *La cultura en la época de Rosas*, 121.
86. "Carta del Viejo Francisco Junco," 121.
87. Whereas the poem associates Rosas and his supporters to various forms of writing, it links the seditious ideas of their enemies with speech: "Miren que son hombres malos / De labia y urbanidar, / Pues con palabras latinas / Nos procuran engañar" [Look at what bad men they are / Of lips and urbane-ity, / Since with Latin words / They try to deceive us] (123). What is striking about this is that it employs the same hierarchy that Julio Ramos detects in *Facundo*, in which "the distance between two forms of speech, one proper (written) and the other alien (oral), is reinscribed as the distance between two hierarchized forms of knowledge" (16). In other words, the prestige of the written word is used by both sides of the ideological divide to affirm their respective projects.
88. "Carta del Viejo Francisco Junco," 122.
89. See John L. Austin's discussion of the term in "Performative Utterances," in *Perspectives in the Philosophy of Language: A Concise Anthology*, ed. Robert J. Stainton (Peterborough, Ont.: Broadview Press, 2000), 239–52.
90. Quoted in Di Meglio, *¡Viva el bajo pueblo!*, 301.

Chapter Two

Graffiti, Public Opinion, and the Poetics of Politics

In the Andean province of San Juan, on the outskirts of its capital city, a monument reads ON NE TUE POINT LES IDEES [One does not kill ideas]. The French phrase, engraved in stone, is a durable reminder of the celebrated act of graffiti Domingo Faustino Sarmiento recounts in the "Advertencia" [Notice] that opens *Civilización y barbarie, vida de Facundo Quiroga y aspecto físico, costumbres y hábitos de la República Argentina* (1845). In this version of the episode, which Sarmiento would recall in various writings throughout his life, he describes the inscription as a hasty, improvised gesture executed as he flees Argentina in 1840, "desterrado por lástima, estropeado, lleno de cardenales, puntazos y golpes recibidos el día anterior en una de esas bacanales sangrientas de soldadesca y mazorqueros" [banished out of pity, broken, covered in bruises, jabs, and punches received the day before in one of those bloody bacchanals of soldiers and thugs].[1] From Chile, the exiled educator and journalist claims authorship of the anonymous scrawl, written in charcoal "bajo las armas de la patria que en días más alegres había pintado en una sala" [beneath the national coat of arms that in happier days I had painted in a room].[2] Appearing twice in the opening of *Facundo*, as a misquoted epigraph and the simulacra of graffiti, *on ne tue point les idées* not only serves as a point of departure for the text it prefaces, it also delimits a locus of enunciation straddling the geographic and discursive limits of Rosas's Argentina, underwriting, as it were, an alternative to the prevailing national order.

In a larger sense, the lapidary inscription is an emblem of the longstanding tendency to monumentalize Sarmiento and his fellow *letrados* of the Generation of 1837 as the founders of Argentine literature and the architects of the modern nation-state. This consecration of a handful of intellectuals promotes a variant of what Jeremy Adelman identifies as "a mainstay of nationalist historiographies, which give to national actors and identities agentic powers in making the world anew and—in their mind's eye—by toppling doomed empires in favor of national successors."[3] According to the terms of this myth, the Rosas regime represents an archaic form of power, grounded in rural traditions and colonial institutions, that has interrupted the path to progress initiated, but left unfinished by the wars of independence. In stark opposition to the premodern or reactionary caudillo, "el progreso argentino es la encarnación en el cuerpo de la nación de lo que comenzó por ser un proyecto formulado en los escritos de algunos argentinos cuya única arma era su superior clarividencia" [Argentine progress is encarnated in the body of the nation that began as a project formulated in the writings of a few Argentines whose only weapon was their superior clairvoyance].[4] These hard-to-kill ideas, prefigured by Sarmiento's anecdote of flight and dissent, predicate nation-building as an exclusive practice determined by the relationship one occupies with respect to writing. In this broader context, the opening of *Facundo* operates as the point of departure for an entire intellectual tradition; it becomes an origin that "makes possible a field of knowledge whose function is to recover it."[5]

On ne tue point les idées demarcates, thus, a nationalist discourse whose boundaries remain relatively stable and impermeable. Such a reading reinforces the central, highly adaptable thesis of *Facundo* that Spanish American society is neatly split between two incompatible modes of existence, between civilization and barbarism. In Ricardo Piglia's words, this opposition "se cristaliza en el contraste entre quienes pueden y quienes no pueden leer esa frase (que es una cita) escrita en otro idioma" [is crystalized in the contrast between those that can and those that cannot read that phrase (which is a quote) written in another language].[6] The binary logic collapses, however, as soon as it becomes apparent that the dictum is a paraphrase or misquotation, which Sarmiento erroneously attributes to Hippolyte Fortoul. Drawing on Paul Groussac and Paul Verdvoye, Piglia argues that the saying does not serve as a shibboleth, but rather articulates the "double bond" of Argentine literature: "on the one hand, its relation to political discourse; on the other, its relation to foreign forms and genres of an already autonomous fiction."[7] Sarmiento's ersatz erudition makes it impossible to fetishize the meaning of the quote; ideas may be untouchable, but they cannot transcend their utterance. The generative force of *on ne tue point les idées* resides in its dislocation, in a narrative that depicts it as hurriedly etched in charcoal beneath the crest of the nation. Though the gesture epitomizes the desire to constitute an independent literary field, it also reveals a conflictive relationship with the public discourse of Rosas's Argentine Confederation, a body of writing that literary and cultural studies have traditionally ignored. In other words, while the words that opens *Facundo* put into relief the fissures of a divided political field, the histrionic act also points to the common, underlying discursive space that made these oppositions mutually intelligible.

This chapter reconsiders the function of writing in the struggle for national organization in mid-nineteenth-century Argentina by rereading the opening of *Facundo* not as a misquotation, but as graffiti. In doing so, it reads Sarmiento's inscription as a contingent response to how the Rosas regime employed visuality, rituals of state power, and public space in order to reconfigure, monitor, and control the expression of public opinion as mechanisms for legitimizing its power. Emphasizing the centrality of gesture in the celebrated anecdote thus reveals strong affinities as well as points of contention that the foundational works of the Generation of 1837 shared with cultural practices employed by supporters of the Rosas regime. This line of interpretation is encouraged by the fact that Sarmiento employs graffiti at two crucial moments in subsequent works, *Viajes* and *Campaña en el Ejército Grande*, to reassert his authority in the overlapping fields of politics and literature. Sarmiento is not alone in using graffiti in this manner: in the historical novel *Amalia*, José Mármol also identifies the inception of his writing career as an act of graffiti in defiance of the *Restaurador de las leyes*. Moreover, as an examination of poetry and pro-Rosas public festivals indicate, as well as earlier examples of postrevolutionary popular protest, these inscriptions—regardless of what their authors may profess—do not belong solely to a semantic field limited to a dissident cultural elite, nor to an alternative body of writing.[8]

Read collectively these graffiti characterize the struggle to define the operative terms of a shared public discourse, a conflict that conditioned political life and cultural activities in postrevolutionary Argentina. In this context, writing operates not as an exclusive or distinguishing activity, but as an individual and apparently spontaneous expression, a surrogate for collective and extra-official declarations of adherence or dissent. What links the diverse writings of this provisional corpus is a common poetics that calls attention to their conspicuous departure from everyday speech; by virtue of a degree of unfamiliarity or illegibility, graffiti seek to produce an affect that either reinforces or disrupts a sense of belonging. At the same time, the site-specific inscriptions and their subsequent representations (in print media, in graphic forms, in narrative) emulate, appropriate, or incite forms of popular protest that emerged in the years following independence, and thus are complicit in constituting the *pueblo* as an indispensable, if imagined recipient of the messages they seek to disseminate.

MARGINALIA OF THE LETTERED CITY

Before engaging in a close reading of Argentine graffiti, let us first consider the key words of our common critical vocabulary. As a survey of recent titles indicates, scholarly inquiries into intellectuals' role in nineteenth-century Latin America continue to grapple with Ángel Rama's concept of *la ciudad letrada* [the lettered city].[9] This is especially the case for this chapter because Rama repeatedly takes an interest in graffiti—as well as other marginal scriptural practices—in his best-known book, *La ciudad letrada* (1984). Rama's consideration of graffiti alludes to the possibility of reorienting (or decentering) the study of Latin American cultural history. A critical rereading of Rama, however, also signals the limits of such an endeavor, because it cautions that we must work with textual and graphic re-presentations of nineteenth-century graffiti, as cultural objects mediated by other, hegemonic forms of writing.

Graffiti illustrates a central and deeply problematic notion that runs through *La ciudad letrada*: throughout the history of Latin America, a class of intellectuals wielded disproportionate power by using writing to assimilate and neutralize alternative cultural activities.[10] Writing is less a treasure house (or a "thesaurus"), than a clearinghouse, through which all demands must pass:

> Todo intento de rebatir, desafiar o vencer la imposición de la escritura, pasa obligadamente por ella. Podría decirse que la escritura concluye absorbiendo toda la libertad humana, porque sólo en su campo se tiende la batalla de nuevos sectores que disputan posiciones de poder. Así al menos parece comprobarlo la historia de los *graffiti* en América Latina.
>
> Por la pared en que se inscriben, por su frecuente anonimato, por sus habituales faltas ortográficas, por el tipo de mensaje que transmiten, los *graffiti* atestiguan autores marginados de las vías letradas, muchas veces ajenos al cultivo de la escritura, habitualmente recusadores, protestatarios e incluso desesperados. (*La ciudad letrada,* 52)
>
> [Any effort to refute, defy or conquer the imposition of writing, must necessary pass through it. It could be said that writing ends up absorbing all human freedom, because only on its terrain can battle be waged by new sectors disputing positions of power. This is, at least, what the history of graffiti in Latin America seems to confirm.
>
> On the walls on which they are inscribed, due to their frequent anonymity, for their habitual spelling errors, for the kinds of messages they transmit, graffiti are a testament of authors marginalized from written protocols, who are frequently alienated from the cultivation of writing, and habitually disregarded, contrarian, and often desperate.]

Graffiti marks the fringe of the lettered city, a space comprised of accredited individuals and accrediting institutions that concede aesthetic and political representation to unrecognized groups. Nameless, subaltern subjects may only make visible their exclusion (or make present their absence) from this domain with unorthodox materials and an improper or borrowed code. The anonymity, impropriety and, often, illegibility of these inscriptions irrupt in public space and interrupt public discourse. In defacing the walls of the physical city, these writings confirm, time and time again, the unshakable hegemony of the lettered city.

To support this broad assertion, Rama offers three instances, drawn from history at intervals of roughly two hundred years: Hernán Cortés's riposte "pared blanca, papel de necios" [white wall, paper of fools]; Alonso Carrió de la Vandera's observations in *El lazarillo de ciegos caminantes* (c. 1776); and the proliferation of political graffiti during the second half of the twentieth century.[11] Each example refers to an unspeakable or forbidden script, which provokes an official reaction that condemns the act and denigrates its faceless author(s). As it spans the full arc of Latin American history, this selection of anecdotes posits a stable, complicit relationship between *letrados* and power. Though it is not an entirely static identity, "the *locus* of the *letrado* in the history of Spanish American cultural history remains immutable, unaltered."[12] Given this configuration, Rama's history of graffiti is refracted through lettered sources. The first two examples he cites are canonical works of colonial literature: Bernal Díaz del Castillo's *Historia verdadera de la conquista de la Nueva España* (1632) and Concolorcorvo's narrative; in the third, Rama and his audience: "todos hemos sido testigos de la invasión de *graffiti* políticos" [we have all been witnesses to the invasion of political graffiti].[13] Precisely at a moment where *La ciudad letrada* seems to attempt "to configure a countercanon that expands our sense of colonial and premodern Latin American textuality" by turning to "graffiti as collective writing," Rama conflates the subject and object of his study.[14] The very strength of the lettered city, paradoxically, restricts the inquiries of a scholar who interrogates the foundation and boundaries of his own place of enunciation.

La ciudad letrada establishes a meta-history of ideas that links figures and intellectual practices from different historical moments and disparate geographies. Julio Ramos attributes this often-emulated reduction to the fact that, "while Rama considers a variety of writers as diverse as Rodó and Sarmiento within the category of the *letrado*, based on the (biographical) fact that they occupied public positions, he downplays the transformation of the place of the *literato*-intellectual before the changing configurations of power."[15] Any given conjuncture is subordinated to an autonomy of letters, whose visibility increases retrospectively. The consequence of orienting cultural history in this fashion, which does not escape Rama, is that alternative practices—including graffiti and other forms of popular expression—tend to be suppressed or omitted from the archival record. *La ciudad letrada* engages the same binary logic that informs the traditional reading of *on ne tue point les idées*, which threatens to limit its scope of inquiry to "el campo semántico e ideológico que corresponde a . . . la ciudad como asiento y origen de proyectos civilizadores, y el letrado como matriz de lo que más globalmente se ha llamado la *intelligentsia* latinoamericana, haciendo énfasis en su condición eurocentrista" [the semantic and ideological field that corresponds to . . . the city as the base and origin of civilizing projects, and *letrados* as the mold for what is more globally known as the Latin American intelligentsia, emphasizing its Eurocentric condition].[16] Graffiti, then, serves only as an analogy that demarcates the outer limits of a restricted discursive field: in the case of Joaquín Fernández de Lizardi, "le ocurre lo mismo que pasaba con los anónimos autores de *graffiti*" [what occurs with him is the same that happened to the anonymous authors of graffiti]; Simón Rodríguez, exiled from lettered city, "como los escritores de *graffiti*, hubiera tenido que introducirse en ella para mejor combatirla" [like graffiti writers, would have had to insert himself into it in order to combat it better].[17]

In a book where Sarmiento figures so prominently, the inscription that opens *Facundo* is conspicuously absent from Rama's considerations about graffiti. At first glance, Sarmiento's gesture appears to make literal the analogy that Rama uses to characterize the efforts of outliers like Lizardi and Rodríguez: Sarmiento protests the brutality of the Rosas regime with words and, in doing so, epitomizes how dissidents "can effectively assail positions of social power only on a two-dimensional battlefield of line and space," to borrow from John Charles Chasteen's elegant translation of *La ciudad letrada*.[18] And, like the graffiti that Rama does mention, it conveys the unspeakable, though not because it contains "desahogos innobles, insultos y amenazas" [ignoble outbursts, insults, and threats] as its initial audience is said to have believed, but because it is written in a foreign language that neither these unnamed officials nor, for that matter, Sarmiento spoke.[19] The anonymous, unintelligible script, which he calls a "hieroglyph," conveys its author's repudiation, protest, and desperation in the face of a prevailing political order.

Although the French maxim—if identified as such—evokes a specific kind of foreignness, a cosmopolitan sophistication that reinforces the binary logic announced in the full title of *Facundo*, the narrative account of its reception strongly suggests that Sarmiento appeals to the power of the written word in a broader sense. In simple terms, the efficacy of his gesture depends on the strangeness and illegibility of its script. This becomes more apparent if we consider other moments when Sarmiento revisits the incident and its setting. Toward the conclusion of his autobiography *Recuerdos de provincia* [Recollections of a Provincial Past] (1850), Sarmiento compresses the anecdote into a series of clauses opening a sentence that narrates his entrée into the intellectual circles of Santiago de Chile. It is not the first time, though, that *Recuerdos de provincia* mentions the Valle de Zonda, the site of the celebrated scrawl. This occurs in "Los huarpes," the third chapter of the book, in which Sarmiento offers a brief history of the precolonial indigenous societies of his native Cuyo. In the absence of an archival source documenting their presence, Sarmiento examines the surrounding landscape and notes a series of petroglyphs that he describes as "vestigios rudos de ensayos en las bellas artes, perfiles de guanacos y otros animales, plantas humanas talladas en la piedra, cual si se hubiese estampado el rastro sobre arcilla blanda" [crude traces of attempts at fine art, profiles of guanacos and other animals, human footprints carved in stone, as if steps had been impressed on soft clay].[20] The traces of a disappeared culture illustrate the precariousness of the author's own civilizing project, symbolically initiated on a nearby wall. Read conjointly, these two moments of the autobiography underscore Francine Masiello's reading of *Facundo*: "presenciamos más que un estudio sobre las ruinas del pasado; también presenciamos la ruina creativa de los objetos que terminamos estudiando" [we witness more than a study about ruins of the past; we also witness the creative destruction of the objects we come to study].[21] Before the painted rocks, Sarmiento assumes a position akin to the befuddled first readers of *on ne tue point les idées*, as he projects his own sensibilities onto the difficult-to-decipher glyphs. Regarded as primitive attempts at representative art, the scrapes in soft clay become signs for the impermanence of both their authors and their medium. Read in the same Romantic mode, the crudeness of Sarmiento's own inscription points to its immediate effect, and also provides a *recuerdo del porvenir* [a memory of the future]: its eventual decomposition or erasure (and hence, the need to re-represent the gesture in another, more lasting and transmissible format).

A later text, titled "Las Piedras Pintadas de Zonda" ["The Painted Rocks of Zonda"] (1864), further emphasizes the physical and functional proximity of Sarmiento's scrawl and the neighboring indigenous drawings. Equal parts scientist and travel guide, Sarmiento charts the topography of the region and catalogues numerous images that cover its rocks. Beyond reporting the sheer quantity of lines scraped on their surfaces, he repeatedly makes an effort to distinguish between prehistoric petroglyphs and more recent additions:

> Piedras enteras están llenas de garabatos, arabescos diría, indescifrables, y por el capricho representarían algo que á geroglíficos se asemejase ó si no son simples juegos sin importancia. Despues vienen los [*sic*] imitaciones modernas, las fechas y los nombres propios que conmemoran lo que no merece recuerdo, de nuestros tiempos, y profanando aquel documento precioso de otros tiempos ha puesto en duda su autenticidad. (*Obras de D. F. Sarmiento* XLVI, 113–14)
>
> [Entire stones are covered with scribbles, indecipherable arabesques I would call them, and might represent something like hieroglyphs or, if not, they are

simple games without purpose. Then come the modern imitations, the dates and proper names that commemorate those who deserve no remembrance, from our times, and, in defiling that precious document of other times they have cast doubt on its authenticity.]

The landscape of Zonda here becomes a palimpsest whose abundance of designs stymies the observer's efforts to tease out their individual meaning. While their original signifying function remains inaccessible, they nonetheless possess a value that is at once historical and aesthetic, one which is threatened by the artless markers of presence left by Sarmiento's contemporaries. The true danger posed by such overwriting is not that it erases reminders of the past, but that it renders them false falsifications. As we will see, this denunciation is not without irony, given Sarmiento's own proclivity to leave his name and an accompanying date on remote landscapes (and then write about it). What distinguishes these present-day inscriptions from the "indecipherable hieroglyphs"—a description that echoes the language Sarmiento employs to describe his own graffiti in *Facundo*—is not simply the antiquity of the latter, but that the former can do no more than convey a banal message of a momentary, individual yet anonymous presence.

Key to Sarmiento's narrative reconstruction of his defiant gesture, then, is the notion that his graffiti possesses a hieratic quality, one which is readily identified by its anonymous first audience. Indeed, even if its first "readers" were illiterate, and even if its translation, requested by the government, produces only incomprehension—"Oída la traducción, '¡y bien!—dijeron—, ¿qué significa esto?'" [Upon hearing the translation, "Well!" they said, "what does that mean?"]—those who first report the graffiti, the government, and the translators who "decipher" the message all immediately—and correctly—recognize it as a direct challenge to the authority represented by the national coat of arms. In these initial interpretations the meaning and language of the inscription are secondary to the act of writing and its specific place of enunciation. Sarmiento's tag thus operates according to the same logic by which "when *montoneros* received only a verbal order, even those who occupied the lowest ranks in the rebellion (the majority of whom were illiterate) pressed their superiors to record it on paper; minimally, they wanted to see the document that, they assumed, contained the order," as Ariel de la Fuente observes in his study of the Province of La Rioja in the 1860s.[22] Writing, as the visible trace of authority (or defiance of that authority), establishes the doubly subaltern position of the anonymous first readers of *on ne tue point les idées*: not only can they not read French nor understand the translated maxim, but their immediate response to the gesture also confirms their subordinate status with respect to the Rosas regime.

By reaffirming the implacability of writing in the struggle for power, Sarmiento's inscription calls attention to the shifting place of the intellectual's position in this process, disrupting the neat trajectory that Rama traces through his three coordinates. For, if Sarmiento is an iconic nineteenth-century intellectual, then the opening of *Facundo* less depicts an author marginalized from the *vías letradas*, than it signals the marginalization of the *vías letradas* themselves. The autobiographical anecdote would represent a restricted, but unified field of cultural production, whose internal conventions disregard all external demands.[23] This neat inversion presupposes that Sarmiento's abandonment of his patria and native tongue symbolizes what we might call a wholesale "brain-drain" from Rosas's Argentina. In doing so, it intimates a tendency that Rama resists in *La ciudad letrada*: "the notion that specific texts our authors can be said to alter this relationship between power and signification, or that we can reconstruct the epistemic period solely based on the transgressive qualities of a given text."[24] For Román de la Campa, Rama's inclusions of noncanonical sources in the posthumous *La ciudad letrada* constitute a sadly truncated effort to resituate the study of Latin American intellectual activity in a broader field of inquiry—the social—where the binary logic that underpins the work is decentered. In other words, Rama calls attention to the civilization/barbarism (writing/speech, etc.) binary, neither to reinforce nor to eliminate it, but "to extend the play of differences and semiotic excess to the broadly social and cultural domains."[25] This sympathetic reading, together with the call for a more rigorously historicized reading of lettered practices, points to a more nuanced understanding of Sarmiento's inscription: *on ne tue point les idées* captures a particular historical moment when conflicting social groups fought to reroute *vías letradas*.[26]

The elitism that the French maxim conveys, after all, is a counterpoint to Sarmiento's abandonment of his native land. This exclusion is not merely geographic or linguistic, but discursive, because, as Josefina Ludmer argues, "con Rosas la patria es *casi* el género [gauchesco]" [with Rosas the fatherland is *almost* the gauchesque genre].[27] I emphasize the qualifier of Ludmer's assertion because, while gauchesque literature is an emblematic body of writing that provided the dominant idiom for the Argentine Confederation, it was but one of many discursive practices that Rosas and his supporters employed to legitimate the regime and maintain power. Contrary to the commonplace image of Rosas as a caudillo who ruled by brute force and disdained intellectual activity, a survey of pro-Rosas journalism reveals that "la oposición simple entre el discurso y las acciones, donde las segundas aparecen juzgadas como verdaderas y el primero como falso, difícilmente pueda sostenerse sin alguna modificación" [the simple opposition between discourse and action, where the latter appears to be judged as true and the former as false, is difficult to uphold without some modification].[28] Sarmiento, in other words, did not flee a barbarism that left its marks solely on the bodies of its victims, but escaped a repressive political climate that, in addition to physical intimidation, depended on writing to a great extent. By opening *Facundo*—written and published in Santiago de Chile—with an account of his scrawl, Sarmiento locates the genesis of his resistance within the territory of the Rosist patria, on the same surface that the regime's iconography occupies, beneath the national coat of arms. It is on this contested space—and not in the metaphoric void of the pampa or *desierto*, as common knowledge would have it—that Sarmiento stakes his claims for authorship and political authority.

Thus, while Sarmiento doubtlessly appeals to a transcendent or transcultural power of writing, he also emphasizes the immediate sociopolitical context that both inspired his transgression and conditioned its reception. The description of his bruised body, the location, and the writing implement suggest how the proscribed *letrado* emulates a strategy employed by other marginalized social actors in the expansion of the political in postrevolutionary society. An earlier example of this phenomenon can be found in an 1822 caricature that shows a black or mulatto boy reaching overhead to write the phrase "*¡Mueran los ereges [sic]!*" [May the heretics die!] on a wall, unaware that Buenos Aires governor Martín Rodríguez and his interior minister Bernardino Rivadavia are watching him (see figure 2.1). Notably, in this depiction of protest against the ecclesiastical reforms carried out by the provincial government in the early 1820s, the writer's face and, hence, his individual identity remain concealed; in contrast to his audience, the representatives of military and civic power who are seen in profile, the boy "parece una representación del bajo pueblo como un todo" [seems a representative of the lower classes as a whole].[29] The broadsheet, which presumably circulated in the same urban space depicted therein, announces the emergence of a social actor and a form of dissent that attract the attention of a republican regime struggling to centralize its power over competing institutions which have outlasted the authority of the Spanish crown, namely the church and the Cabildo. It illustrates how, as the civil conflicts of the 1820s were intensifying, a new form of public opinion emerged that was "associated with a *pueblo* identified in screaming posters, military barracks, and rural canteens seething with unrest."[30] The period immediately preceding Rosas's rise to power thus witnessed "not just a mode of production but a mode of legitimation that was in crisis."[31] By labeling the representatives of the fledgling state as "ereges"—the same word followers of Facundo and Rosas will later use to denounce their Unitarian enemies—the drawing employs religious rhetoric to make a point that is decidedly modern: the bespectacled, portly figure in tails and top hat and his slender companion, decked in formal military regalia, must confront the demands of a subject who calls into question the legitimacy of the secular authorities they embody.

At first glance the caricature seems to constitute a perfect inversion of the episode Sarmiento narrates: an anonymous figure is captured in the act of

Figure 2.1. Anonymous caricature of boy writing graffiti, c. 1822

scrawling a poorly written denunciation in the center of power by the very subjects he seeks to discredit. However, in identifying Sarmiento as the individual author who escapes from the scene of his delinquent erudition in a remote corner of Argentina, *Facundo* takes the space of popular protest as its own, signaling a momentary conflation of the *buen decir* of literary discourse and the impropriety of subaltern writing. Though writing has traditionally been regarded as an instrument for distinguishing "oneself from all of the social classes that did not pertain to the arena of *civitas* which Latin American intellectuals like Domingo Faustino Sarmiento identified as the paradigm of modernity," *Facundo* begins with a moment of indistinction, as if to declare *je est l'autre*.[32] Much like the 1822 caricature, Sarmiento situates his act beneath the gaze of the state; in contesting the Rosas regime, he requires its representatives as his audience. The key difference between these two instances, though, is that Sarmiento reveals his identity ex post facto, seeking to establish his own authority by defying one (Rosas) and declaring his affinity with another (the metropolis). As such, the beginning of *Facundo* dramatizes the need and difficulty of demarcating "a position from which to speak in the face of an assumed horizon of discursivity that assigns a precarious rhetorical authority to the postcolonial interlocutor."[33] The antagonism that graffiti incites thus is not one of pure opposition (between civilization and barbarism, the spoken and written word, foreign and local, sanctioned and prohibited speech, individual and collective, etc.), but instead inscribes itself on the fraught terrain of postrevolutionary public opinion. *Facundo* contests its enemy directly not only by evoking the ghost of its eponymous subject ("¡Sombra terrible de Facundo!" [Terrible specter of Facundo!]), but by conjuring an equally threatening specter of a vague alterity that the standing regime can never fully classify or control.

POLITICAL DISCOURSE AND THE MAGIC OF NAMES

While the opening anecdote of *Facundo* is the most celebrated, it is not the only instance when Sarmiento employs graffiti to emphasize the relevance of his work within a specific conjuncture. *Campaña en el Ejército Grande* (1852) recounts his involvement with General Justo José de Urquiza's army, which defeated Rosas and brought an end to his regime. At one point during the campaign, Sarmiento was returning to army headquarters in Gualeguaychú from Montevideo by boat, when he took advantage of a brief stop to explore the island Martín García, situated at the confluence of the Uruguay and Plate rivers. Sarmiento had identified Martín García as the ideal site for the capital of the "Estados Unidos del Río de la Plata" in his utopian political tract *Agirópolis*, published in 1850. Though Sarmiento sent a box containing copies of the work to Urquiza from Chile, as he recounts in *Campaña en el Ejército Grande*, the general ignored and, on occasion, mocked Sarmiento's offers to counsel him. Setting foot on Martín García for the first time permits Sarmiento to insist once more on the important place he ought to occupy in national politics:

> En un peñasco que está cerca de la playa escribí corriendo estas fechas, para mi cuento muy significativas:
> 1850–Argirópolis
> 1851–Sarmiento (*Campaña en el Ejército Grande*, 152)
>
> [On an outcropping close to the beach I hurriedly wrote these dates, very meaningful to my tale:
> 1850–Argirópolis
> 1851–Sarmiento]

With a gesture that approaches a parody of the colonial act of claiming a territory, Sarmiento employs the title and publication date of *Argirópolis* as a toponym and date of foundation, one that precedes his arrival on the island. Calling attention to an effectively inaccessible—and therefore, unverifiable—sign of past presence, he collapses three distinct moments of writing into one: that of *Agirópolis*, that of the inscription, and that of *Campaña en el Ejército Grande*. By means of an autograph, Sarmiento plots a personal trajectory in discursive and geographic space from the margin to an imaginary center; if *Facundo* is *la ida*, *Campaña* is *la vuelta* of Sarmiento.[34]

Consistent with Sylvia Molloy's reading of *Recuerdos de provincia*, it could be said that the reprinted signature captures a moment when "el individuo que ha venido apuntalándose con lecturas, con citas, con letras, cede lugar a esas letras mismas, desaparece en favor de sus textos" [the individual who has been propping himself up with readings, with quotes, with letters, gives way to these very letters, he disappears in favor of his texts].[35] In a sense, it lays bare the fiction that lends signatures an "absolute singularity": "the pure reproducibility of a pure event."[36] If *Campaña en el Ejército Grande*—published originally in installments in Rio de Janeiro and Santiago—narrates the reinsertion of its author into the national territory and politics, the episode on Martín García alludes to the rewriting and overwriting of this scene. And, while it alludes to Sarmiento's desire to redraw the boundaries of the patria and rename it, the accompanying dates serve as a reminder of the immediate circumstances of the inscription. Thus, as it conveys immediacy and presence, the anecdote underscores Sarmiento's continued efforts to locate himself in the self-elected center of an imagined political community.

The self-referentiality of the episode is heightened when one takes into account that, in *Campaña en el Ejército Grande*, Sarmiento in fact repeats the act of engraving his name on a remote island. In "Mas-a-fuera," a letter to Demetrio Peña from December 14, 1845, which was published in 1849 as part of the first volume of *Viajes por Europa, Africa y América*, Sarmiento narrates a brief excursión to the Archipelago Juan Fernández. Throughout the trip, Sarmiento is mindful of the literary and historical figures associated with the island, namely Captain Cook, the castaways Juan Fernández and Alexander Selkirk, and Selkirk's fictional version, Robinson Crusoe. Toward the end of the day, Williams, an American inhabiting the island, informs Sarmiento and his companions that "en un árbol estaban inscritos más de veinte nombres de viajeros" [more than twenty names of travelers are engraved on a tree].[37] It is late in the day, however, and the men must return to their ship. Sarmiento laments the lost opportunity, then resolves to a leave a trace of his presence, too:

> Acaso hubiéramos tenido el placer al verlos, de quitarnos relijiosamente nuestros gorros de mar en presencia del de Cook i de los de sus compañeros. Pero ya que esto no nos fuese dado, encargáramosle [a Williams] gravase al pié de una roca, *ad perpetuam rei memoriam*, los de
> HUELIN.
> SOLARES.
> SARMIENTO.
> 1845. (*Viajes*, 22)

[Perhaps we would have had the pleasure, when seeing them, to remove our seamen's hats religiously in the presence Cook's name and those of his companions. But since this was not possible, we entrusted Williams with engraving at the foot of a rock, *ad perpetuam rei memoriam*, those of:
HUELIN
SOLARES
SARMIENTO
1845]

Sarmiento here employs a ghostwriter to supplement the unseen name of Cook and his crew with his own. Contrary to *Facundo*, where he claims authorship of an anonymous scrawl, here the inverse occurs: he reveals the inscription bearing his own name to be another's work. While Sarmiento offers his name in (the) place of Cook, he alludes to the fictitious nature of the gesture, as written by a "real-life" Robinson Crusoe. The opening letter of *Viajes* thus locates the work in the interstices of fiction and history, of Latin American, North American, and European forms of cultural production, thus enabling "Sarmiento to situate himself with respect to the multiple cultural referents that impinge upon him."[38] At a glance, then, the inscriptions of *Viajes* and *Campaña* characterize the double bond to which Piglia refers: the centripetal forces of Sarmiento's political aspirations and the centrifugal pull of his literary pretensions.

These are not incompatible impulses in Sarmiento's writing, but, instead, call attention to the fictitious aspect of political rhetoric and the inescapable political dimension of postrevolutionary Latin American literature. Soon after landing, Sarmiento and his shipmates meet the four Anglo-Americans who inhabit the island, and the men agree to hunt wild goats. As Mary Louise Pratt observes, the scene initially appears to be an idyllic, masculine utopia, free of women and government.[39] It does not take long, however, for Sarmiento to notice discord among the men, which leads him to ruminate on the necessarily political nature of human affairs. Rejecting the "sueño vano" of the island hermitage, he ventures that "[s]e nos secaria una parte del alma como un costado a los paralíticos, si no tuviésemos sobre quienes ejercitar la envidia, los celos, la ambicion, la codicia, i tanta otra pasion eminentemente social, que con apariencia de egoista, ha puesto Dios en nuestros corazones, cual otros tantos vientos que inflasen las velas de la existencia para surcar estos mares llamados sociedad, pueblo, estado" [part of our soul would shrivel up, like the side of a paralytic's body, if we did not have those for whom we felt envy, jealousy, ambition, greed, and so many other eminently social passions, which, under the guise of selfishness, God has placed in our hearts, like so many other winds that fill the sails of our existence to cut a path through those seas called society, people, state].[40] What at first appears to be a utopian society, free of state interference, ultimately operates as a kind of case study to examine the central place of politics in human interactions.

Within this model, Sarmiento specifically reflects on the function of language. Prior to embarking on the hunt, the men fashion protective footwear from goat hides, "calzado a la Robinson Crusoe, segun nos complaciamos todos en llamarlo, a fin de cohonestar con una palabra noble, la innoble i bastarda forma que daba a nuestros piés" [footwear à la Robinson Crusoe, as we fancied to name it, so as to cover with a noble word that ignoble and bastard form stuck to our feet]. The appropriation of a "noble" or proper name reminds Sarmiento that the "secreto de los nombres es májico, como usted sabe, en política sobre todo, federacion, americanismo, legalidad, etc., etc., no hai nadie tan avisado que no caiga en el lazo" [secret of names is magic, as you know, in politics above all, federation, Americanism, legality, etc., etc., there is no one so careful as to not fall in the trap].[41] The ostensible thrust of his criticism is that an inadequate form, called by a misleading name, is imposed on a given object: a boot to a foot, a political system to a nation. The phenomenon, for Sarmiento, occurs in multiple contexts, but is most frequent—and perhaps most egregious—in political discourse. The analogy between footwear and politics operates, thus, as a thinly veiled criticism of the Rosas regime and its ubiquitous slogan of ¡Viva la Santa Federación! If "Robinson Crusoe" is too dignified a name for the crude footwear of the hunters of Mas-a-fuera, it follows that the dominant political order of the day has misappropriated the term "Federación." Both cases reveal an ironic meaning that exceeds the intended use of the word because the elevated term ultimately puts into relief the sorry state of the entity it identifies. In this sense, the analogy reaffirms the traditional critique of the disjunction between action and rhetoric, between doing and saying, of Rosas and, in a larger sense, of populist regimes.[42]

This reading is complicated by the fact that Sarmiento admits to using language in the same way and recognizes its practical effectiveness. He concedes to the necessity of political rhetoric and its ineffable "magic," though he protests the misuse of specific words without identifying the guilty parties. There is an incongruence to the analogy, due to the slippage from a proper name ("Robinson Crusoe") and explicit agents to a series of authorless (or unauthorized) concepts. While the first set of terms seem to suggest a deficiency or an equivocation, the political words point to something more arbitrary and radical, akin to what Ernesto Laclau calls an "empty signifier": "a constitutive lack, . . . an impossible object which . . . shows itself through the impossibility of its adequate representation."[43] Words like *federation*, *Americanism*, and *legality* may bring men together, but they do so in a mysterious way, one that seems to defy reason or intelligence, because they are devoid of intrinsic meaning; any authority may use them for its own ends.

Whereas the "calzado Robinson Crusoe" has an easily recognized, preexisting content (a foot), regardless of the inappropriateness or absurdity of the name, the enumerated concepts do not specify or contain a particular form of political association; instead, they seek to constitute it. By establishing his place of enunciation as a remote locale, beyond the reach of the state, Sarmiento places himself at a remove from the contemporary misappropriation of these terms, a posture that the graffiti at the end of the text underscores in dramatic fashion. At the same time, however, by placing his own name alongside those of Crusoe, Cook, Selkirk, and Fernández, Sarmiento also implicates himself in the same system of signification that his political opponents use; at a remove from Rosist hegemony, the letter from Mas-a-fuera signals how he and his opponents employ similar rhetorical strategies to legitimize their respective claims to power. If Sarmiento contests the regime's application of certain terms—such as "legality" and "savage"—and the legitimacy of others—"Federation" instead of "Republic," for example—these differences are semantic, not structural.

POETRY, RITUAL, AND URBAN SPACE IN ROSAS'S BUENOS AIRES

Ironically Juan Manuel de Rosas himself best explains the special brand of "magic" that Sarmiento detects at the core of political discourse. In a letter to the governor of Tucumán, Alejandro Heredia, dated July 16, 1837, Rosas insists on the importance of employing a codified, but boisterous rhetoric to instill a sense of unity throughout the various provinces of the Federation. The government, he argues, must solicit and, at the same time, orchestrate public participation:

> es de absoluta necesidad que en sus oficios y proclamas y en todos los actos oficiales suene siempre la Federación con calor, procurando hacer mención de ella cuantas veces sea posible con especial aplicación al caso o asunto de que se trate, y esto aunque parezca que es con alguna machaca o violencia, porque esa misma machaca prueba ante la generalidad del pueblo que la Federación es una idea que ocupa y reboza el corazón del que habla. (*Correspondencia de Juan Manuel de Rosas*, 168)
>
> [it is of utmost importance that in your charges and proclamations and in all official events [the name of] the Federation sounds with fervor, endeavoring to make mention of it as many times as possible with particular reference to the situation or matter at hand, and though it may seem to be done bluntly or violently, that very bluntness proves to the people as a whole that the Federation is an idea that fills and brims from the heart of he who speaks.]

Rosas reminds Heredia that declarations of patriotism are not ancillary, but integral to the affairs of state. Preceding the fervent cries of the *pueblo* are a chain of written documents, private and public, that seek to regulate the spoken word. Rosas's letter accounts for the production of a signifier that does not merely represent, but enacts hegemonic relations. The purpose of public functions is not to harness spontaneous outbursts, but to produce an illusion of spontaneity that creates an affective bond, which doubles as an apparatus of vigilance.[44] Inciting the passions of its citizenry, the state seeks to create the sense of belonging to a preexisting community. A key element of this operation is repetition. A chorus of *vivas* may generate extreme and even violent passions, but in doing so, it constitutes a biopolitics that engages the hearts, throats, lungs, and ears of its participants. The meaning of patriotic slogans is contingent on a specific action, residing in neither a fixed signified nor a preexisting referent. The collective identity named *federación* is realized precisely when the signifier is crushed ("con alguna machaca o violencia") by its forceful echo.

The antagonism between an intellectual class and the order embodied by Rosas may pit two incompatible ideologies against one another, but both form part of the broader struggle to establish popular sovereignty throughout Spanish America in the turbulent wake of independence. If there was a lack of consensus in terms of the internal configuration of national territory, competing models of sovereignty uniformly regarded the state as indispensable in establishing a supposedly organic connection between a people and a geographic entity. As political elites attempted to establish a new order in the vacuum created by the collapse of imperial authority, they realized that "[a] fin de afirmar los nuevos Estados era necesario, en fin, consolidar lo que no era más que un patriotismo americanista vago en una 'conciencia nacional' a la que subordinaran otras formas de identidad (regionales, de casta, etc.)" [in order to assert the legitimacy of new States, it was ultimately necessary to shape that which was nothing more than a vague Americanist patriotism into a "national consciousness" to which other forms of identity (regional, of social class, etc.) would be subordinated].[45] The failure of the initial, ambitious centralist designs throughout the continent, such as Bolívar's Gran Colombia and Rivadavia's Unitarian government, gave way to decades of internecine conflicts, during which any attempt to establish a national authority required negotiations among caudillos and other local elites.[46] However, the failure of early efforts at the centralization of authority did not imply a reversion to archaic or premodern societies, but instead gave way to a proliferation of nationalist projects. This is, of course, not to ignore the often bloody consequences of conflicts between competing interests, but to emphasize a mutual intelligibility, the common ground that opposing forces fought to partition. In the case of the Argentina at mid-century, Jorge Myers has convincingly demonstrated how pro-regime journalism demonstrates that "los tópicos, símbolos y figuras emblemáticas que servían para articular un sistema de representaciones de lo político conformaban una lengua común, compartido por todas las facciones en pugna" [the emblematic topics, symbols, and figures that served to articulate a system of representing the political conformed to a common language, shared by all competing factions].[47] If "civilization and barbarism" may have been—at the time, at least—an axiomatic dichotomy only for a limited subset of social actors, terms like "federation," "Americanism," and "legality" belonged to a republican discourse employed by multiple groups vying for power. Moreover, its underlying binary structure was universally intelligible and rivals pronounced homologous expressions of loyalty and opposition according to these basic terms.

A pro-Rosas graffiti of sorts provides a salient example of this common language and suggests a more complex, reciprocal relationship between speech and writing, as well as between politics and literature, than "civilization and barbarism" alone would suggest. On September 31, 1836, the regime-friendly newspaper *Gaceta Mercantil* published a poem that had been painted on the walls of the barracks situated on the Plaza de la Victoria (which forms part of the current day Plaza de Mayo). Surrounded by portraits of Rosas, the Santa Fe caudillo Estanislao López, and the recently murdered Facundo Quiroga, the verses celebrated Rosas's return to the governorship of Buenos Aires:

> Yo te saludo, día majestuoso,
> Con el idioma mudo del respeto,
> Lleno de admiración, lleno de gozo;
> Tu recuerdo será siempre el objeto
> Que vivirá grabado en nuestros pechos
> Pues nos distes de libre los derechos.
> (Blomberg 30)
>
> [I salute you, majestic day,
> With the mute language of respect,
> Full of admiration, full of joy;
> Your memory shall always be the object
> That lives on engraved in our hearts
> Since you freely gave us our rights.]

The poem is authorless, but given its places of "publication," it is hardly a graffiti in the sense employed by Rama. It pronounces a state-sanctioned discourse of deference and affection from the symbolic center of the city, literally backed by the military strength of the regime. The poem narrativizes the discursive operation that Rosist hegemony employed to structure relations between the leader and his people: the "I" that communicates through a "mute" language, is a featureless and anonymous national subject that not only fills with admiration and joy, but multiplies into a collective object. The articulation between individual and collective, written on the body (politic), is the figure of the caudillo himself. The *poema mudo* heralds the expansion and resulting changes to a linguistic register formerly restricted to the lettered city. As displayed on a wall in a public plaza, it epitomizes how "la política penetra las relaciones cotidianas, introduciendo otros signos identitarios y otros vínculos que parecen modificar el sentido de los intercambios de la población en los lugares de sociabilidad cotidiana" [politics insinuates itself into everyday relations, introducing other signs of identity and new bonds that seem to modify the exchanges of the population in the places of quotidian sociability].[48] The poem forms part of a discourse that incorporates not only the written and spoken word, but also visual images, dress, and forms of behavior. Everyday life becomes codified in a series of readily apprehensible signs. When compared with the 1822 caricature protesting Rivadavia's reforms, the stately verses of the poem suggest the how the Rosas regime—not unlike Sarmiento—appropriates a potential space for popular protest for its own purposes.

In his historical novel *Amalia*, José Mármol depicts the citywide reaction to a moment of crisis as an outburst of enthusiasm for the Rosas regime, underscoring the use of urban space as a medium for controlling popular expression. In response to rumors that an uprising led by Juan Lavalle is approaching, the inhabitants of Buenos Aires act as if their greatest immediate danger is to be suspected of harboring Unitarian sympathies and make every effort to display proof of their fervor for the Federalist cause:

> En menos de ocho días, la ciudad entera de Buenos Aires quedó pintada de colorado. Hombre, mujeres, niños, todo el mundo estaba con pincel en la mano pintando las puertas, las ventanas, las rejas, los frisos exteriores, de día, y muchas veces hasta en alta noche. Y mientras parte de una familia se ocupaba de aquello, la otra envolvía, ocultaba, borraba o rompía cuanto en el interior de la casa tenía una lista azul o verde. Era un trabajo del alma y del cuerpo, sostenido de sol a sol, y que no daba a nadie, sin embargo, la seguridad salvadora que buscaba. (*Amalia*, II: 369)
>
> [In less than eight days, the entire city of Buenos Aires was painted red. Men, women, children, everyone went about with a brush in hand, painting doors, windows, grates, freizes, by day and often until late into the night. And while part of the family busied itself with that, others wrapped, hid, erased, or broke everything within the house that had a stripe of blue or green. It was a labor of body and soul, kept up from dusk until dawn, and which gave no one, however, the guarantee of protection they sought.]

The general populace engages in unproductive labor, carried out household by household, that blurs family hierarchies and distinctions of social class, gender, and between public and private, exterior and interior space. Complying with the tacit orders of the Rosas regime, Mármol insinuates, reveals the more profound disorder that these demands engender. Nonetheless, the makeover also reveals a certain consistency in the exercise of power, pointing to how urban space and electoral politics functioned as complementary mediums for transmitting the same basic message. In *Amalia*, the visible surfaces of Buenos Aires become a uniform, monochromatic expression of support for the regime; in similar fashion, the results of frequent referendums demonstrated how citizens remained universally in favor of Rosas being endowed with the *suma del poder público*. Walls and votes thus convey what Marcela Ternavasio has argued with respect to the latter: "[l]a unanimidad, identificada ahora a la voluntad general . . . se constituyó, a partir de 1835, en la base de sustentación del nuevo régimen" [unanimity, now identified with the general will . . . became, as of 1835, the base supporting the new regime].[49] Mármol of course indicates how the efforts to efface, destroy, or conceal any possible sign of dissenting opinion are no guarantee of safety, not to mention insincere and incomplete. Regardless of consequences, though, the town painted red presents the image of a populace—indeed, a workforce—cowed by a regime whose official message and iconography it paradoxically repeats with obedient spontaneity.

What *Amalia* critiques, then, is the "monopolización progresiva de todas las instituciones públicas de la provincia [que] haría muy difícil la emisión de un discurso alternativo" [progressive monopolization of all the public institutions of the province, which would make the transmission of an alternative discourse very difficult].[50] Comparing the red city of *Amalia* with a report of the diplomat John Murray Forbes puts into relief how the use of popular expression by the regime constituted a modification of postrevolutionary political culture. Forbes, who served as a charge d'affaires for the United States from 1825 until his death in 1831, relayed news of the unrest following the execution of Governor Manuel Dorrego in 1828. In a letter from the following year, several months prior to Rosas's assumption of the governorship, he reported to Secretary of State Martin Van Buren that "[h]ace pocas noches un grupo de mujeres pegaron carteles en las esquinas de las calles, incitando a los partidarios de Dorrego a nombrar su sucesor a la gobernación, y si Lavalle llegara a sufrir algún revés, sería muy de temer un movimiento popular en la ciudad" [a few nights ago a group of women pasted posters on street corners, inciting Dorrego's supporters to name a successor to the government, and if Lavalle were to suffer some setback, there would be cause to fear a popular uprising in the city].[51] The incident suggests how the walls of the city functioned as a space of expression for sectors of the population excluded from party politics and government because, if women "habían sido incluidas en la politización de espacios públicos y que concurrían habitualmente a las fiestas y otras manifestaciones callejeras, estos testimonios son los primeros con los que contamos acerca de una presencia femenina destacada en la acción política" [had been included in the politicization of public space and had frequented festivals and other street activities, these testimonies are the first we have regarding a conspicuous female presence in political activity].[52] As Forbes's letter indicates, the group of women, unidentified except for allusions to their social status and political sympathies, seek to influence the selection of Dorrego's successor by making public their demand in highly visible locations. Unlike the submissive populace that Mármol describes in his novel, the actions and words of these women not only challenge male politicians to take action, but also function as an indicator of potential unrest among the lower classes of the city. In the postrevolutionary period, then, the specter of the *pueblo* as a destabilizing force was one that would produce trepidation among Mármol and his peers and that the Rosas regime needed to interpellate to consolidate its power. The image of a unified *pueblo* denies Mármol, Sarmiento, and their fellow *letrados* the possibility of mounting a domestic or intramural challenge to the regime that plausibly channels popular will.

While there is nowhere to voice open opposition to Rosas in the Buenos Aires of 1840, as depicted in *Amalia*, Mármol uses a footnote to identify the period as the initial moment of his personal resistance to the regime. Writing from Montevideo, he recalls how, while imprisoned in 1839, "carbonicé algunos palitos de yerba mate para escribir con ellos, sobre las paredes de mi calabozo, los primeros versos contra Rosas" [I burned some twigs of mate in order to write with them, on the walls of my cell, the first verses against Rosas].[53] Mármol constructs an authorial figure on the margins of the printed page and the public space of Buenos Aires. In contrast to the publicly displayed verses in praise of Rosas, this denunciation is, in practical terms, illegible, scribbled with a fettered hand in a space of darkness, confinement, and isolation. The gesture evokes his contemporary Sarmiento's use of similar writing implements and, more remotely, Byron and *The Prisoner of Chillon*. The decidedly Romantic graffiti would seem to distinguish Mármol's literary production from the barbarous practices of his captors.

Read together with the "mute poem," however, the footnote of *Amalia* signals a consistency between public and private writing, between expressions of adhesion and dissent. In both cases, the writing on the wall underscores the privileged place that poetry occupies in a common politico-aesthetic regime.[54] It is important to note that the verses written on the exterior barrack walls do not conform to the conventions of the stylized vernacular poetry that circulated in newspapers throughout the city and province, such as Luis Pérez's *El Gaucho*, *El Negrito*, and *El Torito de los Muchachos*, and that was sung or recited in common settings like *pulperías* and cafés. Instead, their placement, style, and message indicate that, in all likelihood, they were initially employed as part of a public ceremony. The so-called *fiestas federales* were staged in Buenos Aires and throughout the Argentine Confederation with increasing frequency after Rosas assumed the *suma del poder público* in 1835. Typically consisting of speeches, dances, processions, the burning of effigies, and poetry readings, these events formed "part of a communicative exchange between the government and its constituency" that employed "republican ritual practices and symbols."[55] The orchestrated demonstrations occurred in public plazas to commemorate national holidays, offering a ritualized display of Federalist fervor with the regularity of the liturgical calendar. Ceremony thus girded the politicization of everyday life, a relationship that the *poema mudo* embodies: revealed and perhaps recited during a festival, the poem remained on the wall and was subsequently printed in a pro-government daily.

The ceremonial poetry of the *fiestas federales* is characteristic of the populist logic of the Rosas regime in that it implies a democratization of participation, though not of opinion or authorship. In *Rosas y su tiempo* (1907), José Ramos Mejía examines the fiestas that took place in November 1839. He pays particular attention to what Adolfo Saldías refers to as "rimas de federal perversidad" [rhymes of Federal perversity]:[56]

> La lira de "La cautiva" había ido à parar à las manos de los puesteros y abastecedores, como uno de esos preciosos objetos de arte que después de un saqueo, destina à usos domésticos la torpeza del soldado. No era posible prostituir más el arte de quien cantó las desventuras de *Dido* y las osadías del *Pirata* heroico. El nivel de la cultura y el buen gusto que el poeta, si así podía llamarse al herrero de la feroz octava: *Viéraste, ¡oh patria sumergida en llanto!* había obtenido en las parroquias, en medio de las lágrimas de las mujeres la grave admiración de los vecinos y los delirios inconscientes de la turba. (*Rosas y su tiempo*, II: 22–23)

> [The lyre of "The Captive" had fallen into the hands of storekeepers and grocers, like one of those precious works of art, which the soldier's ineptitude consigns to domestic use after looting it. It was impossible to prostitute more the art of he who sung the sorrows of *Dido* and the feats of the brave *Pirate*. The level of culture and good taste that the poet, if the smithy of the ferocious octave could be called that—*Would you see yourself, Oh fatherland submerged in tears!*—had garnered in the parishes, in the midst of women's tears, the grave admiration of neighbors and the mindless ravings of the mob.]

Despite Ramos Mejía's sardonic tone, his appraisal of the scene resonates with Rosas's letter to Heredia regarding the repetition of the name "Federation": both regard language as an effective instrument for forging an affective bond that connects the multitude with a larger political community and its leader, a *primus inter pares*. As he enumerates the professions of the participants—market vendors, purveyors, soldiers, and blacksmiths—Ramos Mejía contends that "subalterns are directly implicated in the subversion of 'natural' social distinctions," consistent with *Amalia*.[57] The "federalist perversion" is that, under the auspices of the state, the masses appropriate the language belonging to poets, such as the Romantics Echeverría and Espronceda. Paradoxically, while the plebe "loots" and "prostitutes" poetry through their participation in the public spectacle, the value of poetry as cultural currency appreciates (and is appreciated). Not in spite of, but because of its subjection and debasement, verse proves capable of provoking the tears, admiration, and deliria of its audience. At a remove of more than sixty years from the events in question, Ramos Mejía makes the implicit claim that his notions about the acceptable uses of poetry are the same as those of the Romantic writers to whom he refers. By gendering poetry and lamenting its indecent public exposure, he excoriates the Rosas regime for using an elevated, private language to sway public opinion.

Ramos Mejía's sense of decorum, however, is somewhat anachronistic in that it presupposes poetry is meant to be an exclusively personal or contemplative form of expression. While the image of Amalia reading Lamartine epitomizes an ideal, Romantic dissidents also regarded poetry as a public discourse capable of forging a collective identity through affect. In this regard, it is notable that Ramos Mejía refers to Esteban Echeverría's *La cautiva*, which Echeverría's peers celebrated as a model for national literature. Read by Juan María Gutiérrez at the Salón Literario that took place in Marco Sastre's bookstore in 1837, the poem offers a sweeping depiction of the pampa. In "Originalidad y caracteres argentinos" ["Originality and Argentine Character"], the celebrated second chapter of *Facundo*, Sarmiento regards this potential site for national progress and poetry with a deep ambivalence:

> Ahora yo pregunto: ¿Qué impresiones ha de dejar en el habitante de la República Argentina el simple acto de clavar los ojos en el horizonte, y ver . . . no ver nada; porque cuanto más hunde los ojos en aquel horizonte incierto, vaporoso, indefinido, más se le aleja, más lo fascina, lo confunde, y lo sume en la contemplación y la duda? ¿Dónde termina aquel mundo que quiere en vano penetrar? ¡No lo sabe! ¿Qué hay más allá de lo que ve? ¡La soledad, el peligro, el salvaje, la muerte! He aquí ya la poesía: el hombre que se mueve en estas escenas, se siente asaltado de temores e incertidumbres fantásticas, de sueños que le preocupan despierto.
>
> De aquí resulta que el pueblo argentino es poeta por carácter, por naturaleza. (*Facundo*, 80)
>
> [Now I ask: What impressions are to be left in the inhabitant of the Argentine Republic from the simple act of fixing his eyes on the horizon and seeing . . . no, not seeing anything; because the more he sinks his gaze into that uncertain, hazy, indefinite horizon, the more distant it grows, the more it fascinates him, confuses him, and plunges him into contemplation and doubt? Where does that world which he vainly wishes to penetrate end? He does not know! What is beyond that which he sees? Solitude, danger, the savage, death! Here I have poetry: the man that moves in these settings, he feels assaulted by fantastic fears and uncertainties, of dreams that worry him when awake.
>
> It is for this reason that the Argentine people is poetic by inclination, by nature.]

The deleterious effect of the poetic character is not merely limited to gauchos or inhabitants of the pampa, but to any "habitante de la República Argentina" who happens to fix his gaze on the sublime vastness of the pampa. Sarmiento looks to poetry as the antidote for this national malaise and quotes the opening of *La cautiva* as an example. He is quick to add that Echeverría's work is *about* the pampa, but not *from* the pampa: "es la poesía culta, la poesía de la ciudad" [it is educated poetry, poetry from the city].[58] The urban(e) verses promise to transform the solitary experience of regarding the pampa into a collective aesthetic experience. Though the authors of this new, national poetry belong to the urban cultural elite, Sarmiento emphasizes its potentially broader appeal and social utility. To emphasize this point, he recounts how Echeverría, during a stay in the countryside, easily overcame gauchos' wariness, because "la fama de sus versos sobre la Pampa le había precedido ya: los gauchos lo rodeaban con respeto y afición, y cuando un recién venido mostraba señales de desdén hacia el *cajetiya*, alguno le insinuaba al oído: 'es poeta', y toda prevención hostil cesaba al oír este título privilegiado" [the fame of his verses about the Pampa preceded him: the gauchos surrounded him with respect and admiration, and when a newcomer showed disrespect for the *city slicker*, someone whispered in his ear: "he's a poet," and all hostile wariness ceased the moment that privileged title was heard].[59] For Sarmiento, the prestige conferred on a poet relaxes, if only momentarily, the social distinctions made immediately apparent by speech and dress, the very conventions that are central to the plot of Echeverría's own *El matadero*. The poet neutralizes the unruly gaucho and, in turn, restores a social hierarchy that rural violence has disrupted. Like Ramos Mejía, Sarmiento notes that the prestige of poetry (and poets) is immediately apparent to even the least educated of people. Where Sarmiento differs, however, is that he regards this privileged status as something that ought to be exploited, precisely because poetry operates so forcefully on human emotion. In this regard, the "national literature" advocated in *Facundo* ironically approximates the pro-Rosas publications that Sarmiento denounces elsewhere in the work: both operate on the principle that a noncolloquial language can make evident an organic, preexisting commonality to those that utter it.

CONCLUSION

Poetry in the hands (or tongues and ears) of the *pueblo* affirms a notion that the graffiti penned by *letrados* intimates: during the dictatorship of Juan Manuel de Rosas, the proponents of competing models for national organization clashed on the terrain of discourse. This was not mere semantic quibbling, but an integral part of the internal conflicts that would continue well after Rosas's deposal in 1852. Reading the "public" writings of Sarmiento and Mármol alongside the "mute poetry" of the *fiestas federales* reinforces the findings of social historians that these adversaries employed a shared republican discourse. It also indicates how these ideas enjoyed a dissemination in media besides books and newsprint and well beyond the small population of literate citizens. Moreover, these inscriptions—and their printed reproductions—evidence a common aesthetic regime that divides this social field into a "we" and an internal other: for Sarmiento, civilization versus barbarism; for Rosas and his supporters, *los federales apostólicos* [the apostolic Federalists] and *los salvajes, inmundos, asquerosos unitarios* [the savage, filthy, disgusting Unitarians]. Ironically, these divisions are most apparent when the signifiers that designate the two camps are deformed by shouting, uttered by illiterate crowds, or written in an unintelligible language or in an inaccessible place. These writings and utterances perform difference by asserting support or discontent on the common, contested ground of public opinion, a discursive space that emerged in postrevolutionary Argentina as various social groups made demands to the representatives of emergent state institutions. Through mockery, mimicry, approximation, and appropriation, these enunciations require the immediate reception of a local audience. Their meaning—not to mention their "magic"—is contingent on the affect that their reiterations produce.

As manifest in graffiti, private correspondence, and publicly circulated documents, as well as the corpus traditionally designated as national literature, writing plays an implacable role in the process by which the relationships between power and collective identities were articulated and reallocated. Against the grain of *La ciudad letrada*, our expanded field of inquiry indicates that, in the context of postrevolutionary Argentina, a variety of social actors contested the propriety (and properness) of scriptural practices. Writing was not the exclusive terrain of a unified lettered class, nor was the relationship between culture and state power stable, in spite of the curiously congruent declarations of political adversaries to the contrary. Even for those subjects who could not read or write, or did so poorly, the writing on the wall operated as a forceful, if unstable signifier of the function of the *pueblo* as both an interlocutor and a legitimizing mechanism for opposing political designs. While neither the identity nor the location of this entity was fixed, graffiti demanded its presence as an active political subject and, in doing so, set in motion a play of differences that would coalesce around equivalent binary opposites as the partisan struggles of the era intensified.

NOTES

1. Domingo Faustino Sarmiento, *Facundo: Civilización y barbarie* (Madrid: Alianza, 1988), 32.
2. Sarmiento, *Facundo*, 32.

3. Jeremy Adelman, *Sovereignty and Revolution in the Iberian Atlantic* (Princeton, N.J.: Princeton University Press, 2006), 344.

4. Tulio Halperín Donghi, "Una nación para el desierto argentino," in *Proyecto y construcción de una nación* (Buenos Aires: Ariel, 1995), 8.

5. Michel Foucault, "Nietzsche, Genealogy, History," in *Language, Counter Memory, Practice: Selected Essays and Interviews*, ed. D. F. Bouchard (Ithaca, N.Y.: Cornell University Press, 1977), 143.

6. Ricardo Piglia, "Notas sobre *Facundo*," *Punto de Vista* 17, no. 3 (1980): 15.

7. Ricardo Piglia, "Sarmiento the Writer," in *Sarmiento: Author of a Nation*, ed. Halperín Donghi, Tulio, Gwen Kirkpatrick, Iván Jaksik, and Francine Masiello (Berkeley: University of California Press, 1994), 131. Since the publication of Piglia's influential essay, David Haberly has further complicated the chain of borrowings and transformations of the *bon mot* Sarmiento attributes to Fortoul. He notes that Paul Verdevoye took Charles Didier at his word that Diderot was responsible for the phrase *on ne tire pas des coups de fusil aux idées*. However, it would seem that the quote in fact originates from a similar phrase written by the eighteenth-century writer Count Antoine de Rivarol ("Reopening *Facundo*," 54–55). Contrary to the notion that Sarmiento misremembers or poorly copies a quote (and hence exemplifies the subordinate relationship Latin American culture occupies with respect to its metropolitan model), Haberly reminds us that the same tendencies to misattribute, plagiarize, paraphrase, and rephrase are intrinsic to the supposed model as well.

8. This would be to take literally another commonplace and potentially insist on yet another false continuity, by taking *on ne tu point les idées* to be the origin of all Argentine graffiti.

9. A selection of such examples: Román de la Campa's "*The Lettered City*: Power and Writing in Latin America" (1999); *Latin American Literature and Mass Media* (2001), edited by Edmundo Paz-Solán and Debra A. Castillo, contains both their introduction, titled "Beyond the Lettered City," and Ignacio Corona's contribution, titled "Contesting the Lettered City: Cultural Mediation and Communicative Strategies in the Contemporary Chronicle in Mexico"; Jean Franco's *The Decline and Fall of the Lettered City: Latin America in the Cold War* (2002); a double issue of *Estudios: Revista de Investigaciones Literarias y Culturales* titled "Homenaje a Ángel Rama" (2003); *Más allá de la ciudad letrada: Crónicas y espacios urbanos* (2003), an anthology edited by Boris Muñoz y Silvia Spitta; Bladimir Ruiz's "*La ciudad letrada* y la creación de la cultura nacional: Costumbrismo, prensa y nación" (2004); Françoise Perus's "¿Qué nos dice hoy *La ciudad letrada* de Angel Rama?" (2005); Juan Pablo Dabove's *Nightmares of the Lettered City: Banditry and Literature in Latin America, 1816–1929* (2007); Juan Ricardo Aparicio and Mario Blaser's "The 'Lettered City' and the Insurrection of Subjugated Knowledges in Latin America" (2008).

10. For Carlos J. Alonso, Rama demonizes writing and, therefore, "there is no way out from the *letrado*'s power, just as there is no way out *for* the *letrado*, should he wish to apply his mastery of the written word to an oppositional or contestatory practice within his society" ("*Rama y sus retoños*: Figuring the Nineteenth Century in Spanish America," *Revista de estudios hispánicos* 28, no. 2 [1994]: 288).

11. Ángel Rama, *La ciudad letrada* (Hanover, N.H.: Ediciones del Norte, 2002), 52–55.

12. Alonso, "*Rama y sus retoños*," 287.

13. Rama, *La ciudad letrada*, 54.

14. Román de la Campa, *Latin Americanism* (Minneapolis: University of Minnesota Press, 1999), 135. This conflation captures the expository mode of *La ciudad letrada* that leads Françoise Perus to level a critique that overlooks its unfinished, provisional status: "procede . . . mediante asociaciones contiguas entre los signos que ella misma postula, sin que el lector pueda discernir la distancia—si es que la hay—entre lo atribuido a estos y otros autores u la ubicación del propio Rama al respecto. Así mismo, tampoco resulta clara la relación—recta o distanciada—que mantiene la voz enunciativa con sus propios enunciados o con los que reproduce y pertenecen a otros" [it proceeds . . . by means of contiguous associations between the signs that it postulates, without the reader being able to determine the distance—that is, if there is one—between that which is attributed to one author or another and the location of Rama himself with respect to them. At the same time, nor is it clear if the relation—direct or

distanced—that the speaking subject maintains with his own enunciations or with those that he reproduces and those that belong to others] (365).

15. Julio Ramos, *Divergent Modernities: Culture and Politics in Nineteenth-Century Latin America*, trans. John D. Blanco (Durham, N.C.: Duke University Press, 2001), 60.

16. Mabel Moraña, "De La ciudad letrada al imaginario nacionalista: Contribuciones de Ángel Rama a la invención de América," in *Políticas de la escritura en América Latina: De la Colonia a la Modernidad*, ed. Francisco Lasarte et al. (Caracas: Monte Ávila, 1994), 49.

17. Rama, *La ciudad letrada*, 59, 67.

18. Ángel Rama, *The Lettered City*, trans. John Charles Chasteen (Durham, N.C.: Duke University Press, 1996), 37.

19. Sarmiento, *Facundo*, 32.

20. Domingo Faustino Sarmiento, *Recuerdos de provincia*, ed. María Caballero Wangüemert (Madrid: Anaya & Mario Muchnik, 1992), 93.

21. Francine Masiello, "Los sentidos y las ruinas," *Iberoamericana: América Latina, España, Portugal* 8, no. 30 (2008): 104.

22. Ariel De la Fuente, *Children of Facundo: Caudillo and Gaucho Insurgency during the Argentine State-Formation Process (La Rioja, 1853–1870)* (Durham, N.C.: Duke University Press, 2000), 87.

23. This language is a rather clumsy pastiche of Pierre Bourdieu's terminology, which serves as a reminder of the chimerical nature of treating the foundational works of Argentine literature as belonging to a self-contained field. See Bourdieu's *The Rules of Art: Genesis and Structure of the Literary Field*, trans. Susan Emanuel (Stanford, Calif.: Stanford University Press, 1996) especially "The Author's Point of View: Some General Properties of Fields of Cultural Production" (214–77).

24. De la Campa, *Latin Americanism*, 132. This would merely repeat the tendency that "can be seen, for instance, in the many dissertations and monographs written in the last ten years that study the role of a particular *letrado* in the process of creating a national discourse; works whose formulaic titles usually run: '(Letrado's name) y la creación del discurso fundacional en (country)'" (Alonso, "*Rama y sus retoños*," 290).

25. De la Campa, *Latin Americanism*, 137–38.

26. This assertion is consistent with Tulio Halperín Donghi's observation that the earliest writings of the Generation of 1837 convey an attitude that is, to an extent, reactionary: an acute sense of loss for the traditional position occupied by *letrados* during the colonial era. Halperín finds that these writings are especially concerned with "la hegemonía de la clase letrada como el elemento básico del orden político al que aspira, y su apasionada y a veces despiadada exploración de las culpas de la elite revolucionaria parte de la premisa de que la principal es haber destruido, por una sucesión de decisiones insensatas, las bases mismas de esa hegemonía, para dejar paso a . . . los jefes del federalismo" ("Una nación para el desierto argentino," 10–11).

27. Josefina Ludmer, *El género gauchesco: Un tratado sobre la patria* (Buenos Aires: Sudamericana, 1988), 111 (italics added).

28. Jorge Myers, *Orden y virtud: El discurso republicano en el régimen rosista* (Buenos Aires: Universidad Nacional de Quilmes, 1995), 14.

29. Gabriel Di Meglio, *¡Viva el bajo pueblo! La plebe urbana de Buenos Aires y la política entre la revolución de Mayo y el rosismo (1810–1829)* (Buenos Aires: Prometeo, 2006), 236.

30. Adelman, *Sovereignty and Revolution*, 383.

31. Adelman, *Sovereignty and Revolution*, 383.

32. Santiago Castro-Gómez, "The Social Sciences, Epistemic Violence, and the Problem of the 'Invention of the Other,'" *Nepantla: Views from South* 3, no. 2 (2002): 274.

33. Carlos J. Alonso, *The Burden of Modernity: The Rhetoric of Cultural Discourse in Spanish America* (New York: Oxford University Press, 1998), 36.

34. This narrative of epic return and, in a sense, Sarmiento's literary career, comes to a neat close at the end of *Campaña*, when immediately following the battle of Caseros, he reports that "tomé papel de la mesa de Rosas y una de sus plumas, y escribí cuatro palabras a mis amigos en Chile, con esta fecha. *Palermo de San Benito, febrero 4 de 1852*" [I took paper from Rosas's desk and one of his pens and I wrote these four words to my friends in Chile. *Palermo de San*

Benito, February 4, 1852] (222). While graffiti reveals the marginalized position of the liberal intellectual, the letter from Palermo, written with more traditional implements, announces Sarmiento's arrival at a place of political power.

35. Sylvia Molloy, "Inscripciones del Yo en *Recuerdos de provincia*," *Revista Iberoamericana* 54, no. 143 (1988): 417.

36. Jacques Derrida, "Signature Event Context," in *A Derrida Reader: Between the Blinds*, ed. Peggy Kamuf (New York: Columbia University Press, 1991), 107.

37. Domingo Faustino Sarmiento, *Viajes por Europa, África y América, 1845–1847 y Diario de gastos*, ed. Javier Fernández (Buenos Aires: Colección Archivos, 1993), 22.

38. Mary Louise Pratt, *Imperial Eyes: Travel Writing and Transculturation* (New York: Routledge, 1992), 191.

39. Pratt, *Imperial Eyes*, 191.

40. Sarmiento, *Viajes*, 14.

41. Sarmiento, *Viajes*, 16–17.

42. "Sarmiento señalaba una oposición diametral entre aquello que decía estar haciendo el rosismo y lo que realmente hacía: sus proclamados sólo podían entenderse mediante el tropo de la ironía . . . y sólo podían explicarse como producto del cinismo" [Sarmiento signaled a diametric opposition between that which Rosism said to be doing and what it really was doing: its proclamations could only be understood by means of the trope of irony . . . and could only be explained as a product of cynicism] (Myers, *Orden y virtud*, 14).

43. Ernesto Laclau, *Emancipation(s)* (New York: Verso, 1996), 40.

44. "El partido federal, siempre atento a medir la extensión de su influencia y popularidad entre la población y a identificar—para hostigar y castigar—a los opositores al régimen, entendía a la política como un compuesto de acciones, voces, rituales y apariencias que . . . debían todas orientarse en un determinado sentido." [The Federalist party, always eager to measure the reach of its influence and popularity among the population and to indentify—in order to harass and punish—the opponents of the regime, understood politics as a complex of actions, voices, rituals, and appearances that . . . all needed to be directed in a specific sense.] (Ricardo Donato Salvatore, "'Expresiones federales': Formas políticas del federalismo rosista," 193.)

45. Elías José Palti, *El tiempo de la política: El siglo XIX reconsiderado* (Buenos Aires: Siglo Veintiuno Editores Argentina, 2007), 151.

46. For a discussion of these various models, see Adelman, *Sovereignty and Revolution*, 344–93.

47. Myers, *Orden y virtud*, 45.

48. Pilar González Bernaldo de Quirós, *Civilidad y política en los orígenes de la Nación Argentina: Las sociabilidades en Buenos Aires, 1829–1862*, trans. Horacio Pons (Buenos Aires: Fondo de Cultura Económica, 2001), 203.

49. Marcela Ternavasio, "Entre la deliberación y la autorización: El régimen rosista frente al dilema de la inestabilidad política," *Caudillismos rioplatenses*, ed. Noemí Goldman and Ricardo Donato Salvatore (Buenos Aires: Eudeba, 1998), 179.

50. Myers, *Orden y virtud*, 22.

51. John Murray Forbes, *Once años en Buenos Aires, 1820–1831: Las crónicas diplomáticas de John Murray Forbes* (Buenos Aires: Emecé, 1956), 520.

52. Di Meglio, *¡Viva el bajo pueblo!*, 302.

53. José Mármol, *Amalia*, vol. 2 (Buenos Aires: El Elefante Blanco, 1997), 64.

54. Graciela Batticuore reminds us that, despite later laments about the ineffectiveness of poetry, "al menos hasta entrados los años 40 (época en que se ambienta *Amalia*) la *poesía* seguirá siendo la forma de la escritura elevada a la que aspiran o se ven tentados aunque sea ocasionalmente los autores y autoras románticas que se precian" [at least until well into the 1840s (the era in which *Amalia* takes place), *poetry* will continue to be the elevated form of writing that Romantic male and female authors aspire to or are tempted by, if occasionally] (*La mujer romántica: Lectoras, autoras y escritoras en la Argentina: 1830–1870* [Buenos Aires: Edhasa, 2005], 58).

55. Ricardo Salvatore, *Wandering Paysanos: State Order and Subaltern Experience in Buenos Aires during the Rosas Era* (Durham, N.C.: Duke University Press, 2003), 363. Salva-

tore engages in a close reading of the documents concerning a fiesta that occurred in the town of Dolores, province of Buenos Aires. It underscores how such events were not spontaneous gatherings, but orchestrated spectacles based on those of the capital: "Far from the center of power, Dolores celebrated a patriotic festivity with a blueprint identical to Buenos Aires'. This shows that the political model embodied in that design was replicable even in mid-size and small towns. The images of the federalist fatherland could circulate in iconic form across the territory of the Confederation" (372).

56. Saldías quoted by Ramos Mejía in *Rosas y su tiempo*, *Rosas y su tiempo*, vol. 2 (Buenos Aires: Félix Lajouane, 1907), 21.

57. Salvatore, *Wandering Paysanos*, 388. In this sense we might argue that Rosism approximates an aesthetic regime that, as Jacques Rancière understands it, "en suspendant l'opposition entre entendement actif et sensibilité passive, veut ruiner, avec une idée de l'art, une idée de la société fondée sur l'opposition entre ceux qui pensent et décident et ceux qui sont voués aux travaux matériel" [in suspending the opposition between active understanding and passive sensibility, it seeks to destroy, along with an idea of art, an idea of society based on the opposition between those who think and decide and those who are fated to do manual labor] (*Le partage du sensible*, 70).

58. Sarimento, *Facundo*, 82.

59. Sarimento, *Facundo*, 83–84.

Chapter Three

Visual Culture and the Limits of Representation

On August 17, 1844, Pascuala Beláustegui de Arana, wife of the Minister of Foreign Affairs for the Confederación Argentina, writes to Tomás Guido, the government's representative in Rio de Janeiro, with news from Buenos Aires. Beláusegui boasts of a newfound prosperity enjoyed in the capital city, but her patriotic enthusiasm is momentarily dampened when she turns her attention to a curious custom of its inhabitants:

> En estos días han puesto un gabinete óptico. Usted sabe que esto es para muchachos, se pagan por cada persona cinco pesos incluyendo los niños; pues se llena el salón todas las noches, y con mucha frecuencia sacan cada noche 900 o mil pesos, de suerte que los bribones franceses que son dueños se han de enriquecer en un momento; si usted va al teatro está lleno, si a las funciones de iglesias, no se cabe en ellas, aún cuando predique el Padre Silva; en fin las gentes se ven en todas partes como que hay contento; le hago a usted esta relación porque como patriota tendrá el gusto de saber algo de su país. (Irazusta, *Vida política de Juan Manuel de Rosas*, IV, 246–47)

> [Recently they've set up an optical cabinet. You know this is for kids, the entry is five pesos per person, including small children; the hall is filled every night, and with great frequency they take in 900 or a thousand pesos, so the French scoundrels who are the owners are going to get rich in an instant; if you go to the theater, it's full, or to church functions, it's hard to find a seat, even when the Father Silva is preaching; in the end, the people seem happy everywhere; I tell you this because as a patriot you must enjoy hearing news of your country.]

Decades before the emergence of what is typically identified as "mass culture" or the "cultural industry," this letter provides a glimpse at visual culture taking shape in postrevolutionary Latin America. A member of the Federalist elite, its author is sure to distance herself from the crowds that attend the spectacle and dismisses it as pueril. Ironically, though, Beláustegui's comment echoes the rhetoric that the promoters of the show likely used to publicize it: throughout 1844 an advertisement appeared in the Buenos Aires daily *La Gaceta Mercantil* promoting a "Cosmorama" that promised to inspire "admiración por su brillante magnificencia capaz de encantar y recrear al espíritu menos intelectual" [admiration for its brilliant magnificence, capable of enchanting and entertaining the least intellectual spirit].[1] As Beláustegui's assumed familiarity indicates, the presence of such a diversion was hardly a novelty in the region: magic lanterns first appeared in Buenos Aires at the end of the eighteenth century, and by the 1840s the local press announced audiovisual spectacles with increasing regularity.[2] Publicized with various and often interchangeable names such as dioramas, cosmoramas, *gabinetes ópticos*, *salones de vistas ópticas*, *tutilimundi*, and phantasmagoria, these forms of popular entertainment offered audiences an array of illuminated, projected, enlarged, and moving images, typically accompanied by music or sound effects. Whether depicting the supernatural, exotic landscapes, battle scenes, or other historical events, their displays made extraordinary pictures (or at least the promise of such images) a part of everyday life in Rosas's Buenos Aires.

It is not, then, the newness of the function nor its content that strikes Beláustegui as noteworthy, but instead something about its recent numerical and commercial success. First, she insinuates that, in exchange for five pesos, its spectators are uniformly transformed into "muchachos" or "niños," irrespective of age. The *gabinete óptico* not only makes considerable money from its audiences, it also organizes a form of collective behavior that runs counter to the author's sense of proper, public conduct. The nightly functions moreover succeed in attracting crowds that are equivalent in size, if not respectability, to those that the church and the theater draw. Even though Beláustegui assures Guido of the general happiness of her compatriots, the passing mention of the *gabinete óptico* hints at a certain anxiety that is not limited to either simple questions of decorum nor a lingering resentment for the French blockade of Buenos Aires (which was lifted in 1840); she adverts to a new, collective desire to see that potentially competes with more established forms of sociability. Might the imported "optic" promote a new kind of spectatorship, a distraction that diverts the eye from official iconography? Or is it a new mode of representation that can maintain the hegemony of the *Restaurador de las leyes*?

Embedded in an exchange of pleasantries between members of the ruling elite, the passing mention of the *gabinete óptico* does not answer these questions, but provokes them by conveying an ambivalent curiosity for a newly popular form of entertainment. This qualified interest in turn bespeaks of an underlying problematic: the relationship between political power in postrevolutionary Argentina and an emerging visual regime. In the broadest terms, we could say that the fragment of Belaústegui's letter provides a testimony of the localized experience of a technological and epistemic shift occurring at the beginning of the nineteenth century throughout the Western world, when "a new set of relations between the body on the one hand and forms of institutional and discursive power on the other redefined the status of an observing subject."[3] Within a new political and scientific paradigm, the modern viewing public becomes its own spectacle, one observed, classified, and disciplined—in short, constituted in the act of seeing.

Belaústegui's xenophobic epithet, however, also serves as a reminder that the imposition of a new scopic regime was occurring at the same time that the new nations of Latin America were negotiating neocolonial arrangements with the metropolis. Audiovisual spectacles hence formed part of the larger transatlantic economy of goods, capital, people, and ideas. If studying Latin American visual culture runs the risk of imagining an "imperial center . . . which displaces itself while remaining the same, always becoming more central, more hidden," Belaústegui's first-person account from the mid-nineteenth century serves to caution us that the status and location of the image, the subject, and, for that matter, power were not homogeneous, universal, or stable.[4] As seen through the lens of visuality, the totalizing force of modernity is experienced locally in various uneven, discontinuous, and interrupted ways.

On its own, Belaústegui's letter merely alludes to these larger phenomena, and one could interpret her reference to the *gabinete óptico* in any number of ways, if not dismiss it, much as this cultural practice has traditionally been disregarded, first by intellectuals in the latter half of the nineteenth century and, until recently, by literary and cultural studies.[5] However, this text is but one of numerous references in the Rosist archive to such shows and devices: in addition to articles and advertisements in contemporary print media, writers including the pro-Rosas gazetteer Luis Pérez, the Uruguayan polymath Andrés Lamas, Esteban Echeverría, José Mármol, Domingo Faustino Sarmiento, Juan Bautista Alberdi, Florencio Varela, and Mariquita Sánchez de Thompson refer to optical devices and audiovisual spectacles in their published works and private correspondence. If the frequency with which these phantasmagorical projections haunt the archive attests to the burgeoning popularity of a specific cultural practice, the references more often than not operate with an over-determined rhetorical force whose persuasive component is ideological.

Like Plato's cave allegory, Locke's *tabula rasa* or Marx's camera obscura, these textual fragments function as double images or "hyper-icons" in the sense that "they are themselves 'scenes' or sites of graphic image-production, as well as verbal or rhetorical images (metaphors, analogies, likenesses)."[6] In the context of a crisis of political legitimation, the hyper-icons of postrevolutionary Argentina articulate and problematize the intersecting gazes that constitute modern vision: the desire to consume images, the concomitant efforts to represent, keep watch over, and order this behavior, and scientific inquiry. If spectacles embody a mode of revealing (that is, the technology) necessary to imagine the simultaneous existence of subjects occupying the national territory, they also point to the omissions constitutive of any national narrative. In this regard, these apparatuses are not proleptic; they do not prefigure the nation-state as a specific form that contains a preexisting people, but rather simultaneously rehearse and resist techniques that make visible the possibility of a *res publica*. Read conjointly, then, these optics represent something akin to what Roland Barthes calls a *punctum*: "a subtle *beyond*—as if the image launched beyond what it permits us to see," to see beyond the desired totality (a nation), because it signals the presence of an alterity that frames a visual field through its exclusion.[7]

In looking at and through optics, the purpose of this chapter is to assemble a "viewing machine," a critical apparatus that reveals how the question of representation informs the antagonisms that partitioned postrevolutionary culture and politics in Argentina. In this sense, it seeks to function as widget for the "máquina para leer el siglo XIX" [machine for reading the nineteenth century] proposed by Josefina Ludmer, which reconfigures literature as "secuencias de palabras, discursos o voces de diferentes culturas, que definen o delimitan posiciones o sujetos" [sequences of words, discourses or voices of different cultures, which define or delimit positions or subjects].[8] Within the internecine conflicts of postindependence Latin America, these reassembled sequences, dislodged from an ensconced place in national literary canons, map the myriad, possible social configurations relentlessly rehearsed during the first half of the nineteenth century. Processed as such, they demonstrate how, "entre sus representaciones (sus culturas-voces politizadas), distribuyen espacios, sitúan a cada uno en su relación con otro, tejen alianzas, poderes y subordinaciones, integran a algunos y excluyen a otros" [among their representations (their politicized cultures-voices), they distribute spaces, situate each other with relation to another, weave alliances, powers, and subordinations, integrating some and excluding others].[9] Thus, if the modern state becomes discernable only "*within* the network of institutional mechanisms through which a certain social and political order is maintained,"[10] the interlocking components of Ludmer's theoretical machine reveal the continuous and conflictive assembly, adoption, and abandonment of such mechanisms, prior to the latter half of the century when institutions and codified forms of knowledge were employed to establish specific forms of state power as "the transcendental condition of the real itself."[11] In other words, in contrast to methods of inquiry that seek to explain the eventual dominance of the liberal state and its national variants, the componentry of Ludmer's device reanimates the prodigious and still-ignored discursive output that is extraneous, superfluous, or contrary to teleological narratives that were retrospectively deployed in later decades.

While the complex workings of Ludmer's theoretical machine borrow from surrealist artifacts (works by Marcel Duchamp, Roberto Matta, and Hedda Stern come to mind), my apparatus also finds inspiration in a model that is simpler and contemporary to the objects studied in this chapter. In 1819 the Uruguayan artist Juan Manuel Besnes e Irigoyen sketched the design for a device labeled *Máquina para sacar vistas* (figure 3.1). Besnes's proposed "view-taking machine" is a portable Dürer grid, consisting of a viewfinder and a segmented glass plate, which would be mounted on a tripod. Looking through such a device, an observer could examine a fixed visual field as divided into small, equal-sized squares. For Besnes, a painter of scenic backdrops and transparent paintings for civic festivals, the *máquina* could serve a practical purpose, providing a systematic method for producing verisimilar, large-scale images.[12] Treated allegorically, Benses's proposed device functions as a conceptual model explaining the objective of this chapter. By momentarily restricting my field of inquiry through an arbitrary partition, I hope to represent with greater accuracy the larger cultural landscape of which optical devices and audiovisual spectacles form but a segment. This is to emphasize that the mode of seeing articulated by optical devices is by no means exclusive to them. However, through this focus it becomes possible to detect a more general "problemática da identidade nacional: a superposição de fragmentos, a ilusão de objetos no interior do quadro, donde, a inexistência da própria obra e do 'assunto' que lhe daria suporte" [problematic of national identity: the superimposition of fragments, the illusion of objects within the frame, where the inexistence of the work itself and the "matter" that would support it coexist].[13] Our view-taking machine, in other words, temporarily disarticulates or interrupts the familiar oppositions of civilization and barbarism, image and text, writing and speech, and so on, that sustain the illusion of the Argentine nation as a totality.

Another forerunner to the audiovisual spectacles of the Rosas era suggests how preexisting apparatuses negotiated these partitions-in-formation and were repurposed in the context of postindependence. In his memoir *Twenty-four Years in the Argentine Republic* (1846), the American John Anthony King tells of his participation in the civil wars of the early 1820s. In 1821 a detachment of José Miguel Carrera's troops capture King and strip him of his possessions, but he and an Englishman named Crasey manage to recover a magic lantern from a ransacked cart. What follows is a kind of picaresque narrative of King's misfortunes: dressed in little more than "a calico rag about my person, scarce sufficient to cover my nakedness," he and Crasey travel to San Luis.[14] Upon entering the town, they acquire "a little cast-off clothing," borrow a sheet and put on a magic lantern show, charging

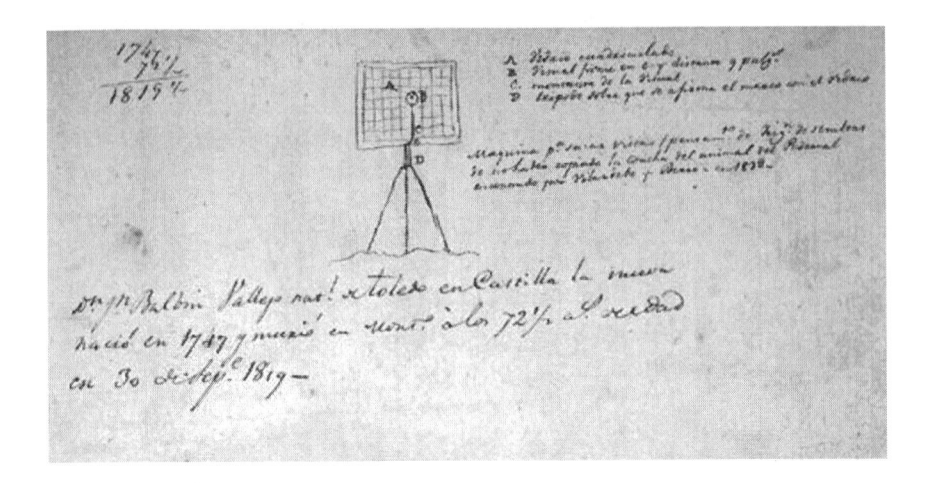

Figure 3.1. "Máquina para sacar vistas," sketch by Juan Manuel Besnes e Irigoyen, 1819

"*un medio chelin entrado*, or sixpence, as the price of admission."[15] Up until this point, King's story approximates folklore, evoking the figure of the impoverished, itinerant Savoyard traversing the rural interior.[16]

What happens the next night, however, alters the tone and significance of the narrative. Following a second profitable evening, an audience member recognizes King in spite of his uncustomary appearance: his acquaintance Coronel José Santos Ortiz, governor of the province and future secretary of the caudillo Facundo Quiroga. Ortiz invites King back to his home, where he warns the American that "as a friend, I advise you to leave the town forthwith" and adds that, "as no disguise is better than your present employment, you can at the same time ensure concealment and obtain subsistence, by exhibiting your lantern in the villages through which you pass."[17] The caudillo himself may view the display of "fantastic figures," but he is not deceived by them. Whereas the magic lantern was traditionally associated with trickery, as it proffered images of the supernatural, here the Coronel reveals a second order concealment, that of the projectionist's identity, only to insist on its practical redeployment. Ortiz delivers this advice "as a friend," which given the larger backdrop of civil war, carries an unmistakable political connotation. Identified by the local ruler—caught in the act, as it were, and interpellated by a sovereign figure—King is permitted to leave a hostile territory and cross enemy lines. He and Crasey, after two months time, reach the city of San Juan, whereupon the author tells a new acquaintance "an *undisguised* account of my history in that country."[18] Deception and undeceiving thus constitute the basic mechanisms of King's narrative. In this respect, the magic lantern episode of *Twenty-four Years in the Argentine Republic* exploits a functional homology between content and expression of phantasmagoria, maintaining its play of oppositions beyond the spectacle itself and extending it into the realm of the social.[19] The purpose or, rather, the repurposing of an old device is something that will be repeated in later depictions of optical devices and optical metaphors. Though the specific terms will vary, the projections set into motion a dynamic between concealing and revealing, one that is mediated by power and that negotiates dividing lines, be they political, cultural, military, or geographic.

The trope evoked by King's magic lantern makes it possible to read his story of the Argentine civil wars as an iteration of the broader crises of political legitimacy and the simultaneous emergence of a new visual regime in the first half of the nineteenth century. It is a relation encapsulated neatly in Marx's celebrated formulation that "in all ideology men and their circumstances appear upside-down as in a *camera obscura*."[20] Marx employs a vehicle that, at the time of writing *The German Ideology* (c. 1846), was by no means new, particularly given the debut of the daguerreotype in 1839. Nor was the camera obscura as a rhetorical figure a novelty; in essence, Marx is offering a farcical repetition of a well-worn trope of European thought.[21] In appropriating a commonplace, the image resists the teleology implicit in the commonsensical notion that "artefacts and technical systems . . . were invented first, then they usurped culture, and in a further step, they brought their influence to bear on the subjects."[22] W. J. T. Mitchell conjectures that Marx "might have noticed that the camera obscura had always had a double reputation as both a scientific instrument and as a 'magic lantern' for the production of optical illusions," but regardless of authorial intent, the analogy, loaded with prior, readily graspable metaphorical meanings, has the paradoxical effect of diminishing the importance of the object itself and, at the same time, puts into relief its multiple uses and the social processes that organize them.[23] In other words, it is necessary to understand the camera obscura in this context (and, by extension, magic lanterns, etc.) as what Delueze calls an *assemblage*: "something that is 'simultaneously and inseparably a machinic assemblage and an assemblage of enunciation', an object about which something is said and at the same time an object that is used."[24] As an overdetermined figure, the camera obscura underscores how ideology is not a discrete, isolatable discourse, but rather a totalizing logic, which can be at the same time scientific and affective, political and aesthetic, serious and ludic.

Read as the variation of a cliché, Marx's analogy signals how the material and discursive proliferation of optical devices in the first half of the nineteenth century evidences a profound epistemological shift. As suggested by simultaneous experiments and inventions in the field of photography, this change did not come about as the result of isolated geniuses, per the standard Romantic script, but as the result of social conditions that led to new applications for preexisting materials and forms of knowledge. In this regard the debut of the daguerreotype does not mark the initiation of the history of photography, but is instead but one conspicuous example of a redistribution of the sensible:

> [T]he epistemological status of all the objects in which protophotographers want to invest their rhetorical desire—landscape, nature, and the camera image on one hand, and space, time, and subjectivity on the other—is at the same moment in the midst of an unprecedented crisis. Each of these concepts is undergoing a radical transformation, as a nascent modern episteme disrupts the stability of its Enlightenment predecessor.[25]

As the limits between subject and object dissolve, the body of the observer becomes involved in the production of the image (or the formation of the proto-photographic object of desire). If these positions with respect to the process of "view-taking" are distinct, they jointly assume an immobility that resembles that which the viewers will later assume when contemplating them. To want to photograph, before (or behind) the camera, not only articulates a crisis on a theoretical plane, but also points to the political and social repercussions that help bring about the decadence of an Enlightenment paradigm. The formal and technical organization to fix or take a picture presupposes and makes possible an order for situating and identifying modern subjects. Or, in Foucauldian terms, it forms part of an emerging regime of discipline.

In the sphere of politics, this "nascent modern episteme" manifested itself in the shift from absolutism to new forms of legitimacy, based on the representation of a people. Toward 1800, as the traditional power arrangements of monarchies eroded, the term "sovereignty," an emblematic neologism of the Enlightenment, "pierde . . . aquel rasgo característico del *imperium*: su ilimitación espacial" [loses that characteristic attribute of the *imperium*: its spatial limitlessness] and the possibility emerges for "concebir la idea de una comunidad que contiene en sí su propio fundamento y principio de legitimidad (la *nación soberana*)" [conceiving of a community that contains within itself its own foundation and principle of legitimacy (the sovereign nation)].[26] Within a territory of established physical boundaries, it becomes necessary to link hegemonic projects with a representation of its inhabitants as a whole. In Latin America, in the absence of the Spanish crown, this process tended to be protracted and violent, as the contingent alliances formed during Independence fragmented without establishing consensual models for political organization.[27] At the same time the previously restricted channels of public opinion proved insufficient, and "new models of representation, developed in the new circles of sociability, outside the privileged gathering points of urban well-to-doers, created new political alliances and affiliations."[28] A phantasmagorical concept, a ghost of future perfect, the concept of the nation slowly gained presence in new social ambits, involving an array of social actors. As we have seen in previous chapters, novel forms of political participation and awareness depended on various cultural practices from within, across, and outside the porous boundaries of the *ciudad letrada* [lettered city]. At the origins of the modern state, nation and people(s) were conjointly articulated in a kind of chiasmic gaze. In other words, postrevolutionary Latin America experienced an ideological inversion that did not simply consist of the substitution of preestablished social positions or privileges.

OPPOSING VISIONS OF "EVERYONES"

If the Rosas regime proved especially adept at enabling various discursive practices to meld creole traditions and sensibilities with the modern political language of republicanism, this did not imply a programmatic or even stable deployment of such practices. Much as its authority on the national level was constructed in piecemeal fashion, its use of different media fluctuated in accordance to the circumstances of a given moment. If the 1840s, as memorably depicted in José Mármol's *Amalia*, marked a period of intense repression of dissident activities through censorship and the *mazorca* police force, the first term of Rosas's governorship witnessed a widespread effort to ensure the vocal adherence of the local populace to the Federalist cause. As we saw in chapter 1, the written and graphic portraits of the newly appointed governor sought to establish through writing, as both a medium and symbol, an affective bond linking the rural and urban poor of the city to a *primus inter pares*.

The prolific if short-lived activity of the gazetteer Luis Pérez is representative of the early years of Rosas's tenure as governor, and a series of satirical texts in his biweekly *El Torito de los Muchachos* (August 19–October 24, 1830) illustrates how optical devices occupied an ambivalent place in the changing cultural landscape. In contrast to some of Pérez's other newspaper, such as *El Gaucho*, *La Gaucha*, and *El Negrito*, which appealed to specific groups by imitating their colloquial speech in verse, *El Torito* presumed to appeal to a broader audience. Edited by Pérez's fictitious alter ego Juancho Barriales (as in "of the barrio" and "muddy," as Julio Schvartzman points out), the periodical is a compendium of various idiolects and registers of the popular classes who populated the unpaved streets of the city's outlying districts, including men and women, gauchos and Afro-Argentines.[29] In addition to poems of praise spoken by fervent supporters of the regime, it also included satirical verses spoken by Unitarians (who would, in turn, be lambasted in other texts in later numbers of the paper). In this sense, the fictitious voices populating its pages formed a motley chorus that aspired to present the city and its environs as a whole. The appeal to totality, however, was couched in the same terms that seven years later Juan Baustista Alberdi would use to present *La Moda*, with an apparent frivolity and lightheartedness. The prospectus of *El Torito* announced that "Mi objeto es divertir / Los mozos de las orillas: / No importa que me critiquen / Los sábios y cagetillas [*sic*]" [My object is to entertain / The boys on the outskirts of town: / I don't care if I'm criticized by / The wise men and the snobs].[30] Destined to be sung or recited aloud in *pulperías*, markets, and other public gathering places, *El Torito de los Muchachos* expressed solidarity with the same audience that Beláustegui refers to disdainfully in her letter to Tomás Guido: the *muchachos* of the capital.[31] The declared purpose of Pérez's newspaper, then, is to appeal to the marginal classes of the city with a language that will provoke and be excoriated by the dandyish Unitarian enemies of the regime. All in good fun, it will help reinforce the social divisions that justify Rosas's mandate.

The September 19 issue of *El Torito de los Muchachos* includes a brief note about another form of entertainment that seeks to attract its readers. Titled simply "Otro," it announces the arrival of an audiovisual spectacle:

> Frente a la Universidad se ha establecido un *Tutilimundi* ò linterna mágica en la que a los que gusten se las enseñará entre otras vistas y perspectivas la del *Purgatorio por dentro*, como es regular se encuentra de toda clase de personas de varios estados, categoría y oficios, hasta escribanos; sin embargo de que estos no son propios de aquel lugar según la opinión de algunos autores clásicos porque no paran en él, y pasan para su destino porque allí no tienen que dar fé, ni hay pleitos.
> La entrada es *gratis* pero la salida no tan fácil. (*El Torito de los Muchachos*, 40)
>
> [A *Tutilimundi* or magic lantern has been established across the street from the University, in which those interested will be shown, among other views and perspectives, that of *Purgatory from within*, and, as is to be expected, there one can find all classes of people of various states, categories, and professions, including scribes; however these do not belong in that place per the opinion of some classical authors because they don't stay put there, and move on as is their destiny since there they don't have to bear witness, there is no dispute.
> The entrance is *free*, but the exit is not so easy.]

Placed on the bottom of the final page of the newspaper, the announcement at its outset mimics the advertisements for audiovisual spectacles that appeared in the dailies of Buenos Aires. As is typical of these promotional texts, Pérez's note calls attention to the variety of exotic images that the *tutilimundi* promises to display. At the same time, it emphasizes the relationship of the spectacle to writing and lettered culture, calling attention to its proximity to the university, the inclusion of scribes in its views of Purgatory, and the opinion of "classical authors." With the darker tone of its final sentence, Pérez's text hints at a kind of entrapment for its audience, too, as if the hidden cost of attending such a spectacle were more than simply economic. Thus, if its first few lines are little more than a light pastiche of the hyperbole of publicity, it closes with a caveat that conflates spectator and content by means of a vague association with the "sábios y cagetillas," who are the professed enemies of the paper.

The alternative names *El Torito de los Muchachos* uses to identify the show serve to reinforce the allegorical implications of its specular quality. Regardless of how one interprets the coordinating conjunction between *tutilimundi* and magic lantern—either the speaker is unsure of the specific apparatus being used, or "or" simply reflects the contemporary habit of using such names interchangeably—the first descriptor alludes to how the diversion may possess a more problematic social dimension in the eyes of *El Torito*. Two contemporary drawings by Francisco de Goya help illustrate this (see figures 3.2 and 3.3). Drawn in Madrid (c. 1818–1820), each image depicts spectators peering through the viewfinders of *tutilimundi*, which the *Diccionario de la Real Academia Española* identifies as a synonym for *mundonuevo*, or a "[c]ajón que contenía un cosmorama portátil o una colección de figuras de movimiento, y se llevaba por las calles para diversión de la gente" [box containing a portable cosmorama or a collection of moving figures, which was carried through the streets for entertaining people].[32] What these drawings make evident is the implied price spectators pay for consuming images of "everyones" or "all the worlds": the unseen pictures captivate an observing subject whose body, in turn, becomes an object of scrutiny (and ridicule). As the faint *pentimenti* visible above the human figures and the placement of the *tutilimundi* suggest, Goya's drawings less concern the specific apparatus than a series of linked gazes, the scenarios that the device facilitates. "Miran lo que no ven" identifies as its subject the shapeless multitude that occupies the background of the image. It is only the figures in the foreground, those who peer into the device and the operator who sets the images in motion, that appear with any kind of detail, distinguished only in relation to the operation of the mechanism. In this sense, "[t]he physical device is simply a figure for a broader psychic, perceptual, and social insularity of the viewer," one which involves "various kinds of self-control and social restraint, particularly for forms of attentiveness that require both relative silence and immobility."[33] The compromising positions the spectators assume—not to mention the bemused gaze of the onlooker (doubled by whomever observes the drawing)—also emphasizes their passivity and vulnerability; in the act of seeing, the body of the observing subject becomes a potential object of scrutiny and subjection.

Returning to Pérez's text, Juancho Barriales cautions the readers of *El Torito de los Muchachos* that the "vistas y perspectivas" of the *tutilimundi*,

Figure 3.2. "Tuti li mundi," Francisco de Goya, c. 1818–1820 (*Courtesy of The Hispanic Society of America, New York*)

Figure 3.3. "Miran lo que no ven," Francisco de Goya, c. 1818–1820

depicting "toda clase de personas de varios estados, categoría y oficios" (another *todo el mundo*), ultimately presents them with a picture of their own passivity and detention. The phantasmagorical images of purgatory, vaguely affiliated with lettered, institutional knowledge, thus constitutes a challenge to the idiosyncratic Federalism embodied by Pérez's frantic journalistic activity in the early 1830s. In a basic sense, the *tutilimundi* represents a direct competitor for the audiences of the newspaper. More importantly, the fantastical images of the otherworld or other worlds that provide the central attraction of audiovisual spectacles undermine the aspirational image of totality as represented by the local figures who populate the pages of *El Torito* and who are the titular protagonists of the constellation of Pérez's other short-lived periodicals. Audiovisual spectacles undermine the affective bonds of this imagined community because they require of their public a form of isolating behavior that stands at odds with the conspicuous and vociferous public performance of support that is central to the discursive strategies of the Rosas regime. In other words, the *tutilimundi* presupposes a representational mode that interrupts the constitutive relations of Rosist hegemony. Lurking behind the *caveat spectator* "[l]a entrada es *gratis* pero la salida no tan fácil" may lurk a Unitarian conspiracy.

This suspicion is all but confirmed in subsequent editions of *El Torito de los Muchachos*, when Pérez devotes two more short texts to the *tutilimundi*. On September 23 the newspaper reports that "se necesitan algunas figuras nuevas porque aun se halla bastante desurtido, y los mejores figurones todavía no se han conseguido; sin embargo, de resultas del viaje, o el crucero de la Sarandí, puede aumentarse la colección" [some new figures are needed because it is already quite repetitive, and the best images have yet to be obtained; however, as a result of the voyage or the cruise of the Sarandí, the collection could be expanded].[34] The note deflates the hyperbole parodied in the previous number and, in doing so, points to the need for the constant renovation of images in order to maintain public interest—in other words, so that the promise of representing an "everyones" remains valid. In this regard, *El Torito* echoes a criticism published July 8, 1826, upon the return of Félix Tiola and his phantasmagoria to Buenos Aires, which concludes by stating that "no es que no nos haya agradado su fantasmagoría; sino sólo que queremos recomendarle . . . que no sea tan avaro con sus fantasmas" [it is not that we found his phantasmagoria to be displeasing; but we want to recommend him to be less stingy with his ghosts].[35] Where Pérez's paper departs from this review is that links the accumulation of images with a local event: the Sarandí was a sailing vessel that had been hijacked the previous week by a group of suspected enemies of the regime. The insinuation of the previous number is thus spelled out more clearly: to view the *tutilimundi* is a gesture of sympathy for the opposition.

The following week *El Torito de los Muchachos* makes one last mention of the *tutilimundi*, informing its readers in an "Aviso" ["Announcement"] of the imminent departure of the spectacle. Again the periodical emphasizes its logistical aspects, announcing that "[e]stimulado el encargado del *Tutilimundi* del negocio que le ha proporcionado la linterna mágica ha dividido la colección, y con una parte de ella marcha el día de hoy en unos *Paylebotes* de dos ruedas, sin saberse su destino, aunque se dice que pone la proa al Sud; y que si le va bien volverá por otra cantidad" [stimulated by the business that it has brought him, the owner of the *Tutilimundi* has divided the collection, and with a part of it is embarking today in some two-wheeled wagons, destination unknown, although it is said he is headed south; and if all goes well he will return for more].[36] In emphasizing the profitability of the venture (despite its free admission) and, for a second time, the accumulation of "figures," *El Torito* further demystifies the mechanisms of the itinerant show. It not only undercuts the rhetoric of uniqueness and the aura of the supernatural cultivated by such shows, but also stresses its fleeting relationship with its audience (and the community at large). If *El Torito de los Muchachos* sought to inspire enthusiastic support for the regime among its audience, then the fragmentary narrative comprised of these three short texts performs a surrogate function, revealing the trickery the *tutilimundi* conceals. Consistent with the express objective of Pérez's newspaper to "divertir / Los mozos de las orillas," in these instances the periodical looks to distract its audience from the arresting images of a competing cultural practice. Ultimately, however, neither the content of audiovisual spectacles nor the forms of behavior and self-discipline they organized would prove incompatible with Rosist hegemony. Whereas Pérez's papers were short-lived and circulated only when needed to rally popular support during Rosas's rise to power, *gabinetes ópticos* and the like continued to operate and eventually began to fulfill an equivalent propagandistic function.[37] A docile public, after all, would ultimately be more compatible with the increased repression that marked the later years of the regime.

If the *tutilimundi* of *El Torito de los Muchachos* obliquely refers to the social costs implicit in the images of "everyones," Andrés Lamas's short fiction "Visiones de la óptica" ["Visions of the Optic"] (1838) deploys a similar optical device to develop an explicit allegory of the kinds of self-restraint that inaugurate as well as those that resist modernity. Lamas published "Visiones de la óptica" in the first number of the Montevideo newspaper *El Iniciador*, which he confounded with Miguel Cané, one of the attendees of Marcos Sastre's literary salon the previous year. During its brief existence *El Iniciador* served as a principal outlet for proscribed dissidents of the Rosas regime, who recently had begun emigrating from Buenos Aires in greater numbers. Juan Bautista Alberdi counted among its collaborators, and its final number (January 1, 1839) consists entirely of an early version of *Dogma socialista*, Esteban Echeverría's programmatic declaration of the liberal doctrine championed by him and his peers.

Narrated in first person, "Visiones de la óptica" begins as an encounter with an enigmatic traveling salesman (much like Borges's "El libro de arena" ["The Book of Sand"]). Struck by the extravagant, disheveled appearance of his unannounced guest, who bears "un cajón a la espalda y un atado de libros en la mano" [a chest on his back and a bundle of books in his arms] the narrator demands "¿quién sois ¿que se os ofrece?" [Who are you? What can I offer you?].[38] The salesman ignores the first question but, in answering the second with a mixture of French and Spanish, he evokes the folkloric figure of the itinerant Savoyard. He identifies the chest on his back as an *optique*, but the nameless narrator quickly insists that "no estoy para opticas" [I'm not interested in optics] and requests that the stranger leave. In voicing his disinclination, the speaker demonstrates his familiarity with the device, not to mention the exaggerated language typically used to promote it. However, the salesman continues his entreaties and insists that this particular *optique* will permit its viewer to see "*el revers de lo que veis todos los dias*" [the reverse of what you see every day].[39] Suspecting he is about to be scammed of a few coins, the narrator reluctantly looks through the viewfinder and witnesses a succession of fantastic images that, effectively, depict an ordered society that contrasts starkly with his own.

Before examining how the narrator verbalizes this experience, however, let us consider the status of the *óptica/optique*. Based on the scant description the text provides (it is a box with a single viewfinder, a "máquina con . . . sus paisajes y vidrios" [a device with . . . its landscapes and lenses]), we can surmise that it is a similar device to those depicted in Goya's drawings, a kind of portable peep show or *tutilimundi*.[40] Without elaborating on the specific workings of the apparatus, however, it is impossible to determine whether its inverted images are produced by artifice or a kind of delirium on the part of the narrator. Suspended between a scientific explanation and a psychological one, between the uncanny and the supernatural, the subsequent enumeration of scenes unfolds on the terrain of fantastic literature. The undecidability of the means by which the visions are produced activates the more expansive meanings of the term: a branch of science or, more generally, a "point of view." In essence, the name of the apparatus underscores the epistemic confusion between the object of desire and the desiring subject.

Peering through the eyepiece of the optic with his right eye, the narrator first witnesses a panorama of an entire continent, of "repúblicas del siglo XIX con costumbres, con hábitos, con tendencias, democráticas, *suyas*, con el sello de la época" [republics of the nineteenth century with customs, with habits, with tendencies that were democratic, *their own*, a mark of the times].[41] By twice mentioning the coetaneity of these utopian states, which he refers to in the following sentence as "unos paises de un mundo nuevo" [some countries of a new world] the speaker insists that the inversion of the Nuevo Mundo is not spatial, but temporal: for a moment the always-deferred modernity of Latin American cultural discourse is actualized and autochthonous, wholly its own.[42] Framed by this spatiotemporal matrix, the observer fixes his gaze on a specific country, "un Pueblo que no alimentaba odios, antipatías nacionales" [a People that did not feed hatred or animosity for other nations], henceforth the visions of the optic will dwell on the ideal national subjects who populate it.[43] First the narrator admires the youths formed in a system of public education, before directing his gaze toward lawyers, judges, and legislators. Later he sees libraries and bookstores, together with intellectuals, whom he portrays as "[l]iteratos considerados, sin mas caudal que sus libros, su cabeza, y su tiempo" [considerate men of letters, with no fortune besides their books, their brains, and their time].[44] The ideal society, then, first becomes visible through the institutions and the public men (not public women) who inhabit the *ciudad letrada*.

As the narrator turns his attention from civic life to the customs of everyday life and the domestic sphere, a simple but substantive change occurs in his narration. Though he continues to report the diverse scenes presented by the optic, his mode of representation shifts from affirmative to negative, as he calls attention to what he does not see:

> Allí vi un teatro que no es un *teatro en ruinas* . . . y su escena la ocupaban actores soportables, no *actores asesinos del poeta y del gusto, ni actores rudos* . . .
> Allí vi gentes que saben que hay un arte moderno . . . gentes que no doblan la rodilla cuando con tono gótico se les nombre ARISTOTELES . . .
> Allí vi unas ruinas . . . en que se leía—FUE UNA PLAZA DE TOROS . . .
> Allí vi padres que no sacrificaban á sus hijas, que no las *vendían* al que más daba . . .
> Allí vi niñas que no eran coquetas, que engañaban à media docena para quedarse después à buenas noches.
> Allí vi niños que no fuman por la calles . . .
> Allí vi gentes que no jugaban al CARNAVAL . . . ("Visiones de la óptica," 103)
>
> [There I saw a theater that wasn't a theater in ruins . . . and its stage was occupied by bearable actors, not actors who murder the poet and good taste, nor vulgar actors . . .
> There I saw people who know that modern art exists . . . people who do not drop a knee when with a gothic tone someone says to them ARISTOTLE . . .
> There I saw ruins . . . that read—THIS WAS A BULLRING . . .
> There I saw fathers that did not sacrifice their daughters, who would not sell them to the highest bidder . . .
> There I saw girls who were not flirts, who cheated a half dozen to stay around after saying goodnight.
> There I saw boys who did not smoke in the streets . . .
> There I saw people that did not take part in CARNIVAL . . .]

The increasingly disembodied voice of the narrator has until this point approximated the idealized, foundational figure of modernity: the universal subject, a "limitless historical actor, who would be able to ensure the fullness of a perfectly instituted social order."[45] Here, however, as the optic suspends the chaos of Carnival, the text effects an ideological inversion that reveals its historical dimension; if its upside-down visions are predicated upon substituting immanence for futurity, a past present continually interrupts it. That is, the accumulating negations make evident that the opposite of "what you see every day" does not consist simply of universalizing the tastes and good manners of a Europhile, bourgeois minority, but also depends on the declared exclusion of the practices, social groups, and institutions associated with the Spanish colonial legacy, the sizable African population of the River Plate, and, more generally, the lower classes. Bullfighting, Carnival, the scholastic intellectual tradition all are visible in the optic, but only as labels marking their prior suppression. In other words, the conspicuous absence of otherness marks the limits of the social as imagined by the optic.

Through the negation of alterity, the spectator shifts from description to commentary. As such, the logic of the narrative ceases to be accumulative and adopts a comparative mode that puts into relief the differences that place the narrator's reality and the visions of the optic in opposition. Though this comparison inevitably conjures the specter of disenchantment, underscoring the distancing separating the speaker himself from the objects he contemplates ("Allí vi . . . Allí vi . . . Allí vi . . ."), it allows the narrative, at least momentarily, to adopt the modernizing, strabismic gaze that Esteban Echeverría will formulate in the *Dogma socialista*: "El mundo de nuestra vida intelectual será a la vez nacional y humanitario; tendremos siempre un ojo clavado en el progreso de las naciones y el otro en las entrañas de nuestra sociedad" [The world of our intellectual life will be at once national and humanistic; we will always have one eye fixed on the progress of nations and the other on the depths of our society].[46] As the narrator emphatically calls attention to his own activity, seeing himself seeing, the optical apparatus fulfills multiple functions: as a machine and a point of view, as an instrument of diversion and discipline, of entertainment and surveillance.[47] Thus, as the speaker enumerates elements of a desired social order, the optic embodies the technological means necessary for realizing it.

However, following the lengthy list of unseen subjects and habits, radical negativity abruptly cuts the national fantasy short. No sooner than the narrator sees the people who do not take part in Carnival, he pulls away from the device and cries, "Oh! amigo, basta, basta: estas son cosas exóticas, caprichos, visiones, de la óptica: cosas que solo en ella he visto, que nadie usa, de que nadie hace caso, que para nada sirven. No quiero perder más tiempo" [Oh!, friend, enough, enough: these are exotic things, caprices, visions of the optic: things that I have only seen in it, that no one uses, that no one pays attention to, that are good for nothing].[48] It is as if, to maintain an affiliation with the modern society whose inhabitants he has cataloged, the narrator must make an extravagant display that the mere specter of an unruly *plebe* repels him. Immediately, however, he identifies himself as a common man, adding "hago lo que hace la mayoría para no tener dolores de cabeza. . . . Todo esto huele a idealismo; nosotros somos positivos, materiales" [I do what the majority does so as to not have headaches. . . . This all reeks of idealism; we are positive, materialists].[49] Expressing a preference for the local and the familiar, the narrator rejects the optic as a grotesque inversion of himself and his circumstances; in other words, he conjures a detailed vision of modernity, only to reject it as alien and inadaptable to his context. In effect, he declares his own inversion, maintaining the rigid dichotomy between reality and fantasy by switching the values assigned to each term.

Reading the narrator's disavowal of the optic in this manner figures Lamas's text as a critique of the popular classes, who were needed to confer legitimacy on the political project championed by Lamas and his peers, but refused to do so. As such, it advances the tenet of *letrados* that only the insight of the intellectual could save the *pueblo* from its blindness; as Echeverría specifies in the *Dogma socialista*, "no es nuestra la fórmula de los ultrademócratas franceses, todo para el pueblo y por el pueblo; sino la siguiente: *todo para el pueblo y por la razón del pueblo*" [our formula is not that of the French ultra-democrats, all for the people and by the people; but the following: *all for the people and for the reason of the people*];[50] or, as Juan Baustista Alberdi declares in *Fragmento preliminar al estudio del derecho* [Preliminary Fragment for the Study of Law] (1837), "[l]os pueblos ciegos no son pueblos, porque no es pueblo todo montón de hombres, como no es ciudadano de una nación, todo individuo de su seno" [blind peoples are not peoples, because not every mass of men is a people, much as every individual within a society is not a citizen of the nation].[51] Forcefully rejecting his own descriptions, the narrator limits his own expressive capacity to maintain the status quo. His voice becomes redundant noise, an articulation of unreason that justifies the lettered elite's stewardship.

At the same time, however, "Visiones de la óptica" serves as an ironic criticism of the dissident liberal thinkers, too, because its featureless speaking subject retains a degree of agency. It is he who elaborates the visions, translating visual images into verbal ones, and he is the subject who resists a further elaboration of the fantasy. As consequence, the neat divide between the utopian and the everyday—a partition that the self-identification of the narrator seemingly sustains—is a false dichotomy. The images are intelligible because the narrator's own optic (that is, his mode of seeing) precedes his encounter with the *óptica*. Though his tastes may differ from those represented by the foreigner's device, his narration signals the capacity (and desire) to interpret the images that flash before his eyes as simultaneous descriptions of an ordered society; in other words, his own imagination is already technological. The self-proclaimed man of the people, despite his outburst, is already on his way to becoming a modern subject prior to the firsthand encounter with the stranger and, we could say, prior to the seeing-eye intervention of an intellectual class. In other words, the text enacts a fundamental rhetorical maneuver of Spanish American cultural discourse, in that it "strenuously argues for modernity, while it signals simultaneously in a number of ways its distance from the demands of modernity's rhetoric as a means of maintaining its discursive power."[52] In more specific terms, the deeply ambivalent fantasy of Lamas's text imagines a specific *todo el mundo* through its *tutilimundi*, only to recoil when confronted with the contradictions that signal the impossibility of its speaker's own inclusion within an idealized image of the social. Beyond the particular content of its spectacle, "Visiones de la óptica" dramatizes not the conflict between diametrically opposed worldviews, but a more fundamental antagonism that is the "negation of a given order [that] is, quite simply, the limit of that order, and not the moment of a broader totality in relation to which the two poles of the antagonism would constitute differential—i.e. objective—partial instances."[53]

Though "Visiones de la óptica" and Pérez's notes about the *tutilimundi* were published in newspapers representing the opposing factions of postrevolutionary Argentina, they articulate a shared tension and irony when presenting representations of "everyones." Both texts reveal a problematic that arises from trying to situate a viewing public before an image that is at once spectacular and specular. The renunciation of these images by *El Torito de los Muchachos* and the narrator-protagonist of "Visiones de la óptica" is not simply an aversion to a modern form of seeing; rather it signals the fundamental incompleteness of images that claim to represent, to quote Pérez's text, "all classes of people in various states, categories and professions." Both texts narrativize this incompletion; the anagnorisis that occurs in Borges "El Aleph" never takes place: "vi el Aleph, desde todos los puntos, vi en el Aleph la tierra, vi mi cara y mis vísceras, vi tu cara, y sentí vértigo y lloré, porque mis ojos habían visto ese objeto secreto y conjetural, cuyo nombre usurpan los hombres, pero que ningún hombre ha mirado: el inconcebible universo" [I saw the Aleph, from all points of view, I saw the earth in the Aleph, I saw my face and innards, I saw your face, and I felt vertigo and cried, because my eyes had seen that sacred and conjectural object, whose name usurps men, but which no man has ever seen: the inconceivable universe].[54] However, though the moment of recognition is averted or aborted in the case of *El Torito* and "Visiones de la óptica," they share a deeper affinity with Borges's text. For the failure of recognition is commensurate with a constitutive absence of difference or, in other words, a kind of "impolitics," as Raúl Antelo employs the term:

> supone una comunidad cuya presencia está habitada, en su centro mismo, en su *aleph*, por una ausencia, ya sea de identidad, de atributos, de proyectos o de acciones. Por ello mismo la impolítica afirma que la comunidad es, en sí

misma, una nada. No es, como pretende la modernización nacionalista, una realidad positiva e identificable, lo cual persigue el objetivo ético y estético de sustraer a la comunidad de toda posible *representación*. ("Borges y la impolítica," 300)

[Impolitics implies a community whose presence is inhabited, in its very center, in its *aleph*, by an absence, which can very well be an identity, attributes, projects, or actions. For this very reason, impolitics affirms that community is, in itself, nothing. It is not, as nationalist modernization insists, a positive and identifiable reality, which pursues the ethic and aesthetic objective of removing the community from all possible *representation*.]

These optical devices of postrevolutionary Argentina, regardless of the obvious partisan allegiances championed by their respective publications, run counter to nationalist narratives. In both cases the encounter with the promised image of totality results in demystification and disavowal, effectively undercutting the representational modality required of a hegemonic relation, "by which a certain particular content overflows its particularity and becomes the incarnation of the absent fullness of society."[55] There is a certain consistency, shared features of a cultural landscape that underpin and, to an extent, undercut the familiar dividing lines that a focus on visuality makes apparent. The allegorical treatment of these devices marks the desire and efforts to represent, order, and maintain vigilance over subjects, but, in doing so, they also signal the contingent nature of such representations. They moreover call attention to the absences, omissions, and exclusions that the rhetoric of politics and publicity seek to conceal. In the end, these encounters with what appear to be foreign objects or a foreign technology are never wholly external, never simply an alien optic that compels a subject to see in a determined way. In other words, if postrevolutionary Argentina experienced the progressive imposition of a modern visual regime at the same time that its political elites were locked in an acrimonious struggle to define a consensual model for organizing the national territory, these apparatuses point to a resistance that is integral to this epistemic shift, as well as a contemporary awareness of this resistance.

APPARATUSES OF THE ROMANTIC IMAGINARY

In the writings of *letrados* of the Generation of 1837, this awareness transmutes into self-awareness, and optical devices operate as metaphors for the conditions and limitations of intellectual activity in postrevolutionary Argentina. Whereas variants of European Romanticism might employ such devices as a way to access history, "ensuring the technological retrieval of the very past that technology has destroyed," their presence in the cultural discourse of their Spanish American contemporaries emphasizes, with equal measures of idealism and skepticism, the possibility of conjugating past and present with a utopian future.[56] In other words, there is a high degree of congruity, a temporal correlation between a future imagined by such an apparatus and the technologized repurposing of this apparatus. The device becomes an instrument for reifying and realizing its own spectacle.

In two early writings Esteban Echeverría essays optical metaphors that hint at the technologized adaptation of these apparatuses. In his epistolary fiction *Cartas a un amigo* (c. 1832), a melancholic narrator likens an episode of insomnia to a magic lantern show.[57] The text constitutes a translation (in the sense of "carrying over"), as it emulates the structure of *Die Leiden des junges Werthers* and incorporates entire passages from Goethe's text.[58] Elaborating on its model, *Cartas a un amigo* draws on the dramatic staging of phantasmagoria:

> Los recuerdos se levantan gigantescos en mi memoria y lo pasado y lo futuro se despliega revestido de diversos colores ante el mágico espejo de mi imaginación. Me detengo a mi arbitrio a examinar y analizar cada objeto que se me presenta, porque soy, a la vez espectador y actor; y luego cuando me fastidio, como los niños, de aquella fantasmagoría apago la lumbre de la linterna mágica y todo es oscuridad y las tinieblas se suceden a las dulces ilusiones de lo pasado y lo porvenir. (*Obras de Esteban Echeverría* V, 46)
>
> [The memories emerge gigantic in my memory and past and present unfold cloaked in diverse colors before the magic mirror of my imagination. With discretion I stop to examine and analyze each object that presents itself to me, because I am, at the same time, spectator and actor; and later when I grow annoyed, like children, with that phantasmagoria I extinguish the light of the magic lantern and all is dark and the sweet illusions of past and future give way to shadows.]

The implied confusion of spectator, apparatus, and illusion implicit in "Visiones de la óptica" is here complete as the poet scrutinizes the objects of his imagination. As the specular, spectral, and spectacular merge, the device morphs from one object to another in a metonymic chain. Thus, in a similar fashion to the narrator of Lamas's text, the speaker subjects himself to a series of images for whose production he is ultimately responsible, yet at the moment of indistinction he exerts agency in the form of negativity, abruptly extinguishing the source of the image. If once again we see the spectacle associated with children and childish behavior, darkness becomes the product of distraction or annoyance, perhaps at the reproduction of familiar images (or the familiar reproduction of images). In other words, the distorted figures produced through self-reflexivity are canceled out when the narrator recognizes the illusory nature of the conjoined images of past and present. *Cartas a un amigo* adopts then discards the analogy of Werther, who muses "what is the world to our hearts without love? What is a magic lantern without light? . . . if love only show us fleeting shadows we are yet happy, when, like mere children, we behold them, and are transported with the splendid phantoms."[59] In this regard, Echeverría does not copy Goethe, but instead takes his imagery as a point of departure for the critique of such musings. Much as the reverie will be cut short by distraction and darkness, the letter in *Cartas a un amigo* is interrupted by the sounds of a strumming guitar; the discourse of futurity appears attenuated when linked with the past, conjured only to be banished.

In "Mefistófeles: Drama-joco-serio, satírico-político" [Mephistopholes: Joco-serious, Satirical-political Drama] (c. 1833), Echeverría engages another of Goethes's works and, in doing so, develops a more sustained and convoluted narrative of interconnected dreams and visions. Like the letter-writer of *Cartas*, its narrator is also prone to melancholic lucubration and, during a spell of insomnia, endeavors to translate the prologue of *Faust*. He is interrupted by a demon that mocks his efforts, telling him "váyase por ese mundo à emplear mejor su tiempo catequizando doncellas, magnetizando viudas, birlando empleos y metiendo su espátula en la olla gorda de la política" [go out in the world and make better use of your time wooing damsels, hypnotizing widows, pinching jobs and mixing it up in the big pot of politics].[60] This derision demonstrates Echeverría's awareness of "una fuerte depreciación de la tarea del traductor" [an intense disregard for the translator's task] in Rosist Argentina and hence operates as a self-critique of Echeverría's previous effort to translate Goethe.[61] Yet, as the narrator employs a series of optical metaphors to describe the content of his vision, it becomes increasingly unclear whether the ultimate object of his critique is himself or the multitude that pays no heed to his intellectual endeavors.

From the Gothic cliché of its first sentence ("La noche estaba oscura, fria y ventosa" [It was a dark, cold, and windy night]), the opening section of the text, titled "La vision," dwells primarily on the setting and the state of the narrator, deferring the exposition of his vision. Having consumed two enormous cups of coffee, the narrator nervously collapses into a chair and "empezaron á pulular en mi mente las formas más estrambóticas y grotescas que hayan entrado en el cráneo humano, á pasar como los espectros de Ricardo III al través de la linterna mágica de mi fantasía" [the most bizarre and grotesque forms that have entered the human skull began to swarm my mind, passing like Richard III's specters across the magic lantern of my fantasy].[62] Though initially overwhelmed by the strange apparitions of his imagination, the narrator resolves to identify them and quickly "[a]plique un mincroscopio [*sic*] ó el disector de infinitamente pequeños corpúsculos, y como por encanto, aquel caos empezó a ordenarse" [applied the microscope or the dissector of infinitely small corpuscles, and as if by charm, that chaos began to order itself].[63] The discourse of science thus permits him to categorize the multiple figures populating his vision, and he identifies them as human beings. Paradoxically, the shift from the supernatural to the scientific effects a disorienting fluctuation of scale, from the enlarged, projected images, to the microscopic, to life-sized.

As the narrator continues his self-scrutiny, little by little he begins to profile the human subjects of his delusion. In spite of himself he continues to "ojear con la fantasía armada de un telescopio de Herchsel aquel mundo de hijos de Adan y Eva" [glimpse with a fantasy assembled with a Hershcel telescope that world of the children of Adam and Eve] until he tumbles headfirst from his chair, "linterna mágica y telescopio en el suelo" [magic lantern and telescope falling to the floor].[64] While the fall and the resulting bruise on his head release him from the visionary state, his narrative pauses and then doubles back on the content of his dream, which resembles an inversion of the inversion of "Visiones de la óptica": telescope in hand (in mind? in writing?) he witnesses "bípedos . . . que hablaban, disputaban y gritaban y escribían como si estuviesen reunidos en asamblea nacional ó en conventículo revolucionario, donde generalmente se discute la política, ciencia lata y profunda " [bipeds who spoke, argued and screamed and wrote as if they were gathered in a national assembly or revolutionary gathering, where politics is the typical topic, that deep and vexing science].[65] The brooding, isolated Romantic figure, regardless of his literary aspirations, has politics on his mind; though the variable optics may signal an effort to distance himself from the public life outside his window, it reveals itself as the persistent object of his obsession. What the narrator fails to identify is the root cause of his vision and the exact nature of its content. Despite applying an "análisis microscópico" [microscopic analysis] he remains undecided whether his sensations are of a material origin or whether, like "Berkley y los idealistas . . . el mundo físico no es mas que una pura ilusion o fantasmagoría" [Berkley and the idealists . . . the physical world was nothing more than a pure illusion or a phantasmagoria].[66] Rhetorical instability underpins ontological uncertainty.

Soon it is nighttime again, and again the narrator's mind wanders as he desires to "abrazar de una mirada la vasta estension del universo!" [observe in a single gaze the vast extension of the universe].[67] The aleph-like reflections drive the narrator to recall his literary namesake, and he attempts to translate its prologue. His efforts are immediately frustrated, however, as the demon interrupts him and urges him to engage in more practical activities, such as getting involved in politics. The spirit prescribes as an antidote to the narrator's flights of fancy the very thing that it likely their cause: melancholy. Though the narrator refuses the demon's assistance, in the following section of the text, titled "Melancolía," he leaves his house, in an admittedly melancholic mood, and walks the Alameda to the banks of the River Plate. Once again a multitude fills his field of vision:

Mugeres y hombres, todos aquellos vivientes, en fin, convirtiéronse para mí en cuerpos diáfanos cuyo cerebro y entrañas veía patentemente la sobrenatural lucidez de mi lente . . . yo pudo [*sic*] leer los pensamientos de aquella turba de seres racionales y analizar sus mas recónditos afectos y pasiones. Asco y horror dióme su primer aspecto y volví a otro lado el rayo visual de mi lente esclamando: O Dios! cuántas miseria en tu creacion! Nada vi entonces sino tristeza y oscuridad . . . alejéme velozmente de aquel sitio placentero para los otros, y para mí melancólico. (*Obras de Esteban Echeverría* V, 198–99)

[Woman and men, all those living souls, in the end became to me transparent bodies whose brains and viscera I saw clearly with the supernatural lucidity of my lens . . . I could read the thoughts of that rabble of rational beings and analyze their most secret passions and affections. At first sight these caused me disgust and horror and I returned to the other side of the lens of my line of sight, exclaiming: Dear Lord! How much misery in your creation! I saw nothing then but sadness and darkness . . . I quickly moved away from that place that is for others pleasing and, for me, melancholic.]

"Mefistófeles" ends as it begins, with an inchoate crowd that provokes the anxiety of an observer whose efforts to scrutinize and classify it produce repugnance and horror. Thus, though Echeverría's Faustian protagonist refuses to make a bargain with the devil, he is nonetheless condemned to face the multitude he despises. What differs about the final scene is that the narrator identifies the masses as an external phenomenon, but one that proves utterly transparent to his knowing eye. The speaker prefers to occlude whatever knowledge the "supernatural lucidity of his lens" has permitted him to see. However, he does so by making himself, once more, the object of his reflexive gaze, suggesting the incompleteness of his withdrawal from the public sphere. The final words of the text underscore how the narrator remains incapable of disassociating himself from the community that has occupied his thoughts throughout the text, effectively stymieing his desired, distinguishing intellectual activity. If, in Freudian terms, melancholy consists of the confusion of subject and object by which the former is implicated in an irretrievable loss, then the various critical lenses of the narrator (phantasmagorical, microscopic, telescopic, etc.) prove incapable of articulating an alternative site, pleasurable or otherwise, where the aspiring translator may labor with total autonomy from the distractions and obsessions of the *plebe* and politics. Nor do these optics equip the intellectual with the necessary instruments to control the otherwise recondite affections and passions of the multitude. Consistent with the rhetorical treatments in *El Torito de los Muchachos* and "Visiones de la óptica," Echverría's proliferating optical metaphors signal how the modernizing gaze compulsively points to an otherness that exceeds its capacity to order. In other words, the unfinished "Mefistófeles" narrativizes the impotency of a literary practice shunned by the ruling regime, one that cannot contribute to "the discourse that delivered individual variations of behavior, shames, and secrets into the grip of power."[68]

While the optical metaphors in Echeverría's writing shuttle between the personal and the public, Domingo Faustino Sarmiento activates another kind of displacement in his rhetorical treatment of these devices. In his extensive corpus, references to *gabinetes ópticos*, panoramas, dioramas, and phantasmagoria most frequently appear in travel writings, consistent with the contemporary publicity that promised potential audiences an array of images depicting exotic and distant locales. In Sarmiento's work these discursive figures are frequently linked to the act of writing and emphasize the utility of verisimilar and immersive imagery in the service of the modernizing projects advocated by their author. They reveal a certain pragmatism, for in calling attention to the illusory nature of images produced through trickery, they contrast with the forceful disavowals dramatized in the other examples examined in this chapter. Since the rhetoric of optics in Sarmiento's writing seeks to juxtapose distant otherness with the site of its readers, the conjugation of the local and the foreign presupposes a homogeneous subjective experience linking these spaces. In synthesis, even if the precise location of the modern is always deferred, Sarmiento's optics present the reader-as-spectator with a provisional simulacrum of modernity's completion.

Throughout the collection of letters that comprise *Viajes por Europa, África y América 1845–1847* (1849–1851), Sarmiento invokes optical devices and audiovisual diversions—particularly the panorama—as if to insist on the deeper coherency of a text that combines "las escenas de que fuí testigo ... con harta frecuencia lo que no ví" [the scenes I witnessed ... so frequently with what I did not see].[69] In admitting that the object of scrutiny always exceeds the traveler's gaze and that his letters endeavor to make up (for) this inevitable surplus, the prologue of *Viajes* stresses the affinities shared by author and reader. It downplays the novelty of its content by asserting its author is yet another consumer of mediated and mediatic sources of knowledge. Within the sphere of modernity, "la vida civilizada reproduce en todas partes los mismos caractéres, los mismos medios de existencia; la prensa diaria lo revela todo; i no es raro que un hombre estudioso sin salir de su gabinete, deje parado al viajero sobre las cosas mismas que él creia conocer bien por la inspeccion personal" [everywhere civilized life reproduces the same characteristics, the same modes of existence; the daily press reveals everything; and it is not unusual for a studious man, without leaving his office, to astonish the traveler about the very things he believed to know well from firsthand experience].[70] Sarmiento's insistence on the homogenizing effect of modern means of production and reproduction reduces the differences of inside/outside, local/foreign, and static/mobile that heretofore distinguished the privileged positions of the learned man and the traveler. If newness is becoming impossible, then the ceaseless accumulation of representations renders the imagined exchange and its mode of sociability superfluous. The homogeneity that assures order in "civilized life," threatens, thus, to produce a systemic excess, an intrinsic alterity that escapes its supposedly all-seeing gaze.

Within this context, Sarmiento proposes a kind of second-order travel writing, one not based solely on unmediated firsthand experience, but rather one that directly engages the discourses reproducing the "same characteristics" and "means of existence." As such, the prologue of *Viajes* rereads the letters that follow as reflections on the mechanisms that constitute the concurrent sensations of sameness and dislocation that are central to "civilized life." Identifying André Dumas as a pioneer of the genre, Sarmiento calls attention to his precursor's embellishments and the compression of chronologically distant events—in short, the techniques of fiction—that promote a pleasurable suspension of disbelief. The novel replaces novelty, animating the reader in a way that mimics other popular diversions: "¡Cuán bellos son los paises así descritos, i cuán animado el movible i corredizo panorama de los viajes!" [How beautiful are landscapes described this way, and how spirited the ever-changing panorama of voyages!].[71] If the dissemination of information through various media renders individual experiences equivalent and diminishes the possibility of surprise, then the principal achievement of Dumas consists of combining events by disrupting the spatiotemporal framework that structures a feeling of disenchantment. It in its place, he offers a vicarious, immersive experience, one whose seamlessly connected passages emulate the all-seeing spectacle of scrolling painted images. Dumas does so in such a fashion that the artifice is not only conspicuous, but becomes a source of enjoyment in and of itself. Effective travel writing becomes a spectacle as much for its mechanisms as for its content:

> ¿quién no dijera que ese es el mérito i el objeto de un viaje, en que el viajero es forzosamente el protagonista, por aquella solidaridad del narrador i la narracion, de la vision y los objetos, de la materia de examen i la percepcion, vínculos estrechos que ligan el alma a las cosas visibles, i hacen que vengan éstas a espiritualizarse, cambiándose en imágenes, i modificándose i adaptándose al tamaño i alcance del instrumento óptico que las refleja? (*Viajes*, 6)
>
> [Who would not say that is the merit and object of a voyage, of which the traveler is in effect the protagonist, due to that solidarity between narrator and narration, between vision and objects, between the materials examined and perception, tight bonds that link the soul to visible things, and cause these things to become spirit, change into images, and modify and adapt to the size and scope of the optical instrument that reflects them?]

While the expense log that Sarmiento kept during his travels provides a material referent for a term that appears over a dozen times in *Viajes*—an entry for August 5, 1847, records he spent two shillings to visit the "Coloseo, Panorama de Londres"—the lengthy question posed in its prologue diminishes the specificity of the metaphor at its close. The implied purpose of the text stands in stark contrast to the naïve tourist who persists in reporting to his peers "the very things" he has inspected personally, for here the modern traveler, as narrator and protagonist of his voyage, instead engages fleeting sensorial experiences. Writing and traveling, conflated so, reveal the connection between the observing subject and the objects he observes. This imbues "visible things" with a spiritual value that allows them to be transmitted and retransmitted in new contexts, albeit modified and adapted to the apparatus that captures them. This "optical instrument" is indefinite and variable, as it refers to multiple operations by which vision and object, matter and perception, soul and things are coupled and recoupled. While "reflejar" may suggest a degree of passivity, it also implies the refracted display of its conditions of production. Travel writing as imagined by Sarmiento narrates, thus, an itinerary not only through physical space, but an encounter between a sensible observer, received ideas, and diverse objects of scrutiny. If the product of this procedure—*Viajes*—is artifice, it theorizes an aesthetic of spectacle, a crucial operation for forming tight bonds among distant participants in the modernizing projects advocated by Sarmiento. What remains unasked in Sarmiento's rhetorical question, however, is whether his instruments can effectively complete this task, or whether they merely emphasize the distance between their reflections and other images of modernity.

In the letters that comprise *Viajes*, as well as in subsequent texts that narrate Sarmiento's eccentric passage from the provincial town of San Juan to exile to a place of power, optical metaphors underscore the precarious but indispensable world-pictures that locate his ambitions and designs in time and space. Thus Sarmiento tells Valentín Alsina that he leaves the United States with "la mitad de mis ilusiones rotas o ajadas, miéntras que otras luchan con el raciocinio para decorar de nuevo aquel panorama imajinario en que encerramos siempre las ideas cuando se refieren a objetos que no hemos visto" [half of my illusions torn or threadbare, while others struggle against reason in order to redecorate that new imaginary panorama where we always keep ideas when they refer to objects we have not seen].[72] No longer capable of idealizing the United States as a supremely efficient machine of progress, he struggles to reconcile the disillusionment of empirical observations with the stubborn hope of the still-distant but contemporary site of actualized futurity, located just beyond his frame of reference. His conceptualization of modernity, as it were, depends on the constantly renewed tension between concealing and revealing, location and disorientation, reason and fantasy. The "imaginary panorama" remains an essential instrument, irrespective of the quality and veracity of images it may display at a given moment.

Writing from Rio de Janeiro several years later, Sarmiento will employ a similar metaphor to describe the sensation of waking from a heavy slumber to a view of the Bay of Guanabara. The bright sun, the sailboats, and the lush, hilly terrain remind him of what Lucio Mansilla has told him of India, but he quickly amends that "yo estaba despierto, y no era recuerdo, ni ilusión, ni pintura, lo que mis ojos veían: las barquillas aquellas se movían, mecíanse las flores, sacudidas por insectos dorados y el ruido de carruajes y el bullicio de población alejaban toda idea de un cuadro de gabinete óptico" [I was awake, and it was not a memory, nor an illusion, nor a painting that my eyes saw: those boats were moving, the flowers were swaying, shaken by golden insects, and the noise of carriages and the bustle of the population dispelled any notion of a scene from an optical cabinet].[73] The metaphor educes the foundational binarisms of Sarmiento's worldview: conflating an oral narrative with an optical cabinet, he emphasizes the exoticness of the scene and his distance from it. But the weak negation barely distinguishes the present scene from Mansilla's tale or a painted transparency; the motions of the boats, flowers, and the accompanying sounds of wagons wheels and the crowd do little to dispel the subsequent evocation of the artificial sights and sounds of an audiovisual spectacle. In other words, the noise and movement serve to underscore the affinity between his current locale and that which "sólo puede verse en la India, en Madras o en Calcuta" [can only be seen in India, in Madras or Calcutta], as he declares in a previous sentence.[74] The portrayal of his locus of enunciation as an animated spectacle thus performs the procedure theorized in *Viajes*: Sarmiento asserts the link between an idea of India (a distant place he has never set foot) with the "visible things" of his surroundings, and proceeds to reify his Orientalist fantasy by converting it into imagery that he adapts and incorporates into another prefatory text (that of the second part of *Campaña*).

Written shortly after Rosas's defeat at the Battle of Caseros, *Campaña en el Ejército Grande* narrates Sarmiento's arrival at the seat of national power—at Rosas's mansion on the outskirts of Buenos Aires, he signs a letter with the dictator's own pen—and his thwarted efforts to assert any immediate authority there. Writing from exile, once again, the negative optical metaphor underscores the implacability of Sarmiento's situation: the forceful disavowal of exotic imagery, the turn toward a familiar quotidian existence, is denied him. Instead of recoiling from an idealized image that threatens his exclusion, it is as if his Orientalized surroundings force him to retreat toward the optical apparatus. In other words, Sarmiento insists on his role of spectator so that he may reassure the reader of his own modernity; in employing the language of spectacle, the traveler-writer treats his immediate environs as pure image, one that is equivalent to the illustrated or verbal descriptions of other exotic locales. The narration exhibits its author's displacement and knowing consumption of repeating views. If the rhetorical turn is ultimately, purposefully ineffective, its deployment nonetheless indicates its versatility. Emblematic of the desire for modernity and its concomitant anxiety, what the optic modifies, adapts, and reflects is ultimately secondary to the technological and social mechanisms it organizes.

CONCLUSION

Like the dissolving views of a diorama, the optical devices of postrevolutionary Argentine cultural discourse present a succession of images that reveal variations of a few basic rhetorical mechanisms. In the most basic sense, they collectively attest to a modern desire to see. Whether referring to actual events or deployed as discursive figures, they embody a visual regime whose diverse techniques ostensibly produce convincing, though conspicuously illusory, illusions of everyone(s). These optical assemblages organize spectacles in which the public not only becomes involved in the elaboration of images and their accompanying theatrics, but in which the public comes to see itself; or more radically, the larger specters of phantasmagoria, magic lanterns, cosmoramas, and the like are not supernatural but specular images of a *pueblo* constituting itself through a subjection to rituals of diversion and codes of conduct. However, as we have seen throughout this chapter, the capacity for self-reflexivity does not immediately translate into an efficient mechanism at the service of one particular ideological project or another. New and repurposed apparatuses alike embody the uneven development of modernity in postrevolutionary Argentina, but less in terms of the specific image one device or another may show, than with respect to the way in which they mediate encounters between foreign influences, local elites, and an audience. This public fulfills a double function as spectator and object of scrutiny, and in this capacity it resists any facile categorization. Which is to say, what optical devices and audiovisual spectacles reveal about the common cultural and political ground of postrevolutionary Argentina is that the discourse of modernity, irrespective of social actors' professed ideological tendencies, is marked by a certain indiscipline. That is, these view-taking machines capture how, in a turbulent, transitional period, provisional nation-pictures produced by competing interests necessarily revealed their incompletion, an alterity that was at the same time constitutive and supplementary to these images. Thus, as we distance ourselves from these ideological *gabinetes ópticos*, it becomes apparent that modern political designs depend on other technologies as well.

NOTES

1. "El Cosmorama. Brillantes fuegos diamantinos," *La Gaceta Mercantil*, May 15, 1844, 4.

2. See Vicente Gesualdo, "Los salones de 'vistas ópticas': Antepasados del cine en Buenos Aires y el interior," *Todo es historia* 21, no. 248 (1988): 70–73, and Beatriz Seibel, *Historia del teatro argentino: Desde los rituales hasta 1930* (Buenos Aires: Corregidor, 2002), 64–145.

3. Jonathan Crary, *Techniques of the Observer: On Vision and Modernity in the Nineteenth Century* (Cambridge, Mass.: MIT Press, 1992), 3.

4. Andrea Noble, "Visual Culture and Latin American Studies," *CR: The New Centennial Review* 4, no. 2 (2004): 225.

5. Graciela Montaldo notes that "[l]a imagen, y especialmente la imagen reproducida, mereció la condena intelectual apenas aparecida en la segunda mitad del siglo XIX" [the image, and especially the reproduced image, received the condemnation of intellectuals no sooner than it appeared in the second half of the nineteenth century] ("Culturas críticas: La extensión de un campo," *Iberoamericana* 4, no. 16 [2004]: 40). The past decade, however, has seen a proliferation of studies attending to questions of nineteenth-century visual cultural, including Jens Andermann's *The Optic of the State: Visuality and Power in Argentina and Brazil*; *Images of Power: Iconography, Culture and the State in Latin America*, edited by Andermann and William Rowe (New York: Berghahn, 2006); *Galerías del progreso: Museos, exposiciones y cultura visual en América Latina*, a volume edited by Andermann and Beatriz González-Stephan (Rosario, Argentina: Beatriz Viterbo, 2006); the forthcoming *Cultura visual e innovaciones culturales en América Latina (desde 1840 a las Vanguardias)*, also edited by González-Stephan. As the dates of this last title suggests, studies on *fin de siglo* phenomena predominate, hinting at the problematic affinity between a new object of study and the traditional teleologies of progress. That being said, studies by Maria Cristina Miranda da Silva and Ernesto Barretta García have shed new light on mid-nineteenth-century Brazil and Uruguay, respectively, and Erica Segre examines the influence of diverse audiovisual spectacles on the illustrated press of mid-century Mexico in *Intersected Identities: Strategies of Visualisation in Nineteenth- and Twentieth-Century Mexican Culture* (New York: Berghahn Books, 2007). In the case of Argentina, phenomena such as magic lantern shows and *gabinetes ópticos* have been primarily examined with respect to the so-called period of "National Organization" following Rosas's deposal, consistent with the notion that the Federalist regime preceded the formation of modern audiences. See, for example, Gesualdo, the presentation of Ana María Telesca and Roberto Amigo, titled "La curiosidad de los porteños: El público y los temas de las vistas ópticas en el Estado de Buenos Aires (1852–1862)" and Pilar González Bernaldo de Quirós's *Civilidad y política* (269–74).

6. W. J. T. Mitchell, *Iconology: Image, Text, Ideology* (Chicago: University of Chicago Press, 1986), 162.

7. Roland Barthes, *Camera Lucida*, trans. Richard Howard (New York: Hill and Wang, 1981), 59.

8. Josefina Ludmer, "Una máquina para leer el siglo XIX," *Revista de la Universidad Nacional Autónoma de México* 530 (1995): n.p. Web November 29, 2012. Ludmer indeed notes an affinity with the artifacts studied in this chapter, and notes that the core of her "machine" "proyecta sobre sí mismo (y aquí funciona como aparato óptico)."

9. Ludmer, "Una máquina para leer el siglo XIX."

10. Timothy Mitchell, "The Limits of the State: Beyond Statist Approaches and Their Critics," *The American Political Science Review* 85, no. 1 (1991): 90.

11. Jens Andermann, *The Optic of the State: Visuality and Power in Argentina and Brazil* (Pittsburgh, Pa.: University of Pittsburgh Press, 2007), 8.

12. Ernesto Beretta García, "Antes del daguerrotipo: Gabinetes ópticos, cosmoramas, máquinas para sacar vistas y experimentaciones con los efectos de luz en Montevideo durante el siglo XIX," in *Artículos de investigación sobre fotografía, 2008*, ed. Ernesto Beretta García, Fernando Miranda, Gonzalo Vicci, Sandra Marroig, and Daniel Elissalde (Montevideo, Uruguay: Ediciones CMDF, 2009), 13.

13. Raúl Antelo, "Lugares do menor," *Latin American Literary Review* 25, no. 50 (1997): 120.

14. John Anthony King, *Twenty-four Years in the Argentine Republic: Embracing Its Civil and Military History, and an Account of Its Political Condition, Before and During the Administration of Governor Rosas* (New York: D. Appleton & Co, 1846), 45.

15. King, *Twenty-four Years*, 46.

16. "The figure of the magic lanternist . . . had folkloric associations. He was linked to a specific popular trade with frequently rural ramifications, in which artisans and their families (conventionally depicted wearing the costume of Savoy) travelled the countryside with a magic lantern strapped to their back" (Segre, *Intersected Identities*, 44).

17. King, *Twenty-four Years*, 47.

18. King, *Twenty-four Years*, 50 (italics added).

19. Performing a close reading of Johann Samuel Halle's brief description of a magic lantern show (1784), in "Lanterna mágica: Fantasmagoria e sincretismo audiovisual," Maria Cristina Miranda da Silva argues that "os planos do conteúdo e da expressão se relacionam entre si a partir de visibilidades e fantasmagorias, explicitadas tanto no plano do conteúdo (ilusão vs realidade) como no da expressão (visibilidade vs ocultamento, claro vs escuro, movimento vs inércia, opacidade vs transparência). Ou seja, visibilidade e fantasmagoria / realidade e ilusão podem ser consideradas categorias do plano do conteúdo que são homologadas semi-simbólicamente pelas categorias do plano de expressão" [the planes of content and expression relate to one another though visibilities and phantasmagorias, explicit both on the level of content (illusion vs. reality) and on that of expression (visibility vs. concealment, light vs. dark, opacity vs. transparency). That is, visibility and phantasmagoria / reality and illusion can be considered categories on the level of content that are homologized in a semi-symbolic fashion by the categories on the level of expression.] (15).

20. Karl Marx, *Selected Writings*, ed. David McLellan (Oxford: Oxford University Press, 2000), 180.

21. Contrary to the way in which the device appears in Romantic discourse, Marx emphasizes how it functions technically, not as an embodiment of poetic inspiration. Samuel Taylor Coleridge, for example, describes the sensation totality produced by Milton's verses as akin to the fleeting visual sensation experienced by a viewing subject: "[t]his is creation rather than a painting, or if painting, yet such, and with such co-presence of the whole picture flashed at once upon the eye, as the sun paints in a camera obscura" (393).

22. Siegfried Zielinski, *Audiovisions: Cinema and Television as Entr'Actes in History* (Amsterdam: Amsterdam University Press, 1999), 20.

23. Mitchell, *Iconology*, 171.

24. Crary, *Techniques of the Observer*, 30–31.

25. Geoffrey Bachten, *Each Wild Idea* (Cambridge, Mass.: MIT Press, 2001), 18.

26. Elías Palti, *El tiempo de la política: El siglo XIX reconsiderado* (Buenos Aires: Siglo Veintiuno Editores Argentina, 2007), 118–19.

27. For a succinct exposition of the different models essayed in the decades following independence and the impediments to making them permanent, see Frank Safford's "Politics, Ideology and Society in Post-Independence Latin America," in *The Cambridge History of Latin America: From Independence to c. 1870*, vol. 3, ed. Leslie Bethell (Cambridge: Cambridge University Press, 2008), especially pages 355–70.

28. Jeremy Adelman, *Sovereignty and Revolution in the Iberian Atlantic* (Princeton, N.J.: Princeton University Press, 2006), 392.

29. Julio Schvartzman, *Microcrítica: Lecturas argentinas, cuestiones de detalle* (Buenos Aires: Biblos, 1996), 121.

30. Luis Pérez, *El Torito de los Muchachos, 1830*, ed. Olga Fernández Latour de Botas (Buenos Aires: Instituto Bibliográfico "Antonio Zinny," 1978), 1.

31. Schvartzman, *Microcrítica*, 121.

32. *Diccionario de la lengua española* (Madrid: Espasa-Calpe, 1994), 2:2248. As we have already seen with Beláustegui's letter and John Anthony King's memoir, it is not the novelty of the device that attracts Goya's interest here. "Tutilimundi" first appears in the *Diccionario de autoridades* in 1739, and "mundinovi" has an entry in the 1734 edition.

33. Jonathan Crary, "Géricault, the Panorama, and Sites of Reality in the Early Nineteenth Century," *Grey Room* 9 (2002): 6, 9.
34. Pérez, *El Torito de los Muchachos*, 44.
35. As quoted in Mauro A. Fernández, *Historia de la magia y el ilusionismo en la Argentina: Desde sus orígenes hasta el siglo XIX inclusive* (Buenos Aires: s.n., 1996), 82.
36. Pérez, *El Torito de los Muchachos*, 52.
37. For example, in 1845 the lithographer Gregory Ibarra put on a phantasmagoria show with his magic lantern to raise funds for the widows of soldiers of the Federation (Fernández 109). Moreover, as Telesca and Amigo and González Bernaldo de Quirós have observed, the images of local events (such as the death of Camila O'Gorman) would increasingly become incorporated into spectacles alongside other, more exotic images in the 1850s.
38. Andrés Lamas, "Visiones de la óptica," in *El Iniciador*, ed. Mariano de Vedia y Mitre (Buenos Aires: Kraft, 1941), 102.
39. Lamas, "Visiones de la óptica," 102.
40. Lamas, "Visiones de la óptica," 104. The *Diccionario de la Real Academia* defines "óptica" as "Aparato compuesto de lentes y espejos, que sirve para ver estampas y dibujos agrandados y como de bulto" [An apparatus comprised of lenses and mirrors, which is used to see plates and drawings enlarged and oversized].
41. Lamas, "Visiones de la óptica," 102.
42. I'm referring here to a central argument of Carlos Alonso's *The Burden of Modernity: The Rhetoric of Cultural Discourse in Spanish America* (New York: Oxford University Press, 1998): "[f]or the Spanish American intellectual the modern has always been 'somewhere else,' regardless of the relative level of advancement of the writer's society at any given time" (32).
43. Lamas, "Visiones de la óptica," 102.
44. Lamas, "Visiones de la óptica," 102.
45. Ernesto Laclau, *Emancipation(s)* (New York: Verso, 1996), 51.
46. Esteban Echeverría, *Dogma socialista*, ed. Alberto Palcos (La Plata, Argentina: Universidad Nacional de la Plata, 1940), 254.
47. In other words, the individual reverie for a brief moment seems to prefigure mass culture at the turn of the century, when audiences "consumed images of an illusory 'reality' [that] was isomorphic to the apparatuses used to accumulate knowledge about an observer," when "Foucault's opposition between spectacle and surveillance becomes untenable" (Crary, *Techniques of the Observer*, 112).
48. Lamas, "Visiones de la óptica," 103.
49. Lamas, "Visiones de la óptica," 104.
50. Echeverría, *Dogma socialista*, 253.
51. Juan Bautista Alberdi, *Fragmento preliminar al estudio del derecho* (Buenos Aires: Biblos, 1984), 127.
52. Alonso, *The Burden of Modernity*, 26.
53. Ernesto Laclau and Chantal Mouffe, *Hegemony and Socialist Strategy: Towards a Radical Democratic Politics* (London: Verso, 2001), 126.
54. Jorge Luis Borges, *El aleph* (Buenos Aires: Alianza, 2002), 194.
55. Laclau, *Emancipation(s)*, 72.
56. Goran M. Blix, *From Paris to Pompeii: French Romanticism and the Cultural Politics of Archaeology* (Philadelphia: University of Pennsylvania Press, 2009), 106.
57. While the headings of several letters bear the date "182 . . .", David Haberly has argued that "the relatively sophisticated language and structure of the 'Cartas,' as well as the influence of the Walpurgisnacht section of Goethe's Faust found in letter 24, lead me to believe that the text itself was written in 1832 or 1833" (Haberly, "Male Anxiety and Sacrificial Masculinity: The Case of Echeverría," *Hispanic Review* 73, no. 3 [2005]: 302).
58. Jorge Myers, "Un autor en busca de un programa: Echeverría en sus escritos de reflexión estética," in *Las brújulas del extraviado: Para una lectura integral de Esteban Echeverría*, ed. Martín Kohan and Alejandra Laera (Rosario, Argentina: Beatriz Viterbo, 2006), 62.
59. Johann W. Goethe, *The Sorrows of Young Werther, and Selected Writings* (New York: New American Library, 1982), 53.

60. *Obras de Esteban Echeverría* V, 193–94.

61. Alejandra Laera, "'Nada se obtiene sin dinero': Pérdidas y ganancias de un hombre de letras," in *Las brújulas del extraviado: Para una lectura integral de Esteban Echeverría*, ed. Martín Kohan and Alejandra Laera (Rosario, Argentina: Beatriz Viterbo, 2006), 88–89.

62. *Obras de Esteban Echeverría* V, 181.

63. *Obras de Esteban Echeverría* V, 182.

64. *Obras de Esteban Echeverría* V, 182–83.

65. *Obras de Esteban Echeverría* V, 185.

66. *Obras de Esteban Echeverría* V, 186.

67. *Obras de Esteban Echeverría* V, 191.

68. Michel Foucault, "Lives of Infamous Men," in *The Essential Foucault: Selections from Essential Works of Foucault, 1954–1984* (New York: New Press, 2003), 289.

69. Domingo Faustino Sarmiento, *Viajes por Europa, África y América, 1845–1847 y Diario de gastos*, ed. Javier Fernández (Buenos Aires: Colección Archivos, 1993), 6.

70. Sarmiento, *Viajes*, 4.

71. Sarmiento, *Viajes*, 3.

72. Sarmiento, *Viajes*, 290.

73. Domingo Faustino Sarmiento, *Campaña en el Ejército Grande*, ed. Tulio Halperín Donghi (Bernal, Argentina: Univ. Nacional de Quilmes, 2004), 102.

74. Sarmiento, *Campaña en el Ejército Grande*, 102.

Chapter Four

The Machine in the Pampa, or Writing as Technology

> La planta de la civilización no se propaga de semilla. Es como la viña, prende de gajo. Este es el medio único de que América, hoy desierta, llegue a ser un mundo opulento en poco tiempo. La reproducción por sí sola es medio lentísimo.
>
> [The plant of civilization is not propagated by seed. It is like the grapevine, it takes to a graft. This is the only way that America, today a desert, may come to be an opulent world in a short amount of time. Reproduction itself is a very slow means.]
>
> —Juan Bautista Alberdi, *Bases y puntos de partida para la organización política de la República Argentina* [Bases and Points of Departure for the Political Organization of the Argentine Republic]

The previous chapters have demonstrated how supporters of Juan Manuel de Rosas and his opponents grappled with fundamental questions of political legitimacy. They debated one another using a common vocabulary and similar rhetorical strategies and cultural forms. Moreover, they shared a basic concern with the *pueblo*, an emerging social actor whose support they sought to secure, represent, and invent. While nationalist historiographies and popular memory alike have long echoed and reinforced the divisive rhetoric of Rosas's Argentina, rendering it transcendent, I have endeavored to recover the common ground that these concurrent, contingent responses helped constitute. What my inquiry indicates is that this discursive terrain, involving multiple participants, was politically and culturally modern, at least in a nascent sense.

Such an argument goes "beyond civilization and barbarism" in two important ways. First, it stresses the importance of examining various cultural artifacts that are contemporary to Sarmiento's *Facundo* and the texts written by his fellow dissident intellectuals, known collectively as Generation of 1837. Second, it contradicts the narrative of progress that these *letrados* formulated in opposition to Rosas and which became official state discourse when they assumed prominent roles in the construction of the nation-state following Rosas's deposal in 1852. At the conclusion of his influential reading on Sarmiento in *Divergent Modernities* (2001), Julio Ramos offers a succinct version of this durable myth:

> we might say that to write, in Sarmiento, is to modernize. We are not dealing with a metaphor here, or an analogy between the field of discourse and the social order "reflected" by it: this "social order," "the rational public sphere," was created (at least in part) by writing. If, at the time *Facundo* was written, modernization had suddenly been interrupted, if the public sphere had been lacking and chaos reigned throughout, then writing—by its generalizing and homogeneizing operation—remained a fundamental model for the ration-al(izing) project.[1]

Consistent with David Viñas's contention that Generation of 1837 maintained an unwavering belief in "la eficacia excepcional de 'las letras'" [the exceptional efficacy of "letters"], Ramos foregrounds Sarmiento's conviction that writing could overcome political and material limitations to institute a new social order.[2] Seen from this perspective, writing and, by extension, modernization were carried out by an enlightened minority that labored in a cultural *desierto*, at a remove from the general chaos that thwarted the immediate realization of their ambitious designs. In more specific terms, Sarmiento and his fellow *letrados* remained the sole agents of a project initiated during independence from Spain and cut short by Rosas's tyranny.

In the context of Ramos's study of nineteenth-century Latin American intellectuals, this restrictive narrative of modernity hinges on the validity of two conditions: in postrevolutionary Argentina modernization had been interrupted, and there was no public sphere to speak of. Limiting his analysis to Sarmiento's own works, Ramos may tacitly uphold these suppositions, but the broader corpus we have considered requires us to question such a conclusion. For while Rosas's Argentina was tumultuous and marked by slow economic and demographic growth, it nonetheless experienced different facets of modernity, including new forms of popular opinion, an emerging visual regime, and the advance of what James E. Sanders refers to as "republican modernity": the dissemination of notions of popular sovereignty and citizenship.[3] This is not to deny the "generalizing and homogenizing operation" of writing in the postrevolutionary period, but rather to insist that this operation involved various participants, including subaltern subjects, and was not limited to a single ideological viewpoint. Substituting "public sphere" for "core idea of nationalism," we could repeat Ernest Gellner's insistence that "the pervasiveness and importance of abstract, centralized, standardized, one to many communication [. . .] itself automatically engenders the core idea of nationalism, *quite irrespective of what in particular is being put into the specific messages transmitted.*"[4] In other words, the designs promoted by Sarmiento and his peers were a portion of what was disseminated through cultural forms that contributed to a "rational(izing) project," one which exceeded intellectuals' expressed objectives. Self-awareness or self-identification with certain dimensions of modernity does not equate with agency.

Reexamining the foundational writings of Generation of 1837 within the broader cultural landscape of postrevolutionary Argentina puts into relief how *letrados* opposed to the Rosas regime came to embrace a particular vision of modernity that privileged technology, machine power, and industrialization over political ideals. This position reflects the diminished aspirations they adopted when their rather halfhearted efforts to participate in the Rosas regime were quickly thwarted: they came to regard themselves not as "los guías sino los intérpretes políticos de los sectores dominantes de la Argentina federal, y en la reorientación hacia objetivos de cambio económico, que el rosismo sirve muy mal, encuentran el camino para una coincidencia con esos sectores" [the guides but as the political interpreters of the dominant sectors of federalist Argentina, and in the reorientation toward objectives of economic change, which *rosismo* addressed poorly, they find points of convergence with these sectors].[5] The path to power required them to seek out a space within the nation that remained outside of Rosas's authority.

Numerous studies have examined the way in which works such as Sarmiento's *Facundo*, Echeverría's *La cautiva*, and Juan Bautista Alberdi's *Bases* constructed the figure of the *desierto*, the empty pampa as the site where nation-building could take place; the purpose of this chapter is to demonstrate how these authors simultaneously called to fill the desert with machines, as if to import wholesale the infrastructure of Western modernity.[6] These machines in the pampa were intended not only to spur economic productivity, but also to accelerate and regulate the "medio lentísimo" of biological reproduction. In other words, the civilizing project of Generation of 1837 was to implement the means for making a modern *pueblo* that would overwhelm and supplant an existing population that had demonstrated little enthusiasm for their political and economic ideas.

Of course, in advocating the use of technology to make a people for the desert-nation, writers such as Alberdi, Echeverría, and Sarmiento had to confront the inescapable fact that, in mid-nineteenth-century Argentina, devices such as the telegraph and the railroad were effectively unavailable. Thus, as occurred throughout Latin America, "the appropriation of the discursive modalities of metropolitan authority" required them "to contend with the absence of its material antagonist in its midst, or more precisely, with its phantasmic presence as the always distant and assumed reality of the metropolis."[7] Faced with its material dearth, dissident *letrados* conjured visions of Western industrial modernity throughout their writings. Hence, as we will see at the end of the chapter, Juan Bautista Alberdi imagined the Paraná River teeming with steamships, shuttling goods past youths swimming nearby. In addition to flights of fantasy, these writers came to regard writing itself as a technology, as an instrument capable of revealing "whatever does not bring itself forth and does yet lie here before us,"[8] as a practice that was to create the conditions for its own obsolescence. Thus, in calling to fill the desert, they proposed transforming writing itself through technological means. For this reason, in describing his travels through the United States in *Viajes por Europa, África y América, 1845–1847*, Sarmiento marvels at the ability of newspapers, the telegraph, and advertisements to instruct and discipline a reading public across a vast territory. In synthesis, the *letrados* of the Generation of 1837 sought to found a literature and, in turn, a modern nation not by situating it within the discursive and temporal limits of Rosas's Argentina, but by insisting on the impossibility of literature in the present moment and sketching a future landscape that would render their own writings at once legible and outdated.

WRITING (IN) THE DESERT

On October 12, 1880, Julio Argentino Roca gave his inaugural address as the newly elected president of the República Argentina. A decorated general, Roca had recently led a military campaign against the indigenous populations of the interior, known as the *Conquista del desierto*. His assumption of the presidency coincided with the federalization of Buenos Aires and—as history books have noted ever since—marked the definitive consolidation of a liberal nation-state that, at least on paper, bore an uncanny resemblance to the one first imagined in works like Sarmiento's *Facundo* and Alberdi's *Bases y puntos de partida para la organización política de la República Argentina*. The symbolism of the moment was not lost on Roca, who boasts at one point in his speech that, at last, "el gobierno podrá ejercer su acción con entera libertad, exento de las luchas diarias y deprimentes de su autoridad que tenía que sostener para defender sus prerrogativas contra las pretensiones invasoras de funcionarios subalternos" [the government will be able to take action with complete freedom, free of the depressing and daily fights for its liberty that it had to wage in order to defend its prerogatives against the invasive pretensions of subaltern functionaries].[9] In other words, the internecine conflicts that plagued Argentina in the decades following independence have finally come to an end; the ruling elite has established a consensus regarding the exclusive use of force.

Yet the Conqueror of the Desert is not content to dwell on the newfound political stability and insists on an immense task that awaits Argentina. The army has removed native tribes standing in the way of progress, but the military presence must be swiftly reinforced by civilian *vías de comunicación*, namely the railroad and the telegraph. The implementation of these technologies will "dejar borradas para siempre las fronteras militares, y a fin de que no haya un solo palmo de tierra argentina que no se halle bajo la jurisdicción de las leyes de la nación" [leave the military boundaries erased forever, such that there will not be a single foot of Argentine territory that does not find itself under the jurisdiction of the laws of the nation].[10] The lines of communication and modes of transport will efface the lingering signs of violence and facilitate the mobility of goods, context-free information, and people. His speech articulates, thus, the nationalist principle of a dominant polity that, in Gellner's terms, wills to extend its boundaries to the limits of its culture, and to impose its culture with the boundaries of its power.[11]

The larger project that is required of the state, then, is to fill the newly emptied, dehistoricized space of the *desierto* with new inhabitants, a people formed and informed by modern means of production. Indeed, Roca is quite direct in stating that the function of the institution he has been elected to lead is not merely to represent an existing constituency, but to create one. He addresses a public that is an imagined community in the sense that it is provisional, reminding them that "[s]omos la traza de una gran nación . . . pero para alcanzar a realizar y completar el cuadro con la perfección de los detalles, es menester entrar con paso firme en el carril de la vida regular de un pueblo" [we are the outline of a great nation . . . but to come to realize and complete the picture in perfect detail, it is necessary to step firmly onto the track of the regular life of a people].[12] Appealing to a "nosotros" situated on a fast track to modernity, somewhere between a crude blueprint and its intricate, finished form, the president conjures an Escher-like image of a *pueblo* constituting itself through writing, one which is both subject and author of its definitive version. Read literally, the metaphor "we are the outline" plots the progressive elaboration of a preconceived image on a two-dimensional surface, one that is not simply the graphic or textual representation of a something else, but, in Jacques Rancière's terms, a distribution of the sensible that inscribes a sense of community.[13] In other words, the image Roca employs is not merely a rhetorical flourish, but an allusion to the cultural forms that have preceded and continue to influence military force, technological innovations, and immigration, which are redrawing the map of the nation.

In vigorously advocating machine power and technology as key instruments for creating a modern nation-people, Roca adopts a cultural discourse of modernity first formulated in Argentina by the Generation of 1837 in opposition to Juan Manuel de Rosas. From their earliest writings, intellectuals such as Esteban Echeverría, Juan Bautista Alberdi, and Domingo Faustino Sarmiento identified the *desierto* as the site for founding both an autonomous literature and a modern nation. Employing the twin discourses of emptiness and erasure, these *letrados* treated the desert as an acultural space where "el Otro que lo habita es visto precisamente como Otro absoluto, hundido en una diferencia intransitable" [the Other that inhabits it is seen precisely as an absolute Other, mired in an unresolvable difference].[14] Their literature thus imagines a site of absolute difference and, at the same time, proposes the means to rationalize it; that which stands in stark opposition to their modernizing goals thus becomes their necessary point of departure. Tracking the emergence of this treatment of the *desierto* reveals how, from its inception, this key discursive figure of Argentine national identity concerned the need to constitute a people, as a workforce and as a source of political legitimacy, and proposed creating it through technological means.

In September 1837, copies of Esteban Echeverría's poetry collection *Rimas* appeared in several bookstores in Buenos Aires. Though the reading of *La cautiva*, its central poem, generated enthusiasm among those present at the Salón Literario in Marcos Sastre's bookstore, the local, pro-Rosas press refused to review the book because of the contrarian political opinions expressed by its author in the Salón's gatherings.[15] As the "Advertencia" or prologue of *Rimas* makes clear, Echeverría ardently wished for his verses to be a catalyst for the eventual socioeconomic transformation of Argentina, a notion that directly defied the Rosas regime's identification with traditional rural culture: "[e]l Desierto es nuestro, es nuestro más pingüe patrimonio, y debemos poner conato en sacar de su seno, no sólo riqueza para nuestro engrandecimiento y bienestar sino también poesía para nuestro deleite moral y fomento de nuestra literatura nacional" [the Desert is ours, it is our greatest patrimony, and we must invest our energies in extracting from its bosom, not only riches for our expansion and well-being, but also poetry for our moral pleasure and the fostering of our national literature].[16] For Echeverría the pampa is a source for poetic inspiration and material progress, where raw materials are to be exploited to make a nation from the desert.[17] Intellectual and manual labor participate in a common undertaking, with the former preceding and directing the latter. Poetry, in other words, initiates an enterprise it cannot fully realize on its own.

Echeverría's poem *La cautiva* establishes a precedent by depicting the pampa as a *desierto* in need of a civilizing force. Centering on the ill-fated escape of the Christian settlers Brian and María from a bloodthirsty Indian tribe, its verses underscore a stark division between society and nature. True to Echeverría's claim that "[e]l principal designio del autor de *La cautiva* ha sido pintar algunos rasgos de la fisonomía poética del Desierto" [the principal aim of the author of *La cautiva* has been to depict some features of the poetic physiognomy of the Desert], the first canto of the poem opens with a panoramic vision of the empty plains:

> El desierto,
> inconmensurable, abierto
> y misterioso a sus pies
> se extiende; triste el semblante,
> solitario y taciturno
> como el mar cuando, un instante,
> al crepúsculo nocturno,
> pone rienda a su altivez.
> (*La cautiva*, 25)
>
> [The desert,
> incommensurable, open
> and mysterious at the feet of the Andes
> extends; sad the figure,
> solitary and taciturn
> like the sea when, in an instant,
> at the falling of night,
> it reins in its haughtiness.]

Viewed from above, the *desierto* lacks any distinguishing features and converts into an ocean-like void. As the poet assumes a heliocentric perspective, he marvels at the plains' inscrutable vastness, their lack of internal divisions and external limits. From such dizzying heights the sun itself becomes disoriented: "Gira en vano, reconcentra / su inmensidad, y no encuentra / la vista en su vivo anhelo / do fijar su fugaz vuelo / como el pájaro en el mar" [it spins in vain, concentrating / its immensity, and does not find / the sight in its vivid desire / on which to set its speedy flight / like a bird in the sea].[18] The poet, speaking as if from these heights, offers a panorama where the entire poem will take place. The staging signals the limits of aesthetic representation: regarding the "maravillas sublimes" [sublime marvels] that "sembró la fecunda mano / de Dios" [sowed by the fecund hand of God] the poet exclaims, "¡Qué pincel podrá pintarlas / sin deslucir su belleza! / ¡Qué lengua humana alabarlas!" [What brush could paint them / without tarnishing their beauty! / What human tongue could praise them!].[19] In the opening lines of *La cautiva*, the desert remains unaltered by human presence and inscrutable to individual comprehension.

After he presents the *desierto* as an abstracted space, Echeverría depicts a group of Indians returning from a raid as a sudden, dramatic interruption. Breaking the stillness of the dawn, a "sordo y confuso clamar" [deafening and confused clamor] accompanies a cloud of dust and the trembling of the earth beneath the hooves of horses. As Mariquita Sánchez de Thompson remarks to Echeverría in a letter dated April 17, 1845, this style moved the German landscape painter Johann Moritz Rugendas to comment that "[es] perfecta la pintura que usted hace de las pampas... usted concibió primero el paisaje y después tomó sus figuras como accesorio para completar aquel" [the painting you make of the pampas is perfect... first you conceived of the landscape and then you treated its figures as an accessory to complete it].[20] The following month, Sarmiento published the first installments of *Facundo* in the Santiago daily *El Progreso* and, in its second chapter, presents Echeverría as a model for aspiring writers, when he recalls how the poet abandoned the classicism of his predecessors:

> [Echeverría] volvió sus miradas al Desierto, y allá en la inmensidad sin límites, en las soledades en que vaga el salvaje, en la lejana zona de fuego que el viajero ve acercarse cuando los campos se incendian, halló las inspiraciones que proporciona a la imaginación el espectáculo de una naturaleza solemne, grandiosa, inconmensurable, callada. (*Facundo*, 78–79)
>
> [Echeverría turned his gaze to the Desert, and there in the limitless immensity, in the solitude where the savage roams, in the distant zone of fire that the traveler sees nearing when the fields burst into flames, he found inspiration in the spectacle of that solemn, grandiose and incommensurable nature provides the imagination.]

As read by Sarmiento and Rugendas, *La cautiva* denies the influence of the indigenous in shaping the pampa and, moreover, dismisses the practical knowledge of its inhabitants for which Sarmiento cannot repress his enthusiasm in the very same chapter of *Facundo*. Like Rugendas's own paintings, *La cautiva* contributes to the prevailing image of an expansive region that overwhelms the capacities of the rational observer and subsumes the savagery of its native inhabitants. At the same time, all three men are quick to insist that *La cautiva* is impressive because of its likeness to a large-scale landscape painting or a panorama; it offers, in other words, an ekphrastic spectacle for an audience who remains at a distance from its vast and disorienting setting. As Neil Smith argues, the nature/society split, which occurs during the formation of social economies based on commodity exchange, "implies the possibility of abstracting from immediate space, and of the conceiving of spatial extension beyond immediate experience."[21] The depiction not only anticipates and encourages the future, violent appropriation of these lands, it also expands, if not explodes the meaning of "pampa" and "desierto." Exceeding its geographical referent, its features abstracted, the *desierto* articulates a logic of expansion, speculation, and centralization.

A comparison of *La cautiva* and its "Advertencia" with a lecture that Echeverría presented to the Salón Literario of 1837 highlights how material wealth, "moral pleasure," and literature tightly cohered in his vision of national progress. Presented in the same forum in which Juan María Gutiérrez read aloud fragments of *La cautiva*, Echeverría's "Segunda lectura" addresses the embryonic cultural life of Buenos Aires and, as Alejandra Laera comments, foregrounds the estancia owner Echeverría's longstanding interest in political economy.[22] Echeverría begins his lecture by urging his listeners to abandon "utopías y . . . teorías quiméricas para el porvenir" [utopias . . . and chimerical theories for the future]; that is, the Argentine *letrado* must discard all pretensions of changing society through the application of universal principles. Instead, one must recognize that "el desarrollo de estos elementos es normal en cada sociedad y sigue una ley necesaria en relación con el espacio y el tiempo" [the development of these elements is normal in each society and follows a necessary law in relation to space and time].[23] At odds with his insistence on attention to the particularities of Argentine life, however, Echeverría employs a trope with airs of a Mediterranean pastoral scene that conflates agriculture and cultural life: "la tierra donde sembrarán y recogerán óptimos y delicados frutos. Los padres plantan el olivo y el dátil para los hijos de sus hijos" [the land where ideal, delicate fruit will be sown and picked. Fathers will plant olives and dates for their sons' sons].[24] What remains consistent is his emphasis on the need to adopt a new *techne* to exploit the countryside, a practice that seeks to convert individual actions into a well-orchestrated enterprise. Like Andrés Lamas's urban utopia in "Visiones de la óptica," Echeverría's pastoral vision depends on synchronization and spatial homogenization.

As the "Segunda lectura" focuses on the question of commercial and industrial growth, Echeverría begins to refer to fields in more concrete terms. He identifies the rural interior as the potential source of the nation's wealth, primarily for grains and hides, and envisions an agglomeration of "capital para llevar con el tiempo nuestra actividad a otra clase de industrias" [the capital that will, in time, direct our activities toward other kinds of industry]. His prophecy, though, is immediately followed by the lament that "nosotros no hemos aprendido todavía a sacar todo el partido que podemos de nuestras vastas llanuras" [we have not yet learned to take full advantage of our vast plains].[25] Concluding his lecture, Echeverría levies a harsh criticism of the anarchy that reigns in the countryside, which is perhaps the most outspoken political statement of the inaugural lectures of the Salón Literario: "lejos de hallar protección en los gobiernos, los labradores, la industria rural no encuentra sino inestabilidad y desaliento" [far from finding protection from the government, the workers and rural industry find nothing but instability and discouragement].[26] He accuses not only the rural workforce for the uncultivated and uncivilized state of the countryside, but also the *jueces de campaña*, the indigenous tribes of the interior, the audience present at the *Salón literario*, and the ravages of war.[27]

The ability to make the pampa productive, however, depends on something that Echeverría skirts in the "Segunda lectura," the very problem that Alberdi will attempt to remedy in his *Bases*: the lack of an adequate workforce. Echeverría asks "¿Y es posible que tierras tan fértiles como las nuestras, consagradas . . . apenas produzcan lo suficiente para el consumo de la Provincia, cuando podía abastecer medio mundo?" [And is it possible that lands as fertile as ours, so blessed, hardly produce what is necessary for the province, when it would supply half the world?].[28] The question is rhetorical because earlier in the *lectura* Echeverría observes that the majority of those who farm the interior are "unos pobres labradores que no cuentan con más capital que el arado y sus bueyes, un campo, las más veces arrendado y su trabajo personal" [poor laborers who cannot count on more capital than their plow and oxen, a field, more often than not leased, and their own labor].[29] For Laera, this represents the lone moment in Echeverría's work where he refers to the "pueblo" not as an abstract entity, but in specific terms, as "el habitante rural, o sea el gaucho; dicho de otro modo: es quien trabaja (produce) la tierra de unos pocos, los ricos, que sólo la poseen (y no producen)" [the rural dweller, that is, the gaucho; in other words, it is he who cultivates the land owned by the few, the rich, who only possess (and do not produce)].[30] In emphasizing their poverty and reduced number, Echeverría less expresses sympathy for the rural poor than he indicates that they alone cannot increase agricultural productivity nor raise the capital necessary for nascent industry. As he denounces the systemic lack of governance in the countryside, Echeverría does not call for the defense of the rural workforce, but its dramatic transformation.

In an oblique manner, the "Segunda lectura," together with *La cautiva*, touch upon a problematic that is central to the poetics of nation-building in Spanish America. Andrés Bello, for example, imagines anonymous laborers subjugating untamed nature in his lengthy poem *La agricultura de la Zona Tórrida* (1826):

> Del obstrüido estanque del molino
> recuerden ya las aguas el camino;
> el intrincado bosque el hacha rompa,
> consuma el fuego; abrid en luengas calles
> la oscuridad de su infructuosa pompa.
> (*Obra literaria*, 45)

> [From the dammed mill pond
> may the waters now remember their course;
> may the ax cut the thick woods,
> may fire consume it; may you open in wide lanes
> the darkness of its fruitless pomp.]

Bello never specifies who, exactly, will provide the manpower necessary to bring about these dramatic changes to the landscape. As Mary Louise Pratt remarks, "[w]hen it comes to concrete relations of labor and property, the seeing-man's powers seem to dissolve into confused noise, distant sounds, a tree cut down by unseen hands. . . . It is on this point that liberal aspirations seem to become unable to represent themselves."[31] And, it must be added, they are unable to represent a people capable of executing these liberal aspirations. Bello's verses read like a preemptive response to "Of Some Sources of Poetry among Democratic Nations," a section of Alexis de Tocqueville's first book of *Democracy in America* (1835). For Tocqueville, poetry and manual labor are two incompatible activities for the typical (North) American:

> Americans . . . are insensible to the wonders of inanimate nature and they may be said not to perceive the mighty forests that surround them till they fall beneath the hatchet. Their eyes are fixed upon another sight: the American people views its own march across these wilds, draining swamps, turning the course of rivers, peopling solitudes, and subduing nature.[32]

What distinguishes Tocqueville's observations from the writings of his Latin American contemporaries is the clear antithesis he asserts between subjective experience and industry. Echeverría's writings, like Bello's, implicitly revel in the promise of "the transformation of natural spontaneity into economic or cultural value through the intervention of the machine," thus conflating *poesis* and *techne*: the transformation of the landscape is a poetic act, and poetry itself serves as a means to this end.[33] The other significant difference, of course, is the question of labor: whereas Tocqueville invokes a social type capable of carrying out this task, Echeverría laments how neither the indigenous tribes nor the "pobres labradores" can modernize the *desierto*.

Indeed, while typically associated with the pampa, the figure of the *desierto* in the Generation of 1837's writings is not limited to a specific geographic region, but rather linked to an uncultured or unproductive other. For Juan Bautista Alberdi in "Predicar en desiertos" [Preaching in Deserts], a short satirical piece published in *La Moda* on March 10, 1838, the city of Buenos Aires is itself a desert in this respect. "Predicar en desiertos" elaborates a familiar complaint of Alberdi's peers, lamenting the lack of a reading public that can appreciate their writings, or, conversely, how the *pueblo* remains oblivious to the civilizing efforts of this literature. Writing under the pseudonym Figarillo, Alberdi resigns to the fact that "[e]scribir español americano es predicar en desiertos. Porque aquí las ideas . . . han de guardar ciertas formas sancionadas, so pena de ser rechazadas en caso de contravención" [writing in Spanish American is to preach in deserts. Because here ideas . . . must maintain certain preordained forms, due to the threat of being rejected in the case of violating them].[34] If writing in American Spanish is the goal of Romantic writers, as Juan María Gutiérrez proposes to the Salón Literario, then for Alberdi it is an undertaking at once futile and exalted, a form of cultural proselytizing that seeks to convert its audience and effect a radical break from its current mode of living.[35] The biblical allusion disassociates it not only from its textual source, but also from its geographic referent. The city and the nation are barren, inhospitable places for a prophet of good literature, taste, and habits: "*La Moda* es un pequeño desierto porque [las mujeres] no leen ni quieren leer" [*La Moda* is a little desert because [women] do not read nor want to read].[36] Wherever he looks, Figarillo finds nothing but *desierto*; each complaint expands the semantic field to which it refers. After mocking the potential female readers of *La Moda*, the article alternates between complaining about the impossibility of using sophisticated language and deriding various sectors of society—shopkeepers, actors, laborers, shepherds, artisans, and the youth—who are all deaf to Figarillo's words, universally incapable of benefiting from the lessons the publication apparently contains.

Alberdi grows impatient as his rant continues; whereas the first figures—women and shopkeepers—receive the attention of full paragraphs, he finally lumps a series of social types into a single sentence, arriving at the conclusion that to write for all of them is to preach in the desert because they learn by instinct, "maquinalmente como los animales" [mechanically like animals].[37] The oxymoronic phrase not only conveys a contempt for the subaltern classes, it dehumanizes and dismisses the notion that their positions in society can constitute, in the aggregate, a unified identity or coherent popular opinion. As he invokes each social type, it becomes increasingly obvious that Alberdi shares a complicit wink with his precious few, supposedly culturally superior readers. In the context of Rosist consensus, which articulates itself via a series of appeals to distinct sectors of society, Alberdi rejects these types as citizens, thus suggesting their participation in politics is illegitimate.

La Moda—from its reports on fashion, its musical compositions and reviews of theater and literature—contains civilized content, but it quickly abandons a tone of civility at the expense of those who are least likely to read the paper.[38] It wavers between addressing its current readers, trying to create more of them, and lamenting the impossibility of such an undertaking. There is a constant tension between instruction and ridicule:

> en *La Moda* el discurso de Alberdi se balancea entre la intención de reformar al pueblo a través de un *arte instructivo* que sancione los vicios y prescriba modelos y comportamientos a imitar, y el impulso por *denostar* a quienes se resisten a entender el nuevo lenguaje con el cual procuran ilustrarlos estos cronistas. (*La mujer romantic*, 33)
>
> [in *La Moda*, Alberdi's discourse wavers between the intention of reforming the people through an *instructive art* that sanctions vices and prescribes models and forms of conduct to imitate, and the impulse to *revile* those that are resistant to understanding the new language with which these chroniclers seek to enlighten them.]

Texts written by Alberdi and his peers at this same point in time suggest that the operation performed in *La Moda* is more radical than simply upbraiding nonreaders for their outmoded customs. *La Moda* employs a conception of the people that does not seek to remake the people according to liberal tastes, but instead emphasizes the unstable and undecided nature of the masses. While Echeverría and others are willing to admit to the multitude's presence as a new social agent, they are quick to negate its capacity as a constructive force. The people is to be at once admired and feared:

> El pueblo, antes de la revolución, era algo sin nombre ni influencia: después de la revolución apareció gigante y sofocó en sus brazos al león de España. La turba, el populacho, antes sumergido en la nulidad, en la impotencia, se mostró entonces en la superficie de la sociedad, no como espuma vil, sino como una potestad destinada por la providencia para dictar la ley, y sobreponerse a cualquier otra potestad terrestre. (Echeverría, *Obra escogida*, 237)
>
> [The people, before the revolution, was something without name or influence: after the revolution it appeared as a giant and suffocated in its arms the lion of Spain. The mob, the rabble, before submerged in nothingness, in powerlessness, showed itself on the surface of society, not as a vile foam, but as a power destined by Providence to establish the law, and impose itself over any other earthly power.]

According to Echeverría's version of the Revolution, the people emerge as a social category in the instant that they expel the crown and establish themselves as the new base of political legitimacy in Spanish America. In the following sentence, however, he undercuts this heroic characterization by employing redundant and negative epithets that, in turn, serve to counter yet another derisive term, a "vile foam." Echeverría conflates in a single sentence three phrases of the people: its nonexistence, its present potency and disorderliness, and its ideal, future-perfect form as the fulfillment of a providential design. What he neglects to explain is how the transition from potentiality to actuality occurs, which is particularly problematic given that Echeverría, like Alberdi's Figarillo, identifies the routines of the general populace as inherited from colonial society. Echeverría's version of history thus contains the two necessary yet incompatible logics that Ernesto Laclau detects in his study of emancipatory discourses, "one that presupposes the objectivity and full representability of the social, the other whose whole case depends on showing that there is a chasm which makes any social objectivity ultimately impossible."[39] In *Dogma socialista*, the people effect an absolute break from a political system, but, at the same time, they function as a metonym (that is, they articulate a causal relationship) for the backwardness of the nation as a whole.

In the imaginary of the Generation of 1837, the people do not possess distinguishing features, neither in the past, nor in the present and future, because this conception accepts and (nominally) absorbs all difference. Thus, as the *Dogma socialista* concludes, Echeverría declares that "todos los argentinos son unos en nuestro corazón, sean cuales fueren su nacimiento, su color, su condición, su escarapela, su edad, su profesión, su clase. Nosotros no conocemos más que una sola facción: la *Patria*" [all Argentines are one in our heart, regardless of birth, color, condition, affiliations, age, profession, or class].[40] It is a highly idealized expression of the role desired by Echeverría and his peers, to be a generation of thinkers capable of reconciling differences between longstanding political factions; here it simply resolves difference in the empty signifier of *patria*, a name still very much lacking a stable referent. Alberdi professes a similar conviction in *Fragmento preliminar al estudio del derecho* (1837), when he declares that "El pueblo no es una clase, un gremio, un círculo: es todas las clases, todos los círculos, todos los roles" [the people is not a class, a guild, a circle: it is all classes, all circles, all roles].[41] In direct opposition to the interpellations and exclusions of Rosist discourse, which involves a constant performance of popular identities, the modernizing discourse of dissident *letrados* instead envisions an unrealized (and impossible) whole, one perceived teleologically, when employing the term *pueblo*. If Rosist writing figures the people as a partial component that represents the whole of society, this is an institutionalist discourse that "attempts to make the limits of the discursive formation coincide with the limits of the community," one in which "differentiality claims to be the only legitimate equivalent: all differences are considered equally valid within a wider totality."[42] Clearly, it is not that the Generation of 1837's notion of the people is all-inclusive, but rather that, unlike Rosist discourse, which depends on the constant invocation of an internal Other, it expels otherness wholly from its imagined community. Consequently, Alberdi can exclude various inhabitants of the national territory and declare in the same text, as he does in *Bases*, that "[l]os americanos hoy somos europeos que hemos cambiado de maestros: a la iniciativa española, ha sucedido la inglesa y francesa" [we Americans of today are Europeans that have changed masters: the Spanish initiative gave way to the English and French].[43] The claims of universality cloak a radical negation of the Other through an acceptance of insignificant (or designified) difference.

Alberdi's *Bases y puntos de partida para la organización política de la República Argentina*, the document that would provide the model for the national constitution of 1853, fuses the concepts of *pueblo* and *desierto*. Beginning with a comparative survey of the constitutions of Spanish American states, *Bases* calls for Argentina to adopt a federal government with a strong executive branch that can stimulate the massive immigration of European laborers, who will help accelerate the modernization of the entire country.[44] Alberdi argues that American constitutions ought to resemble "contratos mercantiles o sociedades colectivas formadas especialmente para dar pobladores a estos desiertos que bautizamos con los nombres pomposos de Repúblicas" [mercantile contracts or collective societies formed especially to bring settlers to these deserts that we baptized with the pompous names of Republics].[45] Consistent with his peers' writings, *desierto* functions in

Bases as a metonym for an entire nation, though here Alberdi employs the term in even broader terms, applying it to the general situation of the states of Spanish America. *Desierto* posits an equivalence between nations' individual struggles to establish themselves, an equivalence that supersedes the colonial heritage, and the struggles for independence; space replaces history.

Beyond its oft-repeated maxim *gobernar es poblar*, the principal objective of the *Bases* is to structure the transition of Argentina from a *desierto* naively labeled "república" to a pragmatic "república posible." Alberdi trenchantly states that the République Argentina must recognize the rights of private property and industry because "el principal elemento de su engrandecimiento y el aliciente más enérgico de la inmigración extranjera" [the principal element of its expansion and the most vigorous incentive for foreign immigration] is nothing more than "el desarrollo y la explotación de los elementos de riqueza" [the development and the exploitation of the elements of wealth] of national territory.[46] He then poses and answers a rhetorical question: "¿Cuál es la constitución que mejor conviene al desierto? La que sirve para hacerlo desaparecer; la que sirve para hacer que el desierto deje de serlo en el menor tiempo posible" [Which is the constitution that best suits the desert? That which makes it disappear; that which makes the desert stop being deserted in the least amount of time possible].[47] Unlike Echeverría, however, for Alberdi there is no poetry in such a task: "[l]a originalidad constitucional es la única a que se pueda aspirar sin inmodestia ni pretensión: ella no es como la originalidad en las bellas artes" [constitutional originality is the only thing to which one can aspire without immodesty or pretension: it is not like the originality of the fine arts].[48] One should not determine the merits of a constitution based on its similarities with other constitutions; one cannot read (or write) one merely by comparing it to existent models, as if constitutions followed the internal conventions of a literary genre. Alberdi wants to divorce aesthetics from politics in *Bases*, as if to deny the decidedly poetic origins of its geospatial imaginary.

Regardless of Alberdi's insistence on the prosaic nature of constitutions, the national state that adopts *Bases* as its founding charter will also make the Generation of 1837's treatment of the *desierto* part of its official discourse. We saw at the beginning of this section how Julio Argentino Roca echoes, if tacitly, the poetry of progress first proposed by Echeverría in his *Rimas*. A predecessor of Roca's provides a more direct link connecting these figures. Indeed, no one better represents the exchanges between literature and politics than Domingo Faustino Sarmiento. In 1871, halfway through his term as president of Argentina, Sarmiento delivered a speech in Rosario, Santa Fe, that encapsulates this carrying over:

> Hemos decretado la abolición de la Pampa. Estamos en el punto de partida de la revolución que nos hará norteamericanos y destronará al estanciero que hace

nacer al gaucho y a la montonera. Va a constituirse una nueva sociedad, una nueva nación, dejando á los muertos, allá, que entierren a sus muertos. La Pampa es una inmensa hoja de papel en que va a inscribirse todo un poema de progreso, de prosperidad y cultura. (*Sarmiento anecdótico*, 245)

[We have decreed the abolition of the Pampa. We are on the verge of the revolution that will make us North Americans and will dislodge the rancher that gives birth to the gaucho and rural militias. A new society is to be constituted, a new nation, leaving the dead, there, to bury their dead. The Pampa is an immense sheet of paper on which an entire poem of progress, prosperity, and culture is going to be written.]

Sarmiento was en route to the inauguration of the Exposición Nacional de Córdoba when he delivered this speech, so in its most immediate context, its purpose was to promote the fair and the state-of-the-art agricultural machines that were to be on display there. In retrospect the oration also can be read as an unofficial declaration of war, as it anticipates the Conquest of the Desert. And, as the reference to North Americans suggests, it alludes to the massive immigration intended to occupy the newly conquered spaces and provide the manpower for this project. Technology and machine power are, in this vision, a kind of poetry that can rewrite an entire landscape as if it were a blank sheet of paper.

If Sarmiento's oratory calls for a decisive break from the past, it also characterizes the shift in spatial perception that structured the process of national organization during the second half of the nineteenth century. If the desert was never fully "abolished," it began to be seen and treated in a new fashion. Partially due to the influence of new trends in cartography, geographers now regarded *desierto* according to a perspective that departed from "la estrategia histórica de ocupación territorial española, que hacía de la ciudad en medio de la *nada* punta de lanza y bastión civilizatorio" [the historic strategy of Spanish territorial occupation, which made the city the spearpoint and bastion of civilization in the middle of *nowhere*].[49] As the metropolis politically and economically subjugated the countryside, it became an extension of urban order, assimilated into the rational, globalized space of a Cartesian grid. Though they remained symbolically opposed, the relationship between city and country assumed a new dimension:

El campo comienza a emular la ciudad. El proceso será largo, sin embargo se cierra el ciclo en el que la llanura había sido tierra de nadie. De aquí en más, las nuevas tierras, al incorporarse como propiedad privada, son inaccesibles como paisaje, como territorio común, y se vuelven desde el inicio condensaciones del pasado de la nación, imagen simbólica. Para la cultura siguen siendo desierto, extensión a la vez íntima y ajena. (Montaldo, *De pronto, el campo* 28)

[The country begins to emulate the city. ... The process will be long, however the cycle in which the plains were a no-man's-land is coming to an end. From here on, the new lands, by being incorporated as private property, are inaccessible as landscape, as common territory, and are from their outset a condensation of the nation's past, a symbolic image. For culture they continue to be desert, an extension at once intimate and distant.]

The ordering of the countryside that Silvestri and Montaldo describe in conceptual and physical terms characterizes what Henri Lefebvre describes as the emergence of "absolute space" in which "a fragment of agro-pastoral space" is "through the actions of masters or conquerors . . . assigned a new role, and henceforward appears as transcendent" while still considered as belonging to nature.[50] The rationalization of the pampa and its transcendence are thus not antithetical, but intimately interrelated; Sarmiento's call for writing a poem of military and technological domination is inscribed on the same discursive terrain, on the same *hoja inmensa*, where the following year his vocal critic José Hernández will publish *El Gaucho Martín Fierro*.

Of course, though Sarmiento anticipates and helps engineer the dramatic changes that Argentina will experience at the close of the nineteenth century and the first decades of the twentieth, he employs a well-worn metaphor to depict the march of progress; if his perspective is oriented toward the future, his rhetoric is clearly a throwback. For Sarmiento's metaphor of epic abolition conjugates the same three elements—pampa, poetry, and progress—that Echeverría invokes in the "Advertencia" to *Rimas*. From the pen of the ill-fated poet, a self-described "artista solitario y caprichoso" [solitary and capricious artist],[51] to the mouth of the president of the Republic, carried over from literature to politics, the ideological kernel of Echeverría's words remains intact: the pampa is a natural resource that provides poetic inspiration and, at the same time, the raw materials for economic growth. Their gaze, then, offers a variant of what Mary Louise Pratt refers to as the "European improving eye" that "produces subsistence habitats as 'empty' landscapes, meaningful only in terms of a capitalist future and of their potential for producing a marketable surplus."[52] What changes over time about the trope—which, to echo Ramos's reading of Sarmiento, is hardly a metaphor at all—is that the vehicle and the tenor have switched places: for Echeverría in 1837, poetry is progress; for Sarmiento in 1871, progress is a poem. The speech in Rosario announces the moment when, to paraphrase Michel Foucault, a spatial, strategic metaphor is deployed that enables us to grasp the point at which a discourse is transformed in, through, and on the basis of power.[53] That is to say, the Generation of 1837's way of looking at the nation becomes hegemonic.

Despite the reiteration *ad infinitum* that the pampa is an empty expanse, its central place in the liberal nationalist imaginary results from its potential as a *social* space—a region that can make new citizens who will, in turn, make a new nation. The creation of the desert is not merely to extract products—raw materials and agricultural goods—nor simply to provide inspiration (or a locus of enunciation) for an emerging literary tradition. The new modes of production—both industrial and cultural—that the Generation of 1837 aspires to implement depend upon and, in turn, promise to institutionalize the social relations that would give lasting legitimacy to a centralized state. In this regard, their aim is not limited to making the polity coincide with the limits of the national territory, nor to make the nation from the state, but to make a nation that *is* the state. Or, to tweak Massimo d'Anzelio's phrase, the Generation of 1837 looks to make the *República Argentina* by making Argentines.[54]

WRITING ACROSS THE DESERT

Throughout his work Domingo Faustino Sarmiento advocates a kind of writing that will not simply be a catalyst for modernizing Argentina, but a scriptural practice that will itself be transformed as part of this process. Indeed, he offers up his own work as a prototype of such technological writing, such as when, in his autobiography *Recuerdos de provincia* (1850), he reproduces a letter from his mentor Domingo de Oro that lavishes praise on Sarmiento's comparative study of educational systems, *De la educación popular* (1849):

> Me parece que usted la concibió con una máquina para empujar a obrar en el sentido de la industria y del movimiento mecánico y material. Su libro es la máquina de dar el mismo impulso al movimiento intelectual, y diré así a la *industria intelectual y moral*, que a su tiempo aumentará con su fuerza el resorte del movimiento material e industrial. (*Recuerdos de provincia*, 180)
>
> [It seems to me that you conceived of it [education] as a machine in order to force work in the sense of industry and mechanical and material movement. Your book is the machine to give the same impulse to intellectual movement, and shall I say *intellectual and moral industry*, which in turn will forcibly spring into action material and industrial movement.]

As Julio Ramos observes, here "[t]he machine is an emblem that condenses the ideal principles of coherence and rationality captured in Sarmiento's notion of the book."[55] Yet, at the same time, Sarmiento is acutely aware of the social conditions that limit the transmission of ideas through the written word: he begins *Recuerdos de provincia* by admitting that "[l]a palabra impresa tiene sus límites de publicidad como la palabra de viva voz" [the printed word has its limits of publicity as does the spoken word].[56] In a similar vein, *Campaña en el Ejército Grande* relates how Sarmiento encounters a resident of Rosario who tells him that "sus escritos de V. los saben de memoria todos. *Argirópolis* lo tienen hasta los soldados" [everyone knows your writings by memory. Even the soldiers have *Argirópolis*].[57] The exaggeration and ambiguity of the phrase (do all the soldiers have copies? or, have they all committed the work to memory?) mark an instability between the written and the spoken word in the text. While the statement smacks of flattery, and its inclusion in *Campaña*, of shameless self-promotion, the anecdote nonetheless prefigures the dilemma faced by aspiring *letrados* in the second half of the nineteenth century, when those who could not access the city of letters by traditional means, began to court (and attempt to mold) a broader public.[58] The risible notion that a programmatic political tract has been transformed into a popular oral narrative epitomizes the problematic nature of disseminating ideas to a broad public across a vast expanse of national territory. Sarmiento confronts this problematic throughout his works, as he considers the role mass media in the service of political unity and material progress. In *Viajes por Europa, África y América, 1845–1847*, particularly in the letters written during his brief travels through the United States, Sarmiento observes the manner in which various forms of communication facilitate economic productivity and ensure a homogeneous national identity. *Campaña en el Ejército Grande*, by contrast, presents on both the level of narration and its formal organization the difficulties of implementing such reforms in Argentina. What remains consistent in the descriptions of the two nations, however, is that Sarmiento advocates the technological improvement of writing as essential for centralizing state power.

As Sarmiento expounds in *Facundo*, a primary obstacle to civilizing Argentina is the distinct form of sociability that results from small, isolated communities that sparsely inhabit the national territory. A sense of geographic determinism, however, permits him to claim optimistically that "hay una organización del suelo, tan central y unitaria en aquel país" [there is an organization of the land, so central and unified in that country] and that, despite the tyranny of Rosas, "otro tiempo vendrá en que las cosas entren en su cauce ordinario" [another time will come when things will return to their normal course of events].[59] Yet five years later, writing in *Argirópolis*, he counters this optimism by arguing that "a la sabia y meditada deliberación del congreso le toca remediar por leyes previsoras este error de la naturaleza" [the wise and thoughtful deliberation of the congress must remedy this error of nature through far-sighted laws].[60] The call for political intervention to rectify an "error" of nature suggests that Sarmiento had become aware of the fact that, though the "necessarily territorial definition of the state might seem to represent a solidification of the bond between geographical space and society," the state must effect an abstraction of space and "justify its authority over society through such abstract principles of social intercourse such as democracy, liberty, moral right, etc."[61] Print media played a central role in producing a sense of simultaneity among members of national communities living in distant places, as per the well-known thesis of Benedict Anderson's *Imagined Communities*, and Sarmiento, as a journalist and educator, enthusiastically advocated new forms of writing.[62]

The United States, as depicted in *Viajes*, presents a model society with regard to its use of technological writing. Given the internal fractures that will soon erupt in the Civil War, it should be noted that Sarmiento's portrayal of the United States is not a study in the tradition of his much admired Tocqueville, but instead a giddy account, grafted with chronicles and studies that he had read prior to setting foot on North American soil. Following the disillusionment of Paris, the United States allows him to project a utopian vision in the New World; in the words of William H. Katra, "parece que Sarmiento, como amante novicio, no quisiera ver o aprender aspectos de la sociedad norteamericana que hubieran desafiado la ilusión rosada que anteriormente había formado" [it seems that Sarmiento, like an inexperienced lover, did not want to see or learn about aspects of United States society that would have challenged the rosy vision that he had previously formed of it].[63] For Sarmiento, progress is evident even in the smallest towns:

> Mi aldea, pues, tiene varios establecimientos públicos, alguna fábrica de cerveza, una panadería, varios bodegones o figonerías, todos con el anuncio en letras de oro, perfectamente ejecutadas por algún fabricante de letras. Este es un punto capital. Los anuncios en los Estados Unidos son por toda la Unión una obra de arte, i la muestra mas inequívoca del adelanto del país. Me he divertido en España i en toda la América de Sud, examinando aquellos letreros donde los hai, hechos con caractéres raquíticos i jorobados i ostentando en errores de ortografía la ignorancia supina del artesano o aficionado que los formó.
>
> El norteamericano es un literato clásico en materia de anuncios, i una letra chueca o gorda, o un error ortográfico espondría al locatario a ver desierto su mostrador. (*Viajes*, 299)
>
> [My town, well, it has various public establishments, a brewery, a bakery, various pubs or taverns, all with signage in gold letters, perfectly executed by some letter maker. Advertisements in the United States are throughout the entire Union a work of art, and the most unequivocal display of progress in the country. I have enjoyed in Spain and throughout Latin America examining those signs wherever they are, made with rickety and hunchbacked letters and with their spelling errors exhibiting the supine ignorance of the artisan or amateur that shaped them.
>
> The North American is a classic literato in matters of advertisements, and a squashed or fat letter, or a spelling error would subject the shopkeeper of the locale to seeing his counter deserted.]

The idealized description of small-town America figures the sign maker as an artist and the consumer as a discerning man of letters. In addition to transmitting commercial information without error or confusion, advertisements operate as models of a homogenized and functional aesthetic. Contrary to Sarmiento's own foundational graffiti, the signs announce their conformity with the social order, articulating it in a comprehensible language and in letters that are standardized and easily reproducible. Culture and commerce reinforce one another mutually, assuring the fluid exchange of goods and information in a stable, national market in which the citizen can move easily about. (In this way, citizens too become objects of exchange: reduced to a set of functions, they can be seamlessly integrated at established points throughout a common market.) Tulio Halperín Donghi additionally detects a pedagogical dimension to Sarmiento's observations, noting that "el omnipresente aviso comercial pareció a Sarmiento, a la vez que un instrumento indispensable para ese nuevo modo de articulación social, una justificación adicional de su interés en la educación popular" [the omnipresent commercial advertisements seemed to Sarmiento an indispensable instrument for that new mode of social articulation and, at the same time, an additional justification of his interest in public education].[64] The ads not only (re)produce a consistent reception, they also render the landscape universally—or, rather, nationally legible, thus comprising a functional form of writing that is symbol and symptom of modern civilization.

Another instrument that Sarmiento greatly admires is the telegraph, an apparatus that allows the direct and instantaneous transmission of messages across great distances. He frequently praises its rapid expansion in the United States, commenting that "sus líneas de telégrafos eléctricos están hoi, únicas en el mundo, puestas a disposición del pueblo, pudiendo en fracciones inapreciables de tiempo, enviar avisos i órdenes de un estremo a otro de la Unión" [its electrical telegraph lines are today unique in the world, at the disposal of the people, capable of sending, in imperceptible fractions of times, announcements and orders from one end of the Union to the other].[65] The telegraph succeeds in synchronizing American territory, in stark contrast to Argentina, where "el siglo XIX y el siglo XII viven juntos: el uno dentro de las ciudades; el otro en las campañas" [the nineteenth and the twelfth century live side-by-side: one in the cities, the other in the country].[66] As David Viñas proposes, the telegraph can also function as a metaphor for Sarmiento's writing:

> Morse is tied specifically to the *writing style* of Sarmiento, particularly if we consider three fundamental aspects: velocity, economy, and penetration. Sarmiento is tantalized by the mighty seduction of those long and frenetic sheets of perforated paper, the product of Morse's telegraph. Indeed that invention carries several connotations: punctuality; the inexorable demands of the clock . . . ; and the relationship of the metallic pen with the white surface of the page.[67]

There is another important aspect of the telegraph that should be mentioned: it annuls the geographic distance between its author and its intended reader. While advertisements exemplify the benefits of popular education, the telegraph embodies the progress of science. In light of the prologue of *Recuerdos de provincia*, which Sarmiento begins by complaining about two purloined letters and, more generally, the inefficient dissemination of writing, Morse's invention allows messages to be read instantly and securely. The telegraphic network, as depicted by Sarmiento, makes possible correspondence where the lag between composition and reception is reduced to fractions of a second.

The vibrant North American press also captures Sarmiento's attention. He praises the United States for being "el único pueblo del mundo que lee en masa, que usa todas sus necesidades, donde 2,000 periódicos satisfacen la curiosidad pública" [the only people of the world that reads en masse, which responds to all of its needs, where 2,000 newspapers satisfy public curiosity].[68] The North American newspaper thus seems to embody the ideals that Sarmiento exposes in "El diarismo," an article published in 1842, in which he declares "[e]l diario es para los pueblos modernos lo que era el foro para los romanos" [the daily paper is for modern peoples what the forum was for the Romans].[69] In the same article, he criticizes the Chilean press for focusing excessively on political mudslinging and not paying enough attention to the customs and broader interests of society. Ultimately, he laments its small base of readers, commenting that "hay pocas, poquísimas personas con relación a la población general que tengan gusto y hábito de leer periódicos" [there are few, so few people in relation to the general population that have the taste and habit of reading newspapers].[70] Here again, we find echoes of Ramos's hypothesis about writing and modernization in Sarmiento's works: the "rational public sphere," a modern forum, is so small as to be rendered insignificant, particularly when compared to an idealized North American model.

Campaña en el Ejército Grande, by contrast, narrates the difficulty of disseminating information to a mass audience across large expanses of territory. Originally published in three installments, the first two in Rio de Janeiro and the third in Santiago de Chile, *Campaña* is a chronicle of Sarmiento's experiences as the official *boletinero* of Urquiza's army during his campaign against Rosas. In the dedicatory letter to Alberdi, he attributes the fragmented publication of the book to the demands of others, including Alberdi himself. He insists in that "era mi ánimo no publicar mi *Campaña* hasta pasado algunos años" [it was my desire not to publish my *Campaña* until several years had passed], a statement that he later reiterates in his polemic with Alberdi.[71] Whether or not the claim is true, the extra-textual intervention calls attention to the "laberinto de fragmentos" [labyrinth of fragments] that comprise the book: a series of letters written by Sarmiento, other participants in the campaign and other political and intellectual figures, excerpts of an earlier book (*Argirópolis*), articles originally published in the newspaper *Sud América*, a prologue to the "Complemento," dedicatory letters to Mitre and Alberdi, and a chronicle of the campaign that contains articles from the bulletin that Sarmiento published in the field, diary entries, correspondence, and official decrees of the Ejército Grande.[72] *Campaña* even records the loss and recuperation of many of these documents; as Sarmiento informs Mitre and later repeats in the chronicle itself, his assistant "había perdido las maletas que contenían el plano topográfico, el diario de la campaña y otros documentos" [had lost the suitcases containing the topographical map, the diary of the campaign, and other documents].[73]

The toponyms that head the various letters (Santiago, Copiapó, Concepción de Uruguay, Rio de Janeiro, Lima. etc.) and divide the chronicle of the campaign (El Rosario, Arroyo del Medio, Caseros, Palermo, Buenos Aires) identify Sarmiento's diverse loci of writing. While with the Ejército Grande, guided by an English topographical map, Sarmiento navigates the Pampa, "que había descrito en *Facundo*, sentida, por intuición" [which I had described in *Facundo*, as I felt it, by intuition] and which "veía por primera vez en la vida" [I was seeing for the first time in my life].[74] Later, after Rosas's defeat at the Battle of Caseros, he expresses the desire to "pasar algunos días en Buenos Aires; quiero conocerla, pues nunca he estado en esta ciudad" [spend a few days in Buenos Aires; I want to get to know it, since I have never been in this city].[75] Thanks to his position in the army, Sarmiento is able to see places that he has only read about in books as he draws closer and closer to the seat of power. *Campaña* thus narrates two distinct itineraries: that of the texts that constitute it, from the international correspondence until its supposedly forced publication; and, contrasting with this confused migration of documents, the chronological account of the trajectory of the Ejército Grande. The text thus accounts for its own disorder and lack of a fixed place of enunciation. In this respect, one can apply to *Campaña* the observation that Graciela Montaldo makes with respect to *Viajes*, albeit in an intracontinental context: "es . . . una forma de dar vuelta el mapa o construir un mapa que tiene un centro móvil" [it is . . . a way of turning the map or constructing a map that has a mobile center].[76] Underscoring the displacement of its author(s) and its publication, Sarmiento puts the precariousness of the text in relief.

In *Campaña* Sarmiento provides an account of the practical difficulties that undermine his efforts to publish the bulletin during the campaign. The episode reveals the degree to which his political persona depends on his capacity to distribute his works to the broadest audience possible. After receiving permission from General Urquiza, Sarmiento purchases a cumbersome printing press in Montevideo. Upon disembarking in Rosario he discovers that there is no carriage to carry it and, additionally, he receives a letter from Elías, personal secretary of Urquiza, that reads, "El General me encarga de decirle que la prensa de Chile ha estado *chillando* en vano contra Rosas" [The General charges me with informing you that the Chilean press has been screeching in vain against Rosas].[77] Furious, Sarmiento considers abandoning the campaign, but later calms himself and decides to continue with what he believes to be "la única novedad, la única fuerza activa del campamento" [the only novelty, the only active force in the encampment].[78] He obstinately attempts to find a mode to transport the press and finally procures "una hermosa carreta para cargar con mis tipos y mis alemanes, la cual marchó siempre a la cabeza del ejército" [a beautiful carriage to carry my types and my Germans [printers], which always marched at the head of the army].[79] The image is eminently comical: Sarmiento, decked in full military regalia, was "el único oficial del ejército argentino que en campaña ostentaba una severidad de equipo, estrictamente europeo" [the only official of the Argentine army that during the campaign displayed a severity of dress, strictly European], crosses the Pampa perched atop a wagon that carries a massive, clunky printing press, forming the vanguard of the invading army.[80] The story of the press, one of the many anecdotes that illustrates the unequal conflict between Sarmiento and Urquiza, reveals how stubbornly Sarmiento attempts to modernize, indeed, to civilize warfare to transform his country politically and socially. Scandalized by Urquiza's insistence that his followers use the crimson insignia made compulsory by the Rosas regime and the illiterate, poorly dressed troops of the army, he reaches the conclusion that "mientras no se cambie el traje del soldado argentino ha de haber caudillos" [as long as the uniform of the Argentine soldier remains the unchanged, there will be caudillos].[81] Thwarted in his attempts to advise Urquiza directly, Sarmiento engages in a symbolic war against the very army in which he is enlisted. The printing press thus possesses a double, symbolic function in addition to its practical use: it represents, at least to Sarmiento, an effort to civilize military force through technology and, in turn, the difficulty of integrating said technology with prevailing customs and habits at both ends of the chain of command (and, for that matter, society).

Both the ordeal of the printing press in *Campaña en el Ejército Grande* and the very structure of the work illustrate the enormous distance between the innovative forms of writing that Sarmiento celebrates in his depiction of the United States and the limitations of the printed word in Spanish America. The community that Sarmiento imagines—in its grandest, most utopian sense, the "Estados Unidos de Sur América," as he designates it in *Argirópolis*—lacks not only modern sociability, but also the effective means to create it. In the context of this ambitious project, his writing stresses the need to modernize its own means of production and distribution, but it also evidences how current modalities of writing, reading, and publishing tend toward dispersion. Traversing the physical space of the *desierto* for the first time, as *Campaña en el Ejército Grande* recounts, Sarmiento must confront the implacable fact that the quixotic efforts of a single intellectual ultimately possess little more than symbolic value and that the "exceptional efficacy of letters" depends at least as much on their distribution as their particular message. In other words, it is not sufficient that the book be a machine in the metaphoric sense; the metaphor must be made literal before the content of any given book can be effectively coherent or rational.

WRITING AWAY (FROM) THE DESERT

While the *desierto* would become the commonplace at the center of most versions of the modernizing projects advanced by members of the Generation of 1837, from time to time some of its members searched out other spaces for locating these designs. In "Impresiones en una visita al Paraná" [Impressions on a Visit to the Paraná River], Juan Bautista Alberdi offers the banks of the Paraná River as one such alternative. Published in Montevideo's *El Iniciador* in 1838, shortly after the closure of *La Moda* and Alberdi's flight into exile, "Impresiones" questions the efficacy of poetry as a means of converting the *desierto* into a productive region. It is not that Alberdi denies the grandeur of the pampa; rather, he offers a recentered map of the nation, pinpointing the Paraná as an ideal point of exchange between the interior and the exterior, between the nation and the global economy. In doing so, he imagines a Faustian fantasy of development, an industrialized utopia in which countless steamships stream past banks teeming with healthy, prosperous citizens.[82]

Prior to recounting his trip to the Paraná, Alberdi begins "Impresiones" with a disavowal of the pampa as a matrix for material progress and an inspiration for national literature. To borrow Schopenhauer's description of the lesser sublime, for Alberdi, the sight of the plains produces a "a recollection of the dependence and wretchedness of the will" that overwhelms the "state of pure knowing in its peace and all-sufficiency."[83] That is, the beauty of the pampa does not compensate for the sense of despair it inspires:

> Yo no amo los lugares mediterráneos, y pienso que este sentimiento es general porque es racional. Si el hombre es un ente social, debe huir de lo que es contrario a su sociabilidad. Me he visto en medio de los portentos de gracia y belleza que abriga el seno de nuestro territorio, me he sentido triste, desasosegado por una vaga impresión de inquietud de no encontrar una playa en que pudiesen derramarse mis ojos: he creído habitar un presidio destinado a los poetas descriptivos. (*Escritos satíricos*, 296)

> [I have no love for land-locked places, and I think that this feeling is general because it is rational. If man is a social entity, he must flee from that which is contrary to his sociability. I have seen myself surrounded by the wonders of grace and beauty in the heart of our territory, and I have felt sadness, disturbed

by a vague impression of disquietude from not finding a shore on which to rest my eyes: I believe to have inhabited a prison destined for descriptive poets.]

Unlike Sarmiento, who views isolation as a condition that makes any form of governance difficult, in which "la municipalidad no existe, la policía no puede ejercerse, y la justicia civil no tiene medios de alcanzar a los delincuentes" [the township does not exist, the police cannot exercise its power, and civil justice has no means of reaching criminals], Alberdi limits his critique to the subjective experience of regarding an area whose limitlessness at once disorients and, paradoxically, confines.[84] The "touch of the sublime" (Schopenhauer) produces a fleeting sense of pleasure that quickly gives way to the unease of being adrift, which, together with the reference to entrapped poets evokes Esteban Echeverría's *Los consuelos* (1834): "El porvenir oscuro / Aparece a mi vista, cual desierto / O borrascoso piélago sin puerto / Donde arribar seguro" [The dark future / Appears before my eyes, like a desert / Or a tempestuous sea without a port / Where to berth safely].[85]

Alberdi proceeds to contrast the heightened awareness that contemplating a great river inspires with the confusion and confinement that the pampa produces. Indeed, whereas the limitless *desierto* overwhelms its observer such that he loses contact with his fellow man, the river, as it cuts its way across the nation and toward the sea, inspires a sense of inclusion and connectivity. As the waters pass him by, Alberdi imagines that they "llevan un destino grande: van a engrosar el vehículo poderoso de la libertad y de la sociabilidad humanitaria: el océano. El océano es la unidad, el progreso, la vida misma del espíritu humano" [bear a great destiny: they will swell the powerful vehicle of liberty and humanitarian sociability: the ocean. The ocean is unity, progress, the very life of the human spirit].[86] The river is an image that immediately defers to a greater whole, an immense ocean full of ports *donde arribar seguro*. Progress becomes a force that develops not from within the boundaries of national territory, but in an international context, through communication and exchange.

In the following paragraph, Alberdi mounts an explicit critique of Echeverría's treatment of the *desierto*. Though he does not use his peer's name, he directly refers to the "Advertencia" of *Rimas*:

> Un poeta americano ha hecho bien en pintar las facciones del desierto. Estas pinturas, a más de su interés de curiosidad, reúnen el interés social. *Aunque el desierto no es nuestro más pingüe patrimonio*, por él, sin embargo, debe algún día, como hoy en Norteamérica, derramarse la civilización que rebosa en las costas. El arte triunfará de nuestros desiertos mediterráneos, pero antes y después de la venida del arte, las costas del Paraná y del Plata serán la silla y el manantial de la poesía nacional. Aunque el arte actual no sea la expresión de lo visible, aunque sea la expresión ideal de la vida social, la profecía del porvenir, él no podrá profetizar un porvenir inmenso sin darle un teatro adecuado, y este

teatro no podrá ser otro que el borde de nuestros opulentos ríos. (*Escritos satíricos*, 297–98; italics added)

[An American poet has done well in painting the features of the desert. These depictions, more for interest than for curiosity, bring together social concerns. *Although the desert is not our greatest patrimony*, because of it someday, as today in North America, civilization must spill over from the coasts where it teems. Art will triumph in our land-locked deserts, but before and after the coming of art, the banks of the Paraná and the Plata will be the seat and fount of national poetry. Although current art may not be the expression of the visible, though it may be the ideal expression of social life, it will not be able to prophesize an immense future without giving it an adequate venue, and this venue will be no other than the shores of our opulent rivers.]

What begins as faint praise for Echeverría's artistic abilities quickly acquires the airs of a manifesto intended to supplant a rival project, as it too calls for a national literature at the service of progress and industry. Alberdi rejects outright the notion that the desert is the nation's greatest patrimony because, for him, it contains no intrinsic quality that will guarantee its transformation; whereas the coasts are sites of constant growth and change, the desert remains static. In other words, though the littoral is presently undeveloped, it reveals its future to a poet attuned to the ideal expression of society. Poetry emerges as a cultural practice that will eventually engage the desert, but the banks of the Paraná, as its source of inspiration, exceed poetry's mimetic capacity. The littoral becomes the origin, the locus of enunciation, the object and the setting of national literature.

Once Alberdi has discredited the desert and its poetic treatment, "Impresiones" acquires a vatic, delirious tone as it presents a utopian vision of the Paraná's future. In deep silence, Alberdi reflects on the significance of the Revolution and resolves that it was "un albor primero y efímero no más" [a first and ephemeral daybreak, no more], an event that left untouched the "teatro espléndido, obra inédita del Criador" [splendid theater, unedited work of the Creator] where he finds himself; here is a site where history has yet to take place.[87] Then, no sooner than he invokes the muses inhabiting the river, Alberdi recalls a sort of epiphany in which he feels himself "sumergir en un éxtasis divino que me transporta a aquellos días afortunados" [submerged in a ecstasy that transports me to those more fortunate days].[88] From the pastoral scene, he moves to describe a vision of the future in which the spires of imposing, sober edifices complement the region's natural beauty. Initially he presents this vision as one of leisure, where girls bathe and youngsters float past in gondolas. Then, in the midst of the idyllic scene, "[a]turde mis oídos el torrente estrepitoso de buques de vapor que suben y bajan la inmensa riqueza de nuestra industria" [the raucous torrent of steamships that bring back and forth the immense riches of our industry startle my ears].[89] The deafening roar of steam engines, however, does not interrupt Alberdi's reverie, but heightens it: he admires the flags of different nations freely navigating the river and can only express admiration for the abundant evidence of progress he witnesses.

In the end, it is neither not the rumble of the steamboat that brings the vision to a close, but instead the far-off clang of a church bell: "[a]quí una campana lúgubre viene a eclipsar mis visiones, la campana de noche que llama a la oración, esta preparación austera de los tiempos futuros" [here a lugubrious bell comes to eclipse my visions, the bell calling to evening prayers, this austere preparation for future times].[90] In spite of the negative modifiers that Alberdi employs to characterize his abrupt return to reality, he attempts to retain Christianity as an agent of progress, conceding that it is one of the few existing institutions in Argentina that provides social cohesion. Ultimately, however, he cannot convert the church bell into a positive symbol because, as it interrupts his daydream, it serves as a bleak reminder that the colonial past continues to impose itself on the national reality. The technological imagination is suppressed when it attempts to assimilate the actual *pueblo* into the utopia it fashions with imported goods (and people, for that matter).

The abrupt switch from the dreamlike ruminations, complete with erotic imagery of young bathers, to the solitary evening underscores the tremendous distance between Alberdi's desired *república verdadera* and his nation's material and cultural backwardness. The church is an emblem of the old order of things, a reminder—not a remainder—of a persistent colonial legacy: at the close of his reverie he imagines that "oigo hablar del siglo XIX como hoy de la edad media" [I hear the nineteenth-century spoken of as today we speak of the middle ages].[91] This observation immediately precedes waking, which suggests that Alberdi "does not wake himself when the external irritation becomes too strong; the logic of his awakening is quite different. First he constructs a dream, a story which enables him to prolong his sleep, to avoid awakening into reality."[92] The rumbling steamships are not simply an extemporaneous image, invented in response to an external irritation (the church bell), but—in a text that represents a dream, or dreamlike state—a manifestation of the Real of Alberdi's desire—the very machine, the industrial motor that permits the realization of the other elements of his fantasy. Žižek reinterprets Freud's dream of the burning child to propose a working concept of ideology, which he defines as "as a fantasy-construction which serves as a support for our 'reality' itself: an illusion which structures our effective, real social relations and thereby masks some insupportable, real, impossible kernel," constituting "a traumatic social division which cannot be symbolized."[93] In this sense, the steamships do not merely stand for progress or industry, but, as they are incompatible with the idyllic elements of Alberdi's vision, they drown out the unexpressed tension between nature and technology.

A contemporary episode in North American literature shares striking similarities with "Impresiones en una visita al Paraná" and elucidates the particular role of technology and industry in the geopolitical imaginary of *letrados* in postrevolutionary Latin America. In his notebooks, Nathaniel Hawthorne recalls a visit made on July 27, 1844, to Sleepy Hollow, a small clearing in the woods near Concord, Massachusetts. Hawthorne sets out to record with precision every possible detail of the scene and, though he concedes that "[w]ere we to sit here all day, a week, a month, and doubtless a lifetime, objects would thus still be presenting themselves as new, though there would seem to be no reason why we should not have detected them all at the first moment," he meticulously describes the setting.[94] First he directs his efforts toward the features of his surroundings that capture his gaze, but then turns his attention to the ambient sounds. In quick succession, he enumerates the rustle of the breeze, a melancholy birdsong, the "chirrup" of a squirrel. It is not long, though, before his ear begins to detect more distant noises, and "[w]ithout any perceptible change of mood or tone, he shifts from images of nature to images of man and society."[95] Like Alberdi, Hawthorne hears a clanging bell, but it is not that of a church, but of the village clock, which "does not disturb the repose of the scene; it does not break our sabbath; for like a sabbath seems this place, and the more so on account of the cornfield rustling at our feet."[96] Immediately thereafter, there follows the sound of "mowers whetting their scythes; but these sounds of labor, when at a proper remoteness, do but increase the quiet of one, who lies at ease, all in a mist of his own musings."[97] The scene Hawthorne paints is one of pastoral bliss, where agricultural activity complements the pleasant setting, at the same time that it underscores the leisure time that makes possible the reflection in the first place. Whereas the church bell heard on the banks of the Paraná evokes a ritualized temporality that interrupts Alberdi's vision, in Hawthorne's recollection the bell measures and regulates the rhythms of secular labor. Though Hawthorne himself sits at a remove from productive activity, he nonetheless reconciles the aural images of industriousness with his sketch of a bucolic scene.

Suddenly, however, a piercing noise interrupts the writer's idyll and forces him to reconsider the tenuous relationship between man and nature that has been maintained throughout his account. Alberdi hears the rumble of the steamships, then the clanging of the church bell; Hawthorne experiences the inverse: the village clock strikes, and then a train speeds past:

> But, hark! there is the whistle of the locomotive—the long shriek, harsh, above all other harshness, for the space of a mile cannot mollify it into harmony. It tells the story of busy men, citizens, from the hot street, who have come to spend a day in a country village, men of business; in short of all unquietness;

and no wonder that it gives such a startling shriek, since it brings the noisy world into the midst of our slumbrous peace.[98]

Hawthorne finds himself unable to integrate the railroad into the space that he has methodically constructed through the accumulation of details. The whistle announces the hurried arrival of city dwellers, all of whom, regardless of their motives for travel, threaten his precious retreat. The locomotive, invisible from Hawthorne's vantage point, disrupts with its cacophonic approach the image of a harmonious balance between nature and society. As Leo Marx argues in *The Machine in the Garden*, his study of the pastoral in nineteenth-century literature of the United States, the episode captures the wariness with which intellectuals regarded the emergence of "technological power, a power that does not remain confined to the traditional boundaries of the city."[99] Whereas Sarmiento laments the invasion of cities by the barbarous forces of the countryside in *Facundo*, Hawthorne, writing less than a year before, laments how the city—as a lived space—overtakes the countryside, filling it with its uncouth inhabitants, its noise, its heat, its restlessness. Marx notes that the scene in fact constitutes a commonplace: "[t]he ominous sounds of machines, like the sound of the steamboat bearing down on the raft or of the train breaking in upon the idyll at Walden, reverberate endlessly in our literature."[100] While attitudes regarding technological power may vary from author to author, Hawthorne's account is emblematic because it narrativizes a central antagonism of North American identity. Technology, on the one hand, makes possible the efficiency that permits Hawthorne to pass an idle Saturday, but, at the same time, it massifies this experience, making it possible for urban inhabitants to "spend a day in a country village." Industrialized society also announces a new form of tourism. The shrieking locomotive does not simply announce a conflict between two modes of life, but augurs a cataclysmic change in the relationship between man and nature and, concurrently, a radical reshaping of the boundaries of North American social space.[101]

In contrast, the rumble of steamboats is strikingly unproblematic in the context of Alberdi's reverie; indeed, the vision reaches its most frenetic, exalted tone when describing their movement. The boats of Alberdi's dream are analogous to the bell of the town clock in Hawthorne's narrative, while the church bell announcing vespers has the same function as the train whistle. The episodes, however, are not perfect inversions of one another because the bell that Alberdi hears is unmistakably religious and that which Hawthorne hears, secular. Also, whereas Hawthorne may hear an actual train, free navigation of the Paraná would not be legislated until 1849. As such, Alberdi's vision narrates a conflict between ideology and a material existence that will not easily conform to it. At the same time, despite their differences, the two texts jointly articulate a significant shift in the perception of space in nineteenth-century America, North and South: nature has acquired a new structure; it is overtaken by industry and, therefore, must be reconstructed as a discrete landscape.

CONCLUSION

The problem central to Echeverría's *La cautiva* and Bello's *Silvas americanas* remains latent in "Impresiones en una visita al Paraná," which becomes increasingly, literally ecstatic as it envisions a future that will not only transform the Paraná, but overrun the boundaries of geographic specificity and effect a nationwide modernization: namely, economic production and biological reproduction; basic questions like "who will build those buildings?" and "who is this multitude that teems on its banks?" remain unposed and unanswered. The steamboats, followed by the image of international flags, represent a desired interruption, the arrival of a massive European immigration that will both conceive and carry out the projects necessary to realize the object of Alberdi's ideology. The river will be the initial site of progress, but Alberdi is at a loss to identify an intrinsic quality either in the ground or in the few inhabitants of the region that could initiate this transformation. In this respect, in spite of its setting, "Impresiones" presents the same basic dilemma at the core of the calls to transform the pampa that Alberdi seeks to look beyond. The technological future remains confined to the fantasy-construction, while the past resounds in the present. The *pueblo* is the common problem of these texts, an empty term that straddles the absolute alterity of the *desierto* and the impossible fullness of a modern national society. In this body of writing, the *deux ex machina* is the machine itself, a foreign apparatus that could overcome the shortage of labor (not to mention popular will) necessary for transforming the desert. As Sarmiento's *Campaña en el Ejército Grande* and Alberdi's *Impresiones* allegorize, literature itself will not suffice to effect the changes so ardently desired by their authors. To write may be to modernize, but only if writing itself is dramatically be altered in the process.

NOTES

1. Julios Ramos, *Divergent Modernities: Culture and Politics in Nineteenth-Century Latin America*, trans. John D. Blanco (Durham, N.C.: Duke University Press, 2001), 20.
2. David Viñas, *De los montoneros a los anarquistas* (Buenos Aires: Carlos Pérez, 1971), 6.
3. James Sanders, "The Vanguard of the Atlantic World," *Latin American Research Review* 46, no. 2 (2011): 105–8.
4. Ernest Gellner, *Nations and Nationalism* (Ithaca, N.Y.: Cornell University Press, 1983), 127 (italics added).

5. Tulio Halperín Donghi, *De la Revolución de Independencia a la Confederación Rosista* (Buenos Aires: Paidós, 2000), 378.

6. Beginning perhaps with Ezequiel Martínez Estrada's classic *Radiografía de la Pampa* (Buenos Aires: Losada, 1968; first published 1933), Argentine cultural criticism has time and time again scrutinized the figure of the *desierto*. More recent studies include Beatriz Sarlo's "En el origen de la cultura argentina: Europa y el desierto. Búsqueda de un fundamento," in *Primer Seminario Latino-Americano de Literatura comparada* (Porto Alegre, Brazil: U Federal do Rio Grande do Sul, 1986); Graciela Montaldo's *De pronto, el campo: Literatura argentina y tradición rural* (Rosario, Argentina: Beatriz Viterbo, 1993); Jens Andermann's *Mapas de poder: Una arqueología literaria del espacio argentino* (Rosario, Argentina: Beatriz Viterbo, 2000); Álvaro Fernández-Bravo's *Literatura y frontera: Procesos de territorialización en las culturas argentina y chilena del siglo XIX* (Buenos Aires: Sudamericana, 1999); and Fermín Rodríguez's "Un desierto de ideas," in *Las brújulas del extraviado: Para una lectura integral de Esteban Echeverría*, ed. Martín Kohan and Alejandra Laera (Rosario, Argentina: Beatriz Viterbo, 2006)

7. Carlos J. Alonso, *The Burden of Modernity: The Rhetoric of Cultural Discourse in Spanish America* (New York: Oxford University Press, 1998), 32.

8. Martin Heidegger, *The Question Concerning Technology and Other Essays*, ed. William Lovitt (New York: Harper Torchbooks, 1977), 13.

9. Julio Argentino Roca, "Discurso ante el Congreso al asumir la presidencia, 12 de octubre de 1880," in *Proyecto y construcción de una nación*, ed. Tulio Halperín Donghi (Buenos Aires: Ariel, 1995), 592.

10. Roca, "Discurso ante el Congreso," 594.

11. Gellner, *Nations and Nationalism*, 55.

12. Roca, "Discurso ante el Congreso," 594.

13. Jacques Rancière, *Le partage du sensible: Esthétique et politique* (Paris: La Fabrique, 2000), 16.

14. Beatriz Sarlo, "En el origen de la cultura argentina: Europa y el desierto: Búsqueda de un fundamento," in *Primer Seminario Latino-Americano de Literatura comparada* (Porto Alegre, Brazil: U Federal do Rio Grande do Sul, 1986), 15.

15. Félix Weinberg, *Esteban Echeverría, ideólogo de la segunda revolución* (Buenos Aires: Taurus, 2006), 86–87.

16. Esteban Echeverría, *La cautiva/El matadero* (Buenos Aires: Emecé, 1999), 17.

17. As Tulio Halerín Donghi comments, the commonplace of nation-building in Argentina has long been the dream of building a nation for the desert ("Una nación para el desierto argentino," in *Proyecto y construcción de una nación* [Buenos Aires: Ariel, 1995], 8). Additionally, adds Fermín Rodríguez, "el gesto de fundar [una nación] en el desierto requiere simultáneamente de fundar el desierto, en la literatura, en la ciencia, en la política: un desierto para la nación" [the gesture of founding [a nation] in the desert simultaneously requires founding the desert in literature, in science, in politics: a desert for the nation] ("Un desierto de ideas," 150).

18. Echeverría, *La cautiva*, 25.

19. Echeverría, *La cautiva*, 26.

20. Mariquita Sánchez de Thompson, *Intimidad y política: Diario, cartas y recuerdos*, ed. María Gabriela Mizraje (Buenos Aires: Adriana Hidalgo, 2003), 332–33.

21. Neil Smith, *Uneven Development: Nature, Capital and the Production of Space* (Cambridge, Mass.: Blackwell, 1991), 80.

22. Alejandra Laera, "'Nada se obtiene sin dinero': Pérdidas y ganancias de un hombre de letras," in *Las brújulas del extraviado: Para una lectura integral de Esteban Echeverría*, ed. Martín Kohan and Alejandra Laera (Rosario, Argentina: Beatriz Viterbo, 2006), 91.

23. Esteban Echeverría, "Segunda lectura," in *El salón literario de 1837*, ed. Félix Weinberg (Buenos Aires: Hachette, 1958), 176, 177.

24. Echeverría, "Segunda lectura," 177.

25. Echeverría, "Segunda lectura," 178.

26. Echeverría, "Segunda lectura," 183.

27. Juan María Gutiérrez writes in "La vida y la obra de Esteban Echeverría," which serves as an introduction to his *Obras completas*, that "[d]el mismo modo que el desierto, añadía en la *Advertencia*, es una riqueza material con que nos brinda la naturaleza, puede ser también fuente de placeres morales como alimento a la literatura argentina: verdades ambas que Echeverría tiene la honra de haber emitido antes que nadie, mostrando con ellas un verdadero pensador en economía social y en el arte, materias que se consideran generalmente divorciadas en una misma cabeza" [in the same way that the desert, he would add in the prologue, is a material richness that nature offers us, it can also be the source of moral pleasures as well as the sustenance for Argentine literature: both truths that Echeverría had the honor of expressing before anyone else, thus revealing him to be a true thinking in social economics and in art, subjects that are generally considered to be divorced in the same head] (31).

28. Echeverría, "Segunda lectura," 183.
29. Echeverría, "Segunda lectura," 182.
30. Laera, "'Nada se obtiene sin dinero,'" 96.
31. Mary Louise Pratt, *Imperial Eyes: Travel Writing and Transculturation* (New York: Routledge, 1992), 179.
32. Alexis de Tocqueville, *Democracy in America*, ed. Harvey C. Mansfield and Delba Winthrop (Chicago: University of Chicago Press, 2002), 461.
33. Ramos, *Divergent Modernities*, 163.
34. Juan Bautista Alberdi, *Escritos satíricos y de crítica literaria* (Buenos Aires: Academia Argentina de Letras, 1986), 66.
35. "Quedamos aún ligados por el vínculo fuerte y estrecho del idioma; pero éste debe aflojarse de día en día, a medida que vayamos entrando en el movimiento intelectual de los pueblos adelantados de la Europa" [We still remain bound by the strong and tight light of language; but this ought to slacken day by day, as we enter into the intellectual currents of the advanced nations of Europe] ("Fisonomía del saber español: Cuál deba ser entre nosotros," 154).
36. Alberdi, *Escritos satíricos*, 63.
37. Alberdi, *Escritos satíricos*, 67.
38. This disdain is also shared by José Mármol in his article "De la prensa periódica": "Emprender la tarea de una publicación periódica, original, americana, bajo las formas más difíciles de la literatura: la poesía, la novela, la historia y la política del momento, es cosa cuya responsabilidad puede pesar mucho sobre nosotros, porque nosotros 'solos' la emprenderemos. Pero, permítasenos este rasgo de franqueza: tenemos más confianza en nosotros mismos para poder cumplir lo que prometemos, que la que nos inspira el público para costear los gastos de nuestras publicaciones" [Undertaking a task like the publication of an original, American periodical publication, under the most difficult conditions for literature: poetry, the novel, history, and politics of the moment, is something whose responsibility weighs much on us, because we "alone" will undertake it. But, let us permit ourselves to be frank: we have more confidence in ourselves to achieve what we promise, than that which the public inspires in us for covering the costs of our publications] (*Manuela Rosas y otros escritos políticos del exilio* [Buenos Aires: Taurus, 2001], 233).
39. Ernesto Laclau, *Emancipation(s)* (New York: Verso, 1996), 5.
40. Esteban Echeverría, *Obra escogida* (Caracas: Ayacucho, 1991), 256.
41. Juan Bautista Alberdi, *Fragmento preliminar al estudio del derecho* (Buenos Aires: Biblos, 1984), 150.
42. Ernesto Laclau, *On Populist Reason* (London: Verso, 2007), 81–82.
43. Juan Bautista Alberdi, *Bases y puntos de partida para la organización política de la República Argentina*, ed. Manuel Fernández López (Buenos Aires: Editorial Losada, 2003), 210.
44. With regards to the problematic of creating a workforce capable of realizing the designs for a liberal state, Alberdi is decidedly more pragmatic and classist than Sarmiento. The last thing Argentina needs, Alberdi argues, is an influx of unproductive, overeducated citizens that resemble the author of these political tracts: "Quiero suponer que la República Argentina se compusiese de hombres como yo, es decir, de ochocientos mil abogados que saben hacer libros. Esa sería la peor población que pudiera tener. Los abogados no servimos para hacer caminos de

fierro, para hacer navegables y navegar los ríos, para explotar las minas, para labrar los campos, para colonizar los desiertos; es decir, que no servimos para dar a la América del Sur lo que necesita" [Let me suppose that the Argentine Republic would be composed of men like me, that is, of eight hundred thousand lawyers that know how to write books. That would be the worst population we could have. We lawyers are good for nothing when it comes to making railways, making rivers navigable and navigating them, exploiting mines, working the fields, colonizing the desert; that is, we serve no purpose in giving South America what it needs] (*Bases*, 231).

45. Alberdi, *Bases*, 203.
46. Alberdi, *Bases*, 221.
47. Alberdi, *Bases*, 228.
48. Alberdi, *Bases*, 61.
49. Graciela Silvestri, "*Errante en torno de los objetos miro*: Relaciones entre artes y ciencias de descripción territorial en el siglo XIX rioplatense," in *Resonancias románticas: Ensayos sobre historia de la cultura argentina 1820–1890*, ed. Klaus Gallo, Graciela Batticuore, and Jorge Myers (Buenos Aires: Eudeba, 2005), 240.
50. Henri Lefebvre, *The Production of Space*, trans. Donald Nicholson-Smith (Oxford: Blackwell, 1991), 234.
51. Esteban Echeverría, *Dogma socialista*, ed. Alberto Palcos (La Plata, Argentina: Universidad Nacional de la Plata, 1940), 347.
52. Pratt, *Imperial Eyes*, 61.
53. Michel Foucault, "Questions on Geography," in *Power/Knowledge: Selected Interviews and Other Writings, 1972–77*, ed. Colin Gordon (New York: Pantheon, 1980), 70.
54. "We have made Italy, now we have to make Italians" (qtd. in Hobsbawm, *Nations and Nationalism since 1780: Programme, Myth, Reality* [Cambridge: Cambridge University Press, 1990], 44).
55. Ramos, *Divergent Modernities*, 164.
56. Domingo Faustino Sarmiento, *Recuerdos de provincia*, ed. María Caballero Wangüemert (Madrid: Anaya & Mario Muchnik, 1992), 77.
57. Domingo Faustino Sarmiento, *Campaña en el Ejército Grande*, ed. Tulio Halperín Donghi (Bernal, Argentina: U Nacional de Quilmes, 2004), 168.
58. Ángel Rama, *La ciudad letrada* (Hanover, N.H.: Ediciones del Norte, 2002), 43–49.
59. Domingo Faustino Sarmiento, *Facundo: Civilización y barbarie* (Madrid: Alianza, 1988), 61.
60. Domingo Faustino Sarmiento, *Argirópolis* (Buenos Aires: A-Z, 1994), 70.
61. Smith, *Uneven Development*, 79–80.
62. Benedict Anderson, *Imagined Communities: Reflections on the Origin and Spread of Nationalism* (London: Verso, 2000), 34–35.
63. William H. Katra, "Sarmiento en los Estados Unidos," in *Viajes por Europa, África y América, 1845–1847 y Diario de gastos*, ed. Javier Fernández (Buenos Aires: Colección Archivos, 1993), 862.
64. Tulio Halperín Donghi, prologue to *Campaña en el Ejército Grande* (Bernal, Argentina: U Nacional de Quilmes, 2004), 50.
65. Sarmiento, *Viajes*, 313.
66. Sarmiento, *Facundo*, 95.
67. David Viñas, "Sarmiento: Madness or Accumulation," in *Sarmiento: Author of a Nation*, ed. Tulio Halperín Donghi, Gwen Kirkpatrick, Iván Jaksik, and Francine Masiello (Berkeley: University of California Press, 1994), 214.
68. Sarmiento, *Viajes*, 313.
69. Domingo Faustino Sarmiento, *Obras de D. F. Sarmiento*, vol. 1 (Santiago de Chile, Gutenberg, 1887), 57.
70. Sarmiento, *Obras de D. F. Sarmiento*, 1:61.
71. Sarmiento, *Campaña*, 118; Juan Bautista Alberdi and Domingo Faustino Sarmiento, *La gran polémica nacional: Cartas Quillotanas/Las Ciento y una*, ed. Lucila Pagliai (Buenos Aires: Leviatán, 2005), 234.
72. Sarmiento, *Campaña*, 112.
73. Sarmiento, *Campaña*, 112, 212.

74. Sarmiento, *Campaña*, 167.
75. Sarmiento, *Campaña*, 228.
76. Graciela Montaldo, *Ficciones culturales y fábulas de identidad en América Latina* (Rosario, Argentina: Beatriz Viterbo, 2004), 68.
77. Sarmiento, *Campaña*, 171.
78. Sarmiento, *Campaña*, 173.
79. Sarmiento, *Campaña*, 187.
80. Sarmiento, *Campaña*, 169.
81. Sarmiento, *Campaña*, 169.
82. Though Alberdi was no great admirer of the socialism of Saint-Simon, "Impresiones en una visita al Paraná" nonetheless resembles those utopian projects that "were far beyond both the financial and the imaginative resources of early nineteenth-century capitalists" (Berman, *All That Is Solid: The Experience of Modernity* [New York: Simon and Schuster, 1982], 72) and prioritized "gigantic energy and transportation projects on an international scale" (74).
83. Arthur Schopenhauer, *The World as Will and Representation*, vol. 1, trans. E. F. J. Payne (New York: Dover, 1966), 204.
84. Sarmiento, *Facundo*, 70.
85. Esteban Echeverría, *Obras completas de D. Esteban Echeverría*, vol. 3 (Buenos Aires: Imprenta y Librería de Mayo, 1871), 24.
86. Alberdi, *Escritos satíricos*, 297.
87. Alberdi, *Escritos satíricos*, 300.
88. Alberdi, *Escritos satíricos*, 301.
89. Alberdi, *Escritos satíricos*, 302.
90. Alberdi, *Escritos satíricos*, 302.
91. Alberdi, *Escritos satíricos*, 302.
92. Slavoj Žižek, *The Sublime Object of Ideology* (London: Verso, 1989), 45.
93. Žižek, *Sublime Object of Ideology*, 45.
94. Nathaniel Hawthorne, *The American Notebooks* (New Haven, Conn.: Yale University Press, 1932), 103.
95. Leo Marx, *The Machine in the Garden: Technology and the Pastoral Ideal* (New York: Oxford, 2000), 13.
96. Hawthorne, *The American Notebooks*, 104.
97. Hawthorne, *The American Notebooks*, 104.
98. Hawthorne, *The American Notebooks*, 104.
99. Marx, *Machine in the Garden*, 32.
100. Marx, *Machine in the Garden*, 15–16.
101. "The specificity of the urban is thus defined not as a separable reality, with its own social and spatial rules of formation and transformation; or merely as a reflection and imposition of the social order" (Edward W. Soja, *Postmodern Geographies: The Reassertion of Space in Critical Social Theory* [London: Verso, 1989], 153).

Conclusion

In 1974 Jorge Luis Borges added a caustic postscript to his prologue for Domingo Faustino Sarmiento's *Recuerdos de provincia*. "Sarmiento," writes Borges, "sigue formulando la alternativa: civilización o barbarie. Ya se sabe la elección de los argentinos. Si en lugar de canonizar el *Martín Fierro*, hubiéramos canonizado el *Facundo*, otra sería nuestra historia y mejor" [keeps formulating the alternatives: civilization or barbarism. If instead of canonizing *Martín Fierro*, we had canonized *Facundo*, our history would be another and better].[1] Borges's remark expresses a profound disenchantment with the state of Argentina under Juan Domingo and Isabel Perón and insinuates that Sarmiento's progressive vision has been rejected in favor of a populism symbolized by the lawless gaucho. Yet the distinction that the counterfactual statement makes between *Facundo* and José Hernández's poem sounds particularly forced coming on the heels of a declaration about Sarmiento's lasting relevance. Between the lines, perhaps in spite of his convictions at the moment, Borges implies that what is truly impossible is not choosing *Facundo* over *Martín Fierro*, or vice-versa, but the idea that the preference for one book over the other—as well as the worldview it ostensibly epitomizes—can be expressed without conjuring and confronting its opposite. The history of Argentina, in other words, consists not of taking one forking path instead of another, but of staging, time and time again, a familiar, unsolvable dilemma. Sarmiento's *Facundo, o civilización y barbarie* articulates a basic condition of the political, an antagonism that structures and exceeds the ontic content it assumes at any given moment. It is not that "the rhetorical ghosts" of the postrevolutionary period survive "because Argentina never agreed on its guiding fictions," but that this disagreement is itself a guiding fiction.[2]

Throughout *Beyond Civilization and Barbarism*, I have demonstrated that the foundational antagonism of Argentine cultural discourse emerged in the postrevolutionary period as various social actors responded to the political crisis left unresolved after the wars of independence. Sarmiento and his fellow lettered elites, writing in opposition to the Rosas regime, forcefully promoted a narrative of this period which the liberal state they later helped found would consecrate as official. In later decades, revisionists would challenge the content of this historiography while reinforcing its underlying structure. Yet, as we have seen, *letrados* were hardly the exclusive authors of these dividing lines, nor was literature the sole medium for inscribing the terms of conflict on a common discursive terrain. Employing a variety of cultural forms, including portraiture, graffiti, and audiovisual spectacles, supporters and opponents of the Rosas regime pronounced and promoted homologous declarations, collectively conceiving of the social as divided in two irreconcilable camps.

These lines were drawn as political opponents sought to link competing projects with the crucial but elusive figure of the *pueblo*. Even if their approaches to this issue vary greatly, this shared concern links two bodies of writing that have long been examined independent of one another. The prolific discursive production of the Rosas regime, on the one hand, deployed a variety of graphic and textual forms, as well as codified public rituals, dress, speech, and behavior to insist on an affectionate and unmediated linkage between diverse sectors of Argentine society and its leader. The intellectual dissidents of the Generation of 1837 were not blind to the popularity Rosas enjoyed among the lower classes of Buenos Aires and beyond, but insisted on the artificiality of this bond. In doing so, they sought to disaggregate the groups the regime aspired to identify as the *pueblo*—such as the women, youth, and workers Alberdi disparages in *La Moda*—and insisted that their expressions of Federalist loyalty were not simply false or coerced, but in fact an inchoate noise that never amounted to a cohesive expression of popular will. The *pueblo* remains for them an unrealized entity, yet one whose formation is, paradoxically, thwarted by the interruption or objection of the subaltern, as Andrés Lamas's "Visiones de la óptica" suggests.

Thus, even as intellectuals insist on the blindness of the masses, they are quick to recognize the need to represent (and, in doing so, appropriate) spontaneous forms of popular expression. *Facundo*'s inaugural graffiti exposes the lengths to which a writer like Sarmiento feels compelled to exhibit his erudition and essential modernity, but it also underscores how writing—and not just a specific literary register—is an indispensible instrument of political power. The language of his scrawl may be French, but the execution of the gesture is wholly consistent with the voice of popular protest. Conversely, writing was ubiquitous in the regime's efforts to establish its hegemony, and the cultural output of the government and its supporters was as integral to its power as were coercion and the reliance on existing, if weak political institutions. Contrary to the accusations of Sarmiento and Mármol, their reliance on writing was not something that the regime tried to conceal. Indeed, portraits of Rosas and public poetry indicate the extent to which writing—painted, printed, handwritten, recited—enacted the sovereign bond between caudillo and *pueblo*.

Indeed, the antagonists of postrevolutionary Argentina demonstrate an acute awareness of the possibilities and limitations of representing a *pueblo* whose consent is, in one form or another, necessary for the legitimacy of any political project. In appealing to the people through a variety of cultural forms and, in the case of the Generation of 1837, in proposing new media and new technologies to (in)form a modern public, they mutually endorsed broad republican ideals. As apparent in the didacticism of certain texts, such as the newspapers of Luis Pérez that contained narrative accounts as to how they should be used, as well as the wariness provoked by certain technologies of seeing (as embodied by optical apparatuses), this conflictive body of writing, cleaved together by common concerns and ideals, collectively map the uneven development of modernity in a more complex sense than is possible when limiting our analysis to an intellectual history told by those who most enthusiastically self-identify as modern.

It is in this respect that I hope *Beyond Civilization and Barbarism* can function as a case study for studying the cultural and political life of the nineteenth century. In focusing on the time and place that gave rise to a commonplace that has had an outsized influence on the Latin Americanist field of reflection, it offers a hypothesis regarding the importance of cultural forms in establishing the terms and conditions for the exercise of power in a postcolonial situation, without taking as inevitable the rise of a specific form of state power. It still remains the case that the default method is to examine postindependence cultural artifacts and phenomena as things that "anticipate" or "look forward to" or "prefigure" those that occur toward the end of the century or in the twentieth. Such framing reiterates and reinforces the "the double movement at the core of the Spanish American text" of a displacement and rejection of modernity.[3] I would suggest that this out-of-jointness embedded in nineteenth-century texts and our study of them is not simply an inevitable symptom of modernity, but, more specifically, an effect of the unresolved struggles to redefine sovereignty in the Western world. What *Civilización y barbarie* and the broader discursive field in which Sarmiento inscribed his graffiti and his impassioned work signals is that, in the protracted struggles "to make states as foundations for nationhood, reterritorializing sovereignty in previously colonized spaces to be filled with nations in the making," the *pueblo* was a crucial, if elusive figure, everywhere and nowhere at once.[4] As Simón Rodríguez observed in his *Defensa de Bolívar* (1828), whereas the governing elite of the United States and France "no tuvieron qué pensar en *crear* pueblos, sino en *dirijirlos*" [did not have to think about *creating* peoples, but *directing them*], a Spanish American counterpart like Bolívar needed to contend with "algunos sujetos [que], A NOMBRE DEL PUEBLO, le hacen resistencia en lugar de ayudarlo" [some subjects [who], IN THE NAME OF THE PEOPLE, resist it/him instead of helping it/him].[5] The Revolution did not effect a complete rupture with Spain, and "[t]he result is an uneven spectacle in which triumph on the battlefield gives way to a political spectacle that is a 'vintage comedy' promising a continuation of colonial rule."[6] This notion ought to be taken quite literally. As we have seen in the case of postrevolutionary Argentina, the struggle to create a people indeed involved spectacle, as well as a variety of other cultural forms. The task of creating the people was an ongoing, constant performance that was prior and indispensible to the rise of the liberal state. Postrevolutionary politics was thus populist, even before such a name existed. Broadening our gaze, then, the question that we will continue to ask is, how did cultural production conjure specters of populism throughout nineteenth-century Latin America?

NOTES

1. Jorge Luis Borges, *Prólogos: Con un prólogo de prólogo* (Buenos Aires: Torres Agüero, 1975), 133.
2. Nicolas Shumway, *The Invention of Argentina* (Berkeley: University of California Press, 1991), 299.
3. Carlos J. Alonso, *The Burden of Modernity: The Rhetoric of Cultural Discourse in Spanish America* (New York: Oxford University Press, 1998), 28–29.
4. Jeremy Adelman, *Sovereignty and Revolution in the Iberian Atlantic* (Princeton, N.J.: Princeton University Press, 2006), 345.
5. Simón Rodríguez, *Obras Completas*, vol. 2 (Caracas: Congreso de la Republica, 1988), 206.
6. Ronald Briggs, *Tropes of Enlightenment in the Age of Bolívar: Simón Rodríguez and the American Essay at Revolution* (Nashville, Tenn.: Vanderbilt University Press, 2010), 50.

Bibliography

Acree, William. "Luis Perez, a Man of His Word in 1830s Buenos Aires and the Case for Popular Literature." *Bulletin of Spanish Studies* 88, no. 3 (2011): 367–86.

Adelman, Jeremy. *Republic of Capital: Buenos Aires and the Legal Transformation of the Atlantic World*. Stanford, Calif.: Stanford University Press, 1999.

———. *Sovereignty and Revolution in the Iberian Atlantic*. Princeton, N.J.: Princeton University Press, 2006.

Agamben, Giorgio. *Homo Sacer*. Translated by Daniel Heller-Roazen. Stanford, Calif: Stanford University Press, 1998.

Alberdi, Juan Bautista. *Bases y puntos de partida para la organización política de la República Argentina*. Edited by Manuel Fernández López. Buenos Aires: Editorial Losada, 2003.

———. *Escritos satíricos y de crítica literaria*. Buenos Aires: Academia Argentina de Letras, 1986.

———. *Fragmento preliminar al estudio del derecho*. Buenos Aires: Biblos, 1984.

Alberdi, Juan Bautista, and Domingo Faustino Sarmiento. *La gran polémica nacional: Cartas Quillotanas/Las Ciento y una*. Edited by Lucila Pagliai. Buenos Aires: Leviatán, 2005.

Alonso, Carlos J. *The Burden of Modernity: The Rhetoric of Cultural Discourse in Spanish America*. New York: Oxford University Press, 1998.

———. "Civilización y barbarie." *Hispania* 72, no. 2 (1989): 256–63.

———. "*Rama y sus retoños*: Figuring the Nineteenth Century in Spanish America." *Revista de estudios hispánicos* 28, no. 2 (1994): 283–92.

Amante, Adriana. "Género epistolar y política durante el Rosismo." In *La lucha de los lenguajes*, edited by Julio Schvartzman, 487–515. Buenos Aires: Emecé, 2003.

Amar Sánchez, Ana María. "Las versiones de la historia: Gauchesca versus periodismo y ensayo histórico." *Filología* 22, no. 1 (1987): 165–82.

Andermann, Jens. *Mapas de poder: Una arqueología literaria del espacio argentino*. Rosario, Argentina: Beatriz Viterbo, 2000.

———. *The Optic of the State: Visuality and Power in Argentina and Brazil*. Pittsburgh, Pa.: University of Pittsburgh Press, 2007.

Andermann, Jens, and Beatriz González-Stephan, eds. *Galerías del progreso: Museos, exposiciones y cultura visual en América Latina*. Rosario, Argentina: Beatriz Viterbo, 2006.

Andermann, Jens, and William Rowe, eds. *Images of Power: Iconography, Culture and the State in Latin America*. New York: Berghahn, 2006.

Anderson, Benedict. *Imagined Communities: Reflections on the Origin and Spread of Nationalism*. London: Verso, 2000.

Antelo, Raúl. "Borges y la impolítica." In *Jorge Luis Borges: Políticas de la literature*, edited by Juan Pablo Dabove, 271–302. Pittsburgh, Pa.: Instituto Internacional de Literatura Iberoamericana, University of Pittsburgh, 2008.
———. "Lugares do menor." *Latin American Literary Review* 25, no. 50 (1997): 109–20.
Aparicio, Juan Ricardo, and Mario Blaser. "The 'Lettered City' and the Insurrection of Subjugated Knowledges in Latin America." *Anthropological Quarterly Anthropological Quarterly* 81, no. 1 (2008): 59–94.
Area, Lelia. *Una biblioteca para leer la Nación: Lecturas de la figura Juan Manuel de Rosas*. Rosario, Argentina: Beatriz Viterbo, 2006.
Austin, John L. "Performative Utterances." In *Perspectives in the Philosophy of Language: A Concise Anthology*, edited by Robert J. Stainton, 239–52. Peterborough, Ont.: Broadview Press, 2000.
Bachten, Geoffrey. *Each Wild Idea*. Cambridge, Mass.: MIT Press, 2001.
Barthes, Roland. *Camera Lucida*. Translated by Richard Howard. New York: Hill and Wang, 1981.
Batticuore, Graciela. *La mujer romántica: Lectoras, autoras y escritoras en la Argentina: 1830–1870*. Buenos Aires: Edhasa, 2005.
Belín Sarmiento, Augusto. *Sarmiento anecdótico*. Buenos Aires: David Soria, 1905.
Bello, Andrés. *Obra literaria*. Edited by Pedro Grases. Caracas: Biblioteca Ayacucho, 1985.
Benjamin, Walter. *Reflections*. Edited by Peter Demetz. Translated by Edmund Jephcott. New York: Schocken, 1986.
Beretta García, Ernesto. "Antes del daguerrotipo: Gabinetes ópticos, cosmoramas, máquinas para sacar vistas y experimentaciones con los efectos de luz en Montevideo durante el siglo XIX." In *Artículos de investigación sobre fotografía, 2008*, edited by Ernesto Beretta García, Fernando Miranda, Gonzalo Vicci, Sandra Marroig, and Daniel Elissalde, 7–38. Montevideo: Ediciones CMDF, 2009.
Berman, Marshall. *All That Is Solid Melts into Air: The Experience of Modernity*. New York: Simon and Schuster, 1982.
Bethell, Leslie. *The Cambridge History of Latin America: From Independence to c. 1870*. Vol. 3. Cambridge: Cambridge University Press, 2008.
Bhabha, Homi K. *The Location of Culture*. New York: Routledge, 1994.
Blix, Göran M. *From Paris to Pompeii: French Romanticism and the Cultural Politics of Archaeology*. Philadelphia: University of Pennsylvania Press, 2009.
Blomberg, Héctor Pedro, ed. *Cancionero Federal*. Buenos Aires: Anaconda, 1934.
Borges, Jorge Luis. *El aleph*. Buenos Aires: Alianza, 2002.
———. *Prólogos: Con un prólogo de prólogos*. Buenos Aires: Torres Agüero, 1975.
Bourdieu, Pierre. *The Rules of Art: Genesis and Structure of the Literary Field*. Translated by Susan Emanuel. Stanford, Calif.: Stanford University Press, 1996.
Bremer, Thomas. "Historia Social de la Literatura e Intertextualidad: Funciones de la lectura en las novelas latinoamericanas del siglo XIX (el caso del 'libro en el libro')." *Revista de crítica literaria latinoamericana* 24 (1986): 31–50.
Briggs, Ronald. *Tropes of Enlightenment in the Age of Bolívar: Simón Rodríguez and the American Essay at Revolution*. Nashville, Tenn.: Vanderbilt University Press, 2010.
Castro-Gomez, Santiago. "The Social Sciences, Epistemic Violence, and the Problem of the 'Invention of the Other.'" *Nepantla: Views from South* 3, no. 2 (2002): 269–85.
Chávez, Fermín. *La cultura en la época de Rosas; aportes a la descolonización mental de la Argentina*. Buenos Aires: Ediciones Theoría, 1973.
Coleridge, Samuel Taylor. *The Major Works*. New York: Oxford University Press, 2000.
"El Cosmorama: Brillantes fuegos diamantinos." *La Gaceta Mercantil*, May 15, 1844.
Crary, Jonathan. "Géricault, the Panorama, and Sites of Reality in the Early Nineteenth Century." *Grey Room* 9 (2002): 5–25.
———. *Techniques of the Observer: On Vision and Modernity in the Nineteenth Century*. Cambridge, Mass.: MIT Press, 1992.
Dabove, Juan Pablo. *Nightmares of the Lettered City: Banditry and Literature in Latin America, 1816–1929*. Pittsburgh, Pa.: University of Pittsburgh Press, 2007.

da Silva, Maria Cristina Miranda. "Lanterna mágica: Fantasmagoria e sincretismo audiovisual." n.p. Web November 29, 2012.
De Angelis, Pedro. *Acusación y defensa de Rosas*. Buenos Aires: La Facultad, 1946.
De la Campa, Román. *Latin Americanism*. Minneapolis: University of Minnesota Press, 1999.
De la Campa, Román. "The Lettered City: Power and Writing in Latin America." In *Foucault and Latin America: Appropriations and Deployments of Discoursive Analysis*, edited by Benigno Trigo. New York: Routledge, 2002.
De la Fuente, Ariel. *Children of Facundo: Caudillo and Gaucho Insurgency during the Argentine State-Formation Process (La Rioja, 1853–1870)*. Durham, N.C.: Duke University Press, 2000.
Derrida, Jacques. "Signature Event Context." In *A Derrida Reader: Between the Blinds*, edited by Peggy Kamuf, 82–111. New York: Columbia University Press, 1991.
de Tocqueville, Alexis. *Democracy in America*. Edited by Harvey C. Mansfield and Delba Winthrop. Chicago: University of Chicago Press, 2002.
Di Meglio, Gabriel. *¡Viva el bajo pueblo! La plebe urbana de Buenos Aires y la política entre la revolución de Mayo y el rosismo (1810–1829)*. Buenos Aires: Prometeo, 2006.
du Gué Trapier, Elizabeth. "Unpublished Drawings by Goya in the Hispanic Society of America." *Master Drawings* 1, no. 1 (1963): 11–20.
Echeverría, Esteban. *Dogma Socialista*. Edited by Alberto Palcos. La Plata, Argentina: Universidad Nacional de la Plata, 1940.
———. *La cautiva/El matadero*. Buenos Aires: Emecé, 1999.
———. *Obra escogida*. Edited by Beatriz Sarlo and Carlos Altamirano. Caracas: Ayacucho, 1991.
———. *Obras completas de D. Esteban Echeverría*. 5 vols. Buenos Aires: Imprenta y Librería de Mayo, 1870–1874.
———. "Segunda lectura." In *El salón literario de 1837*, edited by Félix Weinberg, 175–85. Buenos Aires: Hachette, 1958.
Fernández, Mauro A. *Historia de la magia y el ilusionismo en la Argentina: Desde sus orígenes hasta el siglo XIX inclusive*. Buenos Aires: s.n., 1996.
Fernández Bravo, Álvaro. *Literatura y frontera: Procesos de territorialización en las culturas argentina y chilena del siglo XIX*. Buenos Aires: Sudamericana, 1999.
Fernández de Kirchner, Cristina. "Palabras de la Presidenta en el acto por el Día de la Soberanía Nacional." Accessed May 20, 2013. www.casarosada.gov.ar/discursos/4006.
Forbes, John Murray. *Once años en Buenos Aires, 1820–1831: Las crónicas diplomáticas de John Murray Forbes*. Buenos Aires: Emecé, 1956.
Foucault, Michel. "Lives of Infamous Men." In *The Essential Foucault: Selections from Essential Works of Foucault, 1954–1984*, edited by Paul Rabinow and Nikolas Rose, 279–93. New York: New Press, 2003.
———. "Nietzsche, Genealogy, History." In *Language, Counter Memory, Practice: Selected Essays and Interviews*, edited by D. F. Bouchard, 139–64. Ithaca, N.Y.: Cornell University Press, 1977.
———. "Questions on Geography." In *Power/Knowledge: Selected Interviews and Other Writings, 1972–77*, edited by Colin Gordon, 63–77. New York: Pantheon, 1980.
———. *Society Must Be Defended: Lectures at the Collège de France, 1975–76*. New York: Picador, 2003.
Franco, Jean. *The Decline and Fall of the Lettered City: Latin America in the Cold War*. Cambridge, Mass.: Harvard University Press, 2002.
Gellner, Ernest. *Nations and Nationalism*. Ithaca, N.Y.: Cornell University Press, 1983.
Gesualdo, Vicente. "Los salones de 'vistas ópticas': Antepasados del cine en Buenos Aires y el interior." *Todo es historia* 21, no. 248 (1988): 70–80.
Goethe, Johann W. *The Sorrows of Young Werther, and Selected Writings*. Edited by Catherine Hutter. New York: New American Library, 1982.
Goldman, Noemí, and Ricardo Donato Salvatore, eds. *Caudillismos rioplatenses: Nuevas miradas a un viejo problema*. Buenos Aires: Eudeba, 1998.

González Bernaldo de Quirós, Pilar. *Civilidad y política en los orígenes de la Nación Argentina: Las sociabilidades en Buenos Aires, 1829–1862*. Translated by Horacio Pons. Buenos Aires: Fondo de Cultura Económica, 2001.

———. "Sociabilidad, espacio urbano y politización en la ciudad de Buenos Aires (1820–1852)." In *La vida política en la Argentina del Siglo XIX: Armas, votos y voces*, edited by Hilda Sabato and Alberto Lettieri, 191–204. Buenos Aires: Fondo de Cultura Económica, 2003.

González Echevarría, Roberto. *Myth and Archive: A Theory of Latin American Narrative*. Cambridge: Cambridge University Press, 1990.

González-Stephan, Beatriz. "La construcción espectacular de la memoria nacional: Cultura visual y prácticas historiograficas (Venezuela siglo XIX)." VII Jornadas Andinas de Literatura Latinoamericana. Bogotá, Colombia, 2006.

———. *Fundaciones: Canon, historia y cultura nacional: La historiografía literaria del liberalismo hispanoamericano del siglo XIX*. Madrid: Iberoamericana; Frankfurt am Main: Vervuert, 2002.

Guardino, Peter F. *The Time of Liberty: Popular Political Culture in Oaxaca, 1750–1850*. Durham, N.C.: Duke University Press, 2005.

Guerra, François-Xavier. *Modernidad e independencias: Ensayos sobre las revoluciones hispánicas*. Madrid: MAPFRE, 1992.

Gutiérrez, Juan María. "Fisonomía del saber español: Cuál deba ser entre nosotros." In *El salón literario de 1837*. Weinberg, 145–57.

Haberly, David T. "Male Anxiety and Sacrificial Masculinity: The Case of Echeverría." *Hispanic Review* 73, no. 3 (2005): 291–307.

Haberly, David T. "Reopening Facundo." *Bulletin of Hispanic Studies* 85, no. 1 (2008): 47-62.

Halperín Donghi, Tulio. *De la Revolución de Independencia a la Confederación Rosista: Historia Argentina*. Vol. 3. Buenos Aires: Paidós, 2000.

———. *El revisionismo histórico argentino como visión decadentista de la historia nacional*. Buenos Aires: Siglo Veintiuno, 2005.

———. "Una nación para el desierto argentino." In *Proyecto y construcción de una nación*, 7–107. Buenos Aires: Ariel, 1995.

———, ed. *Proyecto y construcción de una nación*. Buenos Aires: Ariel, 1995.

Halperín Donghi, Tulio, Gwen Kirkpatrick, Iván Jaksik, and Francine Masiello, eds. *Sarmiento: Author of a Nation*. Berkeley: University of California Press, 1994.

Hawthorne, Nathaniel. *The American Notebooks*. New Haven, Conn.: Yale University Press, 1932.

Heidegger, Martin. *The Question Concerning Technology and Other Essays*. Edited by William Lovitt. New York: Harper Torchbooks, 1977.

Hemmings, Clare. "Invoking Affect: Cultural Theory and the Ontological Turn." *Cultural Studies* 19, no. 5 (2005): 548–67.

Hernández, José. *Martín Fierro*. Edited by Eleuterio F. Tiscornia. Buenos Aires: Editorial Losada, 1972.

Hobsbawm, E. J. *Nations and Nationalism since 1780: Programme, Myth, Reality*. Cambridge: Cambridge University Press, 1990.

"La iconografía de Rosas." *Caras y Caretas*, May 13, 1905, n.p.

Irazusta, Julio. *Vida política de Juan Manuel de Rosas: A través de su correspondencia*. Vol. 4. Buenos Aires: Albatros, 1950.

Katra, William H. "Sarmiento en los Estados Unidos." In *Viajes por Europa, África y América, 1845–1847 y Diario de gastos*, edited by Javier Fernández, 853–911. Buenos Aires: Colección Archivos, 1993.

King, John Anthony. *Twenty-four Years in the Argentine Republic: Embracing Its Civil and Military History, and an Account of Its Political Condition, Before and During the Administration of Governor Ross*. New York: D. Appleton & Co., 1846.

Kofman, Sarah. *Camera Obscura of Ideology*. Translated by Will Straw. Ithaca, N.Y.: Cornell University Press, 1999.

Kohan, Martín, and Alejandra Laera, eds. *Las brújulas del extraviado: Para una lectura integral de Esteban Echeverría*. Rosario, Argentina: Beatriz Viterbo, 2006.

Laclau, Ernesto. *Emancipation(s)*. New York: Verso, 1996.
———. *On Populist Reason*. London: Verso, 2007.
———. *Politics and Ideology in Marxist Theory*. Atlantic Highlands, N.J.: Humanities Press, 1977.
Laclau, Ernesto, and Chantal Mouffe. *Hegemony and Socialist Strategy: Towards a Radical Democratic Politics*. London: Verso, 2001.
Laera, Alejandra. "'Nada se obtiene sin dinero': Pérdidas y ganancias de un hombre de letras." In *Las brújulas del extraviado: Para una lectura integral de Esteban Echeverría*, edited by Martín Kohan and Alejandra Laera, 77–112. Rosario, Argentina: Beatriz Viterbo, 2006.
Lamas, Andrés. "Visiones de la óptica." In *El Iniciador*, edited by Mariano de Vedia y Mitre. Buenos Aires: Kraft, 1941.
Lefebvre, Henri. *The Production of Space*. Translated by Donald Nicholson-Smith. Oxford: Blackwell, 1991.
"*El Lucero*: Buenos Ayres, Diciembre 23 de 1829." *El Lucero*, December 23, 1829, 3–4.
Ludmer, Josefina. *El género gauchesco: Un tratado sobre la patria*. Buenos Aires: Sudamericana, 1988.
———. "Una máquina para leer el siglo XIX." *Revista de la Universidad Nacional Autónoma de México* 530 (1995): n.p. Web November 29, 2012.
Lynch, John. *Argentine Dictator: Juan Manuel De Rosas, 1829–1852*. New York: Clarendon, 1981.
———. *Caudillos in Spanish America, 1800–1850*. New York: Clarendon Press, 1992.
Malosetti Costa, Laura. "¿Verdad o belleza? Pintura, fotografía, memoria, historia." *Revista Crítica Cultural* 4, no. 2 (2010): 111–24. Web November 28, 2012.
Marin, Louis. *Portrait of the King*. Minneapolis: University of Minnesota Press, 1988.
Mármol, José. *Amalia*. 2 vols. Buenos Aires: El Elefante Blanco, 1997.
———. *Amalia*. Edited by Doris Sommer. Translated by Helen Lane. Oxford: Oxford University Press, 2001.
———. *Manuela Rosas y otros escritos políticos del exilio*. Buenos Aires: Taurus, 2001.
Martínez Estrada, Ezequiel. *Radiografía de la Pampa*. Buenos Aires: Losada, 1968.
Marx, Karl. *Selected Writings*. Edited by David McLellan. Oxford: Oxford University Press, 2000.
Marx, Leo. *The Machine in the Garden: Technology and the Pastoral Ideal*. New York: Oxford, 2000.
Masiello, Francine. "Los sentidos y las ruinas." *Iberoamericana: América Latina, España, Portugal* 8, no. 30 (2008): 103–12.
Méndez, Cecilia G. *The Plebeian Republic: The Huanta Rebellion and the Making of the Peruvian State, 1820–1850*. Durham, N.C.: Duke University Press, 2005.
Mitchell, Timothy. "The Limits of the State: Beyond Statist Approaches and Their Critics." *The American Political Science Review* 85, no. 1 (1991): 77–96.
Mitchell, W. J. T. *Iconology: Image, Text, Ideology*. Chicago: University of Chicago Press, 1986.
———. "Interdisciplinarity and Visual Culture." *The Art Bulletin* 4 (1995): 540–44.
Mitre, Bartolomé. *Galería de celebridades argentinas: Biografías de los personajes más notables del Río de la Plata*. Buenos Aires: Ledoux y Vignal, 1857.
Molloy, Sylvia. "Inscripciones del Yo en *Recuerdos de provincia*." *Revista Iberoamericana* 54, no. 143 (1988): 407–18.
Montaldo, Graciela. "Culturas Críticas: La extensión de un campo." *Iberoamericana* 4, no. 16 (2004): 35–48.
———. *De pronto, el campo: Literatura argentina y tradición rural*. Rosario, Argentina: Beatriz Viterbo, 1993.
———. "La desigualdad de las partes." *A Contracorriente: Revista de Historia Social y Literatura en América Latina* 7, no. 1 (2009): 14–44.
———. *Ficciones culturales y fábulas de identidad en América Latina*. Rosario, Argentina: Beatriz Viterbo, 2004.
Moraña, Mabel. "De La ciudad letrada al imaginario nacionalista: Contribuciones de Ángel Rama a la invención de América." In *Políticas de la escritura en América Latina: De la*

Colonia a la Modernidad, edited by Francisco Lasarte et al., 41–52. Caracas: Monte Ávila, 1994.

Moreiras, Alberto. *The Exhaustion of Difference: The Politics of Latin American Cultural Studies*. Durham, N.C.: Duke University Press, 2001.

Muñoz, Boris, and Silvia Spitta. *Más allá de la ciudad letrada: Crónicas y espacios urbanos*. Pittsburgh, Pa.: Biblioteca de América, Instituto Internacional de Literatura Iberoamericana, University of Pittsburgh, 2003.

Myers, Jorge. "Un autor en busca de un programa: Echeverría en sus escritos de reflexión estética." In *Las brújulas del extraviado: Para una lectura integral de Esteban Echeverría*, edited by Martín Kohan and Alejandra Laera, 57–75. Rosario, Argentina: Beatriz Viterbo, 2006.

———. *Orden y virtud: El discurso republicano en el régimen rosista*. Buenos Aires: Universidad Nacional de Quilmes, 1995.

Noble, Andrea. "Visual Culture and Latin American Studies." *CR: The New Centennial Review* 4, no. 2 (2004): 219–38.

O'Donnell, Pacho. *La gran epopeya: El combate de la Vuelta de Obligado*. Buenos Aires: Grupo Editorial Norma, 2010.

Palti, Elías José. *El tiempo de la política: El siglo XIX reconsiderado*. Buenos Aires: Siglo Veintiuno Editores Argentina, 2007.

Paz Soldán, Edmundo, and Debra A. Castillo. *Latin American Literature and Mass Media*. New York: Garland Pub., 2001.

Pérez, Luis. *El Torito de los Muchachos, 1830*. Edited by Olga Fernández Latour de Botas. Buenos Aires: Instituto Bibliográfico "Antonio Zinny," 1978.

———. "La lira de los negros." In *Cancionero Federal*, edited by Héctor Pedro Blomberg. Buenos Aires: Anaconda, 1934.

———. *Poesía biográfica de Rosas titulada "El Gaucho."* Edited by Roberto Rodríguez Molas. Buenos Aires: Clio, 1957.

Perus, Françoise. "¿Qué nos dice hoy *La ciudad letrada* de Ángel Rama?" *Revista Iberoamericana* 72, no. 211 (2005): 363–72.

Piglia, Ricardo. "Notas sobre *Facundo*." *Punto de Vista* 17, no. 3 (1980): 14–18.

———. "Sarmiento the Writer." In *Sarmiento: Author of a Nation*, edited by Tulio Halperín Donghi, Gwen Kirkpatrick, Iván Jaksik, and Francine Masiello, 127–44. Berkeley: University of California Press, 1994.

Pratt, Mary Louise. *Imperial Eyes: Travel Writing and Transculturation*. New York: Routledge, 1992.

Prieto, Adlofo. *Proyección del rosismo en la literatura argentina; seminario del Instituto de Letras*. Rosario, Argentina: Universidad Nacional del Litoral, 1959.

Quattrocchi-Woisson, Diana. *Un Nationalisme de déracinés: L'Argentine, pays malade de sa mémoire*. Paris: Editions du Centre national de la recherche scientifique, 1992.

Rama, Ángel. "Argentina: Crisis de una cultura sistemática." *Inti: Revista de Literatura Hispánica* 1, no. 10 (1979): 49–60.

———. "El sistema literario de la poesía gauchesca." In *Poesía gauchesca*, edited by Jorge B. Rivera, 9–53. Caracas: Ayacucho, 1977.

———. *La ciudad letrada*. Hanover, N.H.: Ediciones del Norte, 2002.

———. *The Lettered City*. Translated by John Charles Chasteen. Durham, N.C.: Duke University Press, 1996.

Ramos, Julio. *Divergent Modernities: Culture and Politics in Nineteenth-Century Latin America*. Translated by John D. Blanco. Durham, N.C.: Duke University Press, 2001.

Ramos Mejía, José María. *Rosas y su tiempo*. 2 vols. Buenos Aires: Félix Lajouane, 1907.

Rancière, Jacques. *Disagreement: Politics and Philosophy*. Minneapolis: University of Minnesota Press, 1999.

———. *Le partage du sensible: Esthétique et politique*. Paris: La Fabrique, 2000.

Real Academia Española. *Diccionario de la lengua española*. 2 vols. Madrid: Espasa-Calpe, 1994.

Ríos, Alicia, ed. "Homenaje a Ángel Rama." Special issues, *Estudios: Revista de investigaciones literarias y culturales* 10–11 (2003–2004).

Rivera, Jorge B., ed. *Poesía gauchesca*. Caracas: Biblioteca Ayacucho, 1977.
Roca, Julio Argentino. "Discurso ante el Congreso al asumir la presidencia, 12 de octubre de 1880." In *Proyecto y construcción de una nación*, edited by Tulio Halperín Donghi, 591–95. Buenos Aires: Ariel, 1995.
Rodríguez, Fermín. "Un desierto de ideas." In Kohan and Laera, *Las brújulas del extraviado*, 149–70.
Rodríguez, Simón. *Obras Completas*. Caracas: Congreso de la Republica, 1988.
Root, Regina A. *Couture and Consensus: Fashion and Politics in Postcolonial Argentina*. Minneapolis: University of Minnesota Press, 2010.
Rosas, Juan Manuel de. *Correspondencia de Juan Manuel de Rosas*. Edited by Marcela Ternavasio. Buenos Aires: Eudeba, 2005.
Ruiz, Bladimir. "La ciudad letrada y la creación de la cultura nacional: Costumbrismo, prensa y nación." *Chasqui* 33, no. 2 (2004): 75–89.
Safford, Frank. "Politics, Ideology, and Society in Post-Independence Latin America." In *The Cambridge History of Latin America: From Independence to c. 1870*, vol. 3, edited by Leslie Bethell. Cambridge: Cambridge University Press, 2008.
Salvatore, Ricardo Donato. "'Expresiones federales': Formas políticas del federalismo rosista." In Goldman and Salvatore, *Caudillismos rioplatenses*, 189–222.
———. *Wandering Paysanos: State Order and Subaltern Experience in Buenos Aires during the Rosas Era*. Durham, N.C.: Duke University Press, 2003.
Sánchez de Thompson, Mariquita. *Intimidad y política. Diario, cartas y recuerdos*. Edited by María Gabriela Mizraje. Buenos Aires: Adriana Hidalgo, 2003.
Sanders, James E. "The Vanguard of the Atlantic World: Contesting Modernity in Nineteenth-Century Latin America." *Latin American Research Review* 46, no. 2 (2011): 104–27.
Sarlo, Beatriz. "En el origen de la cultura argentina: Europa y el desierto: Búsqueda de un fundamento." *Primer Seminario Latino-Americano de Literatura comparada*. Porto Alegre, Brazil: U Federal do Rio Grande do Sul, 1986.
Sarmiento, Domingo Faustino. *Argirópolis*. Buenos Aires: A-Z (Secretaria de Cultura de la Nación), 1994.
———. *Facundo: Civilización y barbarie*. Madrid: Alianza, 1988.
———. *Facundo: Edición crítica y documentada*. Edited by Alberto Palcos. La Plata, Argentina: U Nacional de La Plata, 1938.
———. *Facundo: Civilization and Barbarism: The First Complete English Translation*. Translated by Kathleen Ross. Berkeley: University of California Press, 2003.
———. *Campaña en el Ejército Grande*. Edited by Tulio Halperín Donghi. Bernal, Argentina: U Nacional de Quilmes, 2004.
———. *La correspondencia de Sarmiento: Primera serie: Tomo I Años 1838–1854*. Edited by Carlos S. A. Segretti. Córdoba, Spain: Poder Ejecutivo de la Provincia de Córdoba, 1988.
———. *Obras de D. F. Sarmiento*. 52 vols. Santiago de Chile, Gutenberg, 1885–1902.
———. *Recuerdos de provincia*. Edited by María Caballero Wangüemert. Madrid: Anaya & Mario Muchnik, 1992.
———. *Viajes por Europa, África y América, 1845–1847 y Diario de gastos*. Edited by Javier Fernández. Buenos Aires: Colección Archivos, 1993.
Schopenhauer, Arthur. *The World as Will and Representation*. Vol. 1. Translated by E. F. J. Payne. New York: Dover, 1966.
Schvartzman, Julio. *Microcrítica: Lecturas argentinas, cuestiones de detalle*. Buenos Aires: Biblos, 1996.
Segre, Erica. *Intersected Identities: Strategies of Visualisation in Nineteenth- and Twentieth-Century Mexican Culture*. New York: Berghahn Books, 2007.
Seibel, Beatriz. *Historia del teatro argentino: Desde los rituales hasta 1930*. Buenos Aires: Corregidor, 2002.
Shumway, Nicolas. *The Invention of Argentina*. Berkeley: University of California Press, 1991.
Silvestri, Graciela. "*Errante en torno de los objetos miro*: Relaciones entre artes y ciencias de descripción territorial en el siglo XIX rioplatense." In *Resonancias románticas: Ensayos sobre historia de la cultura argentina 1820–1890*, edited by Klaus Gallo, Graciela Batticuore, and Jorge Myers, 225–43. Buenos Aires: Eudeba, 2005.

Smith, Neil. *Uneven Development: Nature, Capital and the Production of Space*. Cambridge, Mass.: Blackwell, 1991.
Soja, Edward W. *Postmodern Geographies: The Reassertion of Space in Critical Social Theory*. London: Verso, 1989.
Sommer, Doris. *Foundational Fictions: The National Romances of Latin America*. Berkeley: University of California Press, 1991.
Sorensen, Diana. *Facundo and the Construction of Argentine Culture*. Austin: University of Texas Press, 1996.
Szuchman, Mark D. "Imagining the State and Building the Nation: The Case of Nineteenth-Century Argentina." *History Compass* 4, no. 2 (2006): 314–47.
Taylor, Diana. *Disappearing Acts: Spectacles of Gender and Nationalism in Argentina's "Dirty War."* Durham, N.C.: Duke University Press, 1997.
Telesca, Ana María, and Roberto Amigo. "La curiosidad de los porteños: El público y los temas de las vistas ópticas en el Estado de Buenos Aires (1852–1862)." In *Quinto Congreso de Historia de la Fotografía: 17 y 18 de agosto de 1996*, 33–36. Buenos Aires: Comité Ejecutivo Permanente, 1997.
Ternavasio, Marcela. "Entre la deliberación y la autorización: El régimen rosista frente al dilema de la inestabilidad política." In *Caudillismos rioplatenses*, Goldman and Salvatore, 159–87.
———. "Estudio preliminar." In *Correspondencia de Juan Manuel de Rosas*. Buenos Aires: Eudeba, 2005.
———. "Hacia un régimen de la unanimidad: Política y elecciones en Buenos Aires, 1828–1850." In *Ciudadanía política y formación de las naciones: Perspectivas históricas de América Latina*, edited by Hilda Sábato, 119–41. Mexico City: Fondo de Cultura Económica, 1999.
Trigo, Abril. "The Exhaustion of Difference: The Politics of Latin American Cultural Studies de Alberto Moreiras." *Revista Iberoamericana* 69, no. 205 (2003): 1024–28.
Viñas, David. *Literatura argentina y política: De los jacobinos porteños a la bohemia anarquista*. Vol. 1. Buenos Aires: Santiago Arcos, 2005.
———. *De los montoneros a los anarquistas*. Buenos Aires: Carlos Pérez, 1971.
———. "Sarmiento: Madness or Accumulation." In *Sarmiento: Author of a Nation*, edited by Halperín Donghi, Tulio, Gwen Kirkpatrick, Iván Jaksik, and Francine Masiello, 213–19. Berkeley: University of California Press, 1994.
Weinberg, Félix. *Esteban Echeverría, ideólogo de la segunda revolución*. Buenos Aires: Taurus, 2006.
———. "El periodismo en la época de Rosas." *Revista de Historia* 2 (1957): 81–100.
———. *El salón literario de 1837*. Buenos Aires: Hachette, 1958.
Weiss, Ignacio, ed. *Archivo Americano y Espíritu de la Prensa del Mundo*. 2 vols. Buenos Aires: Americana, 1946.
Zielinski, Siegfried. *Audiovisions: Cinema and Television as Entr'Actes in History*. Amsterdam: Amsterdam University Press, 1999.
Žižek, Slavoj. *The Sublime Object of Ideology*. London: Verso, 1989.

Index

Adelman, Jeremy, 8–9, 60; *Republic of Capital: Buenos Aires and the Legal Transformation of the Atlantic World*, 8–9; *Sovereignty and Revolution in the Iderian Atlantic*, 9
Afro-Argentines, 19
Agamben, Giorgio, 58n80
La agricultura de la Zona Tórrida (Bello), 132–133
Alberdi, Juan Bautista, 3, 7, 36, 98, 103, 160; *Bases y puntos de partida para la organización política de la República Argentina*, 126, 136–137; *Campaña en el Ejército Grande* and, 144; *desierto* and, 147–148; *Fragmento preliminar al estudio del derecho*, 136; Hawthorne and, 151–152; "Impresiones en una visita al Paraná," 147–152; "Predicar en desiertos," 133–134; Sarmiento and, 144, 155n44
"El Aleph" (Borges), 108–109
Alsina, Valentín, 116
Amalia (Mármol), 7; Rosas in, 38–40; urban space and, 77–80
American Archive and Spirit of the World Press. See Archivo Americano y Espiritu de la Prensa del Mundo
Arana, Felipe, 19
Archivo Americano y Espiritu de la Prensa del Mundo (*American Archive and Spirit of the World Press*), 6–7

Argentina: *Bases y puntos de partida para la organización política de la República Argentina*, 126, 136–137; Buenos Aires, 74–82, 90, 126; civilizing, 141; divisions, 1; modernity in, 124, 159; nineteenth-century, 8; progress in nineteenth-century, 139; República, 137; Rosas's, 124; transition from colony to nation-state, 9
Argentine Confederation, 60
Argentine Dictator: Juan Manuel De Rosas, 1829–1852 (Lynch), 22–23
Argentine independence, 1
Argentine literature, 85n23; Generation of 1837 and, 10–11, 59–60; postrevolutionary, 72
Argentine politics, 5–6; postrevolutionary, 11
audiovisual spectacles: "Cosmorama," 90; forerunners to, 93–95; function of, 91; magic lanterns, 93–95, 120n19; phantasmagoria, 110, 121n37; Rosas regime and, 13, 91; in *El Torito de los Muchachos*, 98–103; *tutilimundi*, 98–103, 100, 101

barbarism, 60; civilization and, 4–5
Barriales, Juancho, 99
Bases y puntos de partida para la organización política de la República Argentina (Alberdi), 126, 136–137

Batticuore, Graciela, 86n54–86n55
Battle of Caseros, 6, 145
Battle of Vuelta de Obligado, 4; defeat at, 1
Beláustegui de Arana, Pascuala, 89–91
Bello, Andrés: *La agricultura de la Zona Tórrida*, 132–133; *Silvas americanas*, 153
Besnes e Irigoyen, Juan Manuel, 93, 94
Bhabha, Homi K., 25
Borges, Jorge Luis: "El Aleph," 108–109; *Recuerdos de provincia* prologue, 159
Bourbon Reforms, 8
Buenos Aires, Argentina, 74–82; federalization of, 126; French blockade of, 90; *Republic of Capital: Buenos Aires and the Legal Transformation of the Atlantic World*, 8–9

Cambridge History of Latin America (Safford), 8
camera obscura, 95. *See also* optical devices
Campaña en el Ejército Grande (Sarmiento), 70–72, 85n34, 140–141, 144–147; Alberdi and, 144; Ejército Grande and, 145; itineraries narrated in, 145; optical metaphors in, 117–118; story of press in, 145–146
Cané, Miguel, 103
Carrió de la Vandera, Alonso, 63
"Carta del viejo Francisco Junco de la Guardia de la Monte, al viejo Gregorio Chaparro de la ciudad" (Letter from old Francisco Junco of Guardia de la Monte, to old Gregorio Chaparro of the city), 49–51; woodcut image accompanying, 51–52, 52
Cartas a un amigo (Echeverría), 110–111
caudillo: clientelism and power of, 23; power of, 23; *pueblo* and, 19; Rosas's image and power of, 24. *See also* Rosas, Juan Manuel de
La cautiva (Echeverría), 7, 128–130, 153; poetry, 7, 81–82; public discourse through poetry and, 81–82
citizens, rulers and, 31
La ciudad letrada (Rama), 62–64, 66–67, 84n14–85n15; cultural history in, 63–64; graffiti and, 62–63; Sarmiento and, 64
La ciudad letrada (the lettered city), 62, 83, 97
Civilización y barbarie, vida de Facundo Quiroga i aspecto físico, costumbres y ábitos de la República Argentina (*Facundo*, Sarmiento), 2–3, 7, 40–44, 126; "Advertencia," 59–60; character of Facundo in, 41–42; civilizing Argentina and, 141; graffiti in, 66–70, 160; modernity in, 159; Rosas regime and, 12–13; Rosist discourse in, 42–43
civilization, 60; barbarism and, 4–5
civilizing Argentina, 141
clientelism, caudillo power and, 23
colonialism, 11; Argentina's transition to nation-state and, 9
Conquista del desierto (Conquest of the Desert), 126, 138
conservatism, 23
Constitution of 1853, 3
Los consuelos (Echeverría), 148
Cortés, Hernán, 63
"Cosmorama" (audiovisual spectacles), 90
cultural criticism, *desierto* in, 154n6
cultural discourse, 108; optical devices in, 118
cultural history, in *La ciudad letrada*, 63–64
cultural landscape: optical devices in, 97; Rosas regime and, 36
culture, Rosas depictions and national, 22

De Angelis, Pedro, 20, 27; "Ensayo histórico," 31–33, 56n54; Pérez's portrayal of Rosas and, 33–35; Rosas and, 35–36
Defensa de Bolívar (Rodríguez), 161–162
Democracy in America (Tocqueville), 133
descamisados, 2
desierto (pampa), 125; Alberdi and, 147–148; in Argentine cultural criticism, 154n6; in *Bases y puntos de partida para la organización política de la República Argentina*, 136–137; city's relationship to, 138–139; *Conquista del desierto*, 126, 138; in cultural criticism, 154n6; in

Index

Echeverría's work, 128–129; in Generation of 1837 writing, 133; indigenous people of, 130; *letrados* and, 127–128; new inhabitants in, 127; "Predicar en desiertos," 133–134; productivity of, 131–132; *pueblo* and, 136; *Radiografía de la Pampa*, 154n6; Roca and, 137; in Sarmiento's work, 137–138; as social space, 140
discourse: cultural, 108, 118; political, 74–75, 108, 118, 160; public, 81–82; Rosist, 42–43
Divergent Modernities (Ramos), 124
Dogma socialista (Echeverría), 135–136
Dorrego, Manuel: execution of, 9, 54, 78–79; funerary procession, 17–19
Dumas, André, 115

Echeverría, Esteban, 15n18, 103; *Cartas a un amigo*, 110–111; *La cautiva*, 7, 81–82, 128–130, 153; *Los consuelos*, 148; *desierto* in work of, 128–129; *Dogma socialista*, 135–136; "El matadero," 46; "Mefistófeles: Dramajoco-serio, satírico-político," 111–114; optical metaphors in work of, 110–114; Revolution and, 135; *Rimas*, 128, 148–149; "Segunda lectura," 130–131; "La vida y la obra de Esteban Echeverría," 155n27; works of, 13
De la educación popular (Sarmiento), 140
elections, 24
"Ensayo histórico" (De Angelis), 31–33, 56n54
"Las esclavas de Buenos Aires muestran que son libres," 52–54
Exhaustion of Difference: The Politics of Latin American Cultural Studies (Moreiras), 5

Facundo. See Civilización y barbarie, vida de Facundo Quiroga i aspecto físico, costumbres y ábitos de la República Argentina
federación, 75
federalistas doctrinarios, 24
federalistas netos, 24
Federalists, 9–10, 25; writings, 15n18
federalization of Buenos Aires, 126

Fernández de Kirchner, Cristina, 1–2
fiestas federales, 79–80, 86n55; ceremonial poetry of, 80–82
Forbes, John Murray, 17–19, 54n3; as Charge d'Affaires for United States, 78–79
Fragmento preliminar al estudio del derecho (Alberdi), 136
French, Buenos Aires blockade by, 90
Fuente, Ariel de la, 66

gabinete óptico (optical device), 89–90
La Gaceta Mercantil (newspaper), 35–36, 55n25; pro-Rosas poem, 76–77
Galería de celebridades argentinas (Mitre), 57n73
El Gaucho (newspaper), 27, 79; "Correspondencia," 56n45; Rosas image on, 51, 52
El Gaucho Martín Fierro (Hernández), 139
Gellner, Ernest, 124–125
Generation of 1837, 4; Argentine literature and, 10–11, 59–60; *desierto* in writings of, 133; modernity and, 13–14; nation-state and, 59; the people to, 135–136; *pueblo* and, 160; Rosas and, 10, 37, 40; writings of, 85n26, 133
The German Ideology (Marx, K.), 95
Goethe, Johann W., 111
Goldman, Noemí, 10, 23
González Bernaldo, Pilar, 10
González-Stephan, Beatriz, 15n19
Goya, Francisco de, 99, 100, 101
graffiti, 59–83; caricature, 68–70, 69; *La ciudad letrada* and, 62–63; in *Facundo*, 66–70, 160; Mármol and, 61, 79; *ON NE TUE POINT LES IDEES*, 59–61, 67; pro-Rosas, 76–77; Sarmiento's employment of, 61, 64–74; sociopolitical context of, 67–68
Groussac, Paul, 60
Guerra, François-Xavier, 9
Guido, Tomás, 89
Gutiérrez, Juan María, 155n27

Haberly, David, 84n7
Halperín Donghi, Tulio, 143, 154n17
Hawthorne, Nathaniel, 151–152

Heredia, Alejandro, 74–75
Hernández, José, 159
history: cultural, 63–64; revisionist, 4

Ibarra, Gregory, 121n37
iconography, Rosist, 21–26
"Impresiones en una visita al Paraná" (Impressions on a Visit to the Paraná River, Alberdi), 147–152; nature and technology in, 150; Revolution and, 149; steamboats in, 150–152
"indiscipline," 15n14
industry, 131
El Iniciador, 103
intellectuals: nineteenth-century Latin American, 124; popular classes and, 107; Rosas and, 33–35, 75–76. See also *letrados*

jueces de paz, 24

King, John Anthony, 93–95

Laclau, Ernesto, 11, 20, 73; populism as defined by, 25–26; *On Populist Reason*, 56n37
Lamas, Andrés, 13, 103–108, 160
Latin America: *Cambridge History of Latin America*, 8; intellectuals in nineteenth-century, 124; literature in, 8; models of sovereignty in, 75; visual culture of, 91
Latin Americanism, contemporary, 5
Lavalle, Juan, 17, 20, 78; uprising, 32
letrados, 5, 124; *desierto* and, 127–128; modernity and, 125–126
the lettered city. See *La ciudad letrada*
Letter from old Francisco Junco of Guardia de la Monte, to old Gregorio Chaparro of the city. See "Carta del viejo Francisco Junco de la Guardia de la Monte, al viejo Gregorio Chaparro de la ciudad"
literature: definitions of, 15n19; in Latin America, 8; postrevolutionary, 72. See also Argentine literature
El Lucero (newspaper), 27
Ludmer, Josefina, 92–93
Lynch, John, 22–23

The Machine in the Garden (Marx, L.), 152
Mackau-Arana treaty, 46
magic lanterns, 93–95, 120n19
"Máquina para sacar vistas," 93, 94
Mármol, José, 19; *Amalia*, 7, 38–40, 77–80; graffiti and, 61, 79; "De la prensa periódica," 155n38; Rosas and, 20
Martínez Estrada, Ezequiel, 154n6
Marx, Karl, 95, 120n21
Marx, Leo, 152
"Mas-a-fuera" (Sarmiento), 71–73
"El matadero" (Echeverría), 46, 58n80
May Rosas Die!. See *¡Muera Rosas!*
media: print, 27; Rosas regime and, 97
"Mefistófeles: Drama-joco-serio, satírico-político" (Mephistopholes: Joco-serious, Satirical-political Drama, Echeverría), 111–114
Mitchell, W. J. T., 15n14
Mitre, Bartolomé, 3, 14n7; *Galería de celebridades argentinas*, 57n73
La Moda (newspaper), 7, 36, 98, 134–135, 160
modernity, 116; Argentine, 124, 159; *Divergent Modernities*, 124; in *Facundo*, 159; Generation of 1837 and, 13–14; *letrados* and, 125–126; *pueblo* and, 125; Roca and, 127–128; Sarmiento and, 140
Montaldo, Graciela, 119n5, 145
Moreiras, Alberto, 5
Moulin, Hippolyte, 45
¡Muera Rosas! (May Rosas Die!, magazine), 37
Myers, Jorge, 10, 75–76

national identity, 8; establishing, 75–76
nationalism, 4
national organization: visual culture and, 119n5; writing in struggle for, 61
nation-building, 132, 154n17
nation-state: Argentina's transition to, 9; construction of, 124; Generation of 1837 and, 59
El Negrito (newspaper), 79
newspapers: *La Gaceta Mercantil*, 35–36, 55n25, 76–77; *El Gaucho*, 27, 51, 52,

56n45, 79; *El Lucero*, 27; *La Moda*, 7, 36, 98, 134–135, 160; *El Negrito*, 79; during Rosas regime, 36–37; sanctioned, 36–37; *Semanario de Buenos Aires*, 36; *Sud América*, 145; *El Torito de los Muchachos*, 13, 79, 97–103
nineteenth-century: Argentina in, 8, 139; Latin American intellectuals in, 124; visual culture in, 119n5

ON NE TUE POINT LES IDEES (One does not kill ideas, graffiti), 59–61; elitism conveyed by, 67
On Populist Reason (Laclau), 56n37
optical devices, 95–96; allegorical treatment of, 109; camera obscura, 95; in changing cultural landscape, 97; in cultural discourse, 118; *gabinete óptico*, 89–90; photography and, public representation through, 96–97. *See also* audiovisual spectacles
optical metaphors: in *Campaña en el Ejército Grande*, 117–118; in *Cartas a un amigo*, 110–111; in Echeverría's work, 110–114; in "Mefistófeles: Drama-joco-serio, satírico-político," 111–114; in Sarmiento's work, 114–118; in *Viajes por Europa, África y América 1845–1847*, 114–116

"The Painted Rocks of Zonda". *See* "Las Piedras Pintadas de Zonda"
Palti, Elías, 9
pampa. *See desierto*
patriotism, 75
Pérez, Luis, 13, 20, 27, 79, 161; De Angelis's portrayal of Rosas and, 33–35; imprisonment of, 58n84; Rosas biographical poem by, 27–31; Rosas portrayed by, 33–35; Rosas regime and, 58n84; *El Torito de los Muchachos*, 97–99
phantasmagoria, 110, 121n37
photography, public representation through, 96–97
"Las Piedras Pintadas de Zonda" ("The Painted Rocks of Zonda," Sarmiento), 65–66

Piglia, Ricardo, 60; "Sarmiento the Writer," 84n7
Plot, D. del, 53
poetry, 74–82; *La cautiva* and, 7, 81–82; *fiestas federales'* ceremonial, 80–82; Pérez's Rosas biographical poem, 27–31; pro-Rosas, 76–77; public discourse through, 81–82; *pueblo* and, 82–83; Sarmiento and, 82
political discourse, 74–75; *pueblo* and, 160. *See also* Argentine politics
popular classes, intellectuals and, 107
popular expression, 78
populism, 11, 21–26, 159; definitions of, 25–26; Laclau and, 25–26; *On Populist Reason*, 56n37; postrevolutionary period and, 11–12; Rosas regime and, 25
postrevolutionary period: archive of, 4–8, 6; creating a people in, 162; literature of, 72; politics in, 11; populism and, 11–12; visual culture in, 89–90; writing in, 124–125
Pratt, Mary Louise, 72, 132, 139
"De la prensa periódica" (Mármol), 155n38
print media, Rosas and, 27. *See also* newspapers
public discourse, poetry and, 81–82
public education, 3
public opinion, 61
public representation through photography, 96–97
pueblo, 153; *desierto* and, 136; Generation of 1837 and, 160; image of, 24; image of unified, 79; modern, 125; poetry and, 82–83; political discourse and, 160; representing, 161; Rosas and, 19, 19–20; Rosas regime and, 24

Quiroga, Facundo, 3

Radiografía de la Pampa (Martínez Estrada), 154n6
railroad, 127
Rama, Ángel, 62; *La ciudad letrada*, 62–67
Ramos, Julio, 124
Ramos Mejía, José, 80–81

Rancière, Jacques, 24
Recuerdos de provincia (Recollections of a Provincial Past, Sarmiento), 64–65, 140; Borges's prologue to, 159
République Argentina, 137
república verdadera, 150
Republic of Capital: Buenos Aires and the Legal Transformation of the Atlantic World (Adelman), 8–9
resistance, 2
Restaurador de las leyes (Restorer of Laws). *See* Rosas, Juan Manuel de
revisionist history, 4
Revolution, 3; Echeverría and, 135; "Impresiones en una visita al Paraná" and, 149. *See also* postrevolutionary period
Rimas (Echeverría), 128, 148–149
ritual, 74–82
Rivera Indarte, José, 37
Roca, Julio Argentino, 126–127; *desierto* and, 137; modernity and, 127–128
Rodríguez, Simón, 161–162
Romanticism, 109
Root, Regina, 10
Rosas, Juan Manuel de (*Restaurador de las leyes*, caudillo), 1–2, 4, 18; in *Amalia*, 38–40; Arana's correspondence with, 19; *Argentine Dictator: Juan Manuel De Rosas, 1829–1852*, 22–23; attacks on, 37; audiovisual spectacles and, 13; as author, 46–49, 48; authoritarianism, 23; biographies, 12; "Carta del viejo Francisco Junco de la Guardia de la Monte, al viejo Gregorio Chaparro de la ciudad," 49–51, 52; conservatism and, 23; De Angelis and, 33–36; depictions of, 20; different literary representations of, 33–35, 44; Dorrego's funerary procession and, 17–19; elections and, 24; in "Ensayo histórico," 31–33; "Las esclavas de Buenos Aires muestran que son libres," 52–54; in *Facundo*, 40–44; as "fenómeno *totalitario*," 37; figure of, 20; *El Gaucho* and image of, 51, 52; Generation of 1837 and, 10, 37, 40; governorship, 9–10; graffiti, 76–77; iconography, 21–26; image of, 19, 22, 35, 49; image of, caudillo power and, 24; image of, ubiquity of, 54; intellectuals and, 33–35, 75–76; legacy of, 4; male inhabitants of countryside and, 52–54; as man of action, 22; Mármol and, 20; *¡Muera Rosas!*, 37; national culture and depictions of, 22; Pérez's biographical poem about, 27–31; Pérez's portrayal of, 33–35; poetry pro-, 76–77; portraits, pro-regime, 18, 44–49; postrevolutionary archive and, 6; power of, 20; print media and, 27; *pueblo* and connection with, 19–20; reading, 37–44; reading and, 6–8; representations of, 26; in revisionist history, 4; rise to power, 24; *Rosas y su tiempo*, 80–81; Rosist discourse, in *Facundo*, 42–43; Roxas y Patrón's correspondence with, 6–8; Sarmiento and, 20; social networks, 19; supporters, 10, 36; vilification of, 3; visual depictions of, 12, 19; in writing, 27–37; writing and, 6–8, 44; writing and, image-text of, 44–54
Rosas regime: Argentina during, 124; audiovisual spectacles and, 13, 91; cultural landscape during, 36; *Facundo* and, 12–13; hegemony, 24, 26; images of Rosas and, 35, 49; media used by, 97; newspapers during, 36–37; opposition to, 79; Pérez and, 58n84; popular expression used by, 78; populism and, 25; pro-regime portraits of Rosas, 18, 44–49; *pueblo* and, 24; Sarmiento and, 12–13
Rosas y su tiempo (Ramos Mejía), 80–81
Rosist discourse, in *Facundo*, 42–43
Roxas y Patrón, José María, 6–8
rulers, citizens and, 31

Safford, Frank, 8
Salón Literario, 36, 128
Salvatore, Ricardo, 10, 23
Sanders, James E., 124
Sarmiento, Domingo Faustino, 2, 3; "Advertencia," 59–60; Alberdi and, 144, 155n44; *Campaña en el Ejército Grande*, 70–72, 85n34, 117–118, 140–141, 144–147; *La ciudad letrada* and, 64; *desierto* in work of, 137–138;

in *Divergent Modernities*, 124; *De la educación popular*, 140; *Facundo*, 2–3, 7, 40–44, 66–70, 141; function of language and, 73; *Galería de celebridades argentinas* contribution by, 57n73; graffiti employed by, 61, 64–74; "Mas-a-fuera," 71–73; modernity and, 140; optical metaphors in work of, 114–118; "Las Piedras Pintadas de Zonda," 65–66; poetry and, 82; progressive vision of, 159; *Recuerdos de provincia*, 64–65, 140, 159; in revisionist history, 4; Rosas and, 20; Rosas regime and, 12–13; "Sarmiento the Writer," 84n7; travel writing, 114–116; United States and, 142–143, 144, 146–147; *Viajes por Europa, África y América 1845–1847*, 114–116, 126, 141, 142–143; works of, 13; worldview, 117
"Sarmiento the Writer" (Piglia), 84n7
Sastre, Marcos, 128
"Segunda lectura" (Echeverría), 130–131
Semanario de Buenos Aires (newspaper), 36
Silvas americanas (Bello), 153
sovereignty: Latin American models of, 75; representation of people and, 96–97
Sovereignty and Revolution in the Iderian Atlantic (Adelman), 9
state power, 8
Sud América (newspaper), 145
Szuchman, Mark D., 46

technology, 125–126; in "Impresiones en una visita al Paraná," 150; nature and, 150–152
telegraph, 127, 143–144
Ternavasio, Marcela, 10, 24

El tiempo de la política: el siglo XIX reconsiderado (Palti), 9
Tiola, Félix, 102
Tocqueville, Alexis de, 133
El Torito de los Muchachos (newspaper), 13, 79, 97–99; *tutilimundi*, 98–103
Trigo, Abril, 14n13
tutilimundi, 98–103
Twenty-four Years in the Argentine Republic (King), 93–95

Unitarians, 25
United States: Forbes as Charge d'Affaires for, 78–79; Sarmiento and, 142–143, 144, 146–147; in *Viajes por Europa, África y América 1845–1847*, 142–143
urban space, 74–82, 157n100; *Amalia* and, 77–80
Urquiza, Justo José de, 70, 144

Van Buren, Martin, 54n3, 78
Verdvoye, Paul, 60
Viajes por Europa, África y América 1845–1847 (Sarmiento), 114–116, 141; prologue, 115; technology in, 126; United States in, 142–143
"La vida y la obra de Esteban Echeverría" (Gutiérrez), 155n27
Viñas, David, 143
"Visiones de la óptica" ("Visions of the Optic," Lamas), 13, 103–108, 160; narrative in, 106; *óptica/optique* in, 104
visual culture: of Latin America, 91; national organization and, 119n5; nineteenth-century, 119n5; in postrevolutionary period, 89–90

workforce, 155n44

About the Author

Brendan Lanctot received his PhD from Columbia University and is an assistant professor of Hispanic studies at the University of Puget Sound. He specializes in nineteenth-century Latin American cultural studies and is particularly concerned with how a variety of cultural forms represented, formed, and informed new political subjects. Lanctot has published articles on contemporary Argentine literature and film, and is currently working on a book project titled *Specters of Populism in Nineteenth-Century Latin American Culture*.